Get the eBook FREE!

(PDF, ePub, Kindle, and liveBook all included)

We believe that once you buy a book from us, you should be able to read it in any format we have available. To get electronic versions of this book at no additional cost to you, purchase and then register this book at the Manning website.

Go to https://www.manning.com/freebook and follow the instructions to complete your pBook registration.

That's it!
Thanks from Manning!

Probabilistic Deep Learning

Probabilistic
Deep Learning

WITH PYTHON, KERAS, AND
TENSORFLOW PROBABILITY

OLIVER DÜRR
BEATE SICK
WITH ELVIS MURINA

MANNING
SHELTER ISLAND

Manning Publications Co.
20 Baldwin Road
PO Box 761
Shelter Island, NY 11964

Development editor:	Marina Michaels
Technical development editors:	Michiel Trimpe and Arthur Zubarev
Review editor:	Aleksandar Dragosavljević
Production editor:	Deirdre S. Hiam
Copy editor:	Frances Buran
Proofreader:	Keri Hales
Technical proofreader:	Al Krinker
Typesetter:	Dennis Dalinnik
Cover designer:	Marija Tudor

ISBN: 9781617296079
Printed in the United States of America

brief contents

PART 1 BASICS OF DEEP LEARNING...1

    1 ▪ Introduction to probabilistic deep learning 3

    2 ▪ Neural network architectures 25

    3 ▪ Principles of curve fitting 62

PART 2 MAXIMUM LIKELIHOOD APPROACHES FOR
        PROBABILISTIC DL MODELS 91

    4 ▪ Building loss functions with the likelihood approach 93

    5 ▪ Probabilistic deep learning models with TensorFlow
           Probability 128

    6 ▪ Probabilistic deep learning models in the wild 157

PART 3 BAYESIAN APPROACHES FOR PROBABILISTIC
        DL MODELS...195

    7 ▪ Bayesian learning 197

    8 ▪ Bayesian neural networks 229

contents

preface xi
acknowledgments xii
about this book xiv
about the authors xvii
about the cover illustration xviii

PART 1 BASICS OF DEEP LEARNING 1

1 Introduction to probabilistic deep learning 3

1.1 A first look at probabilistic models 4

1.2 A first brief look at deep learning (DL) 6

    A success story 8

1.3 Classification 8

    Traditional approach to image classification 9 ▪ Deep learning approach to image classification 12 ▪ Non-probabilistic classification 14 ▪ Probabilistic classification 14 Bayesian probabilistic classification 16

1.4 Curve fitting 16

    Non-probabilistic curve fitting 17 ▪ Probabilistic curve fitting 18 ▪ Bayesian probabilistic curve fitting 20

1.5   When to use and when not to use DL?   21

When not to use DL   21 ▪ *When to use DL   22* ▪ *When to use and when not to use probabilistic models?   22*

1.6   What you'll learn in this book   23

2   Neural network architectures   25

2.1   Fully connected neural networks (fcNNs)   26

The biology that inspired the design of artificial NNs   26 Getting started with implementing an NN   28 ▪ *Using a fully connected NN (fcNN) to classify images   38*

2.2   Convolutional NNs for image-like data   44

Main ideas in a CNN architecture   44 ▪ *A minimal CNN for edge lovers   47* ▪ *Biological inspiration for a CNN architecture   50 Building and understanding a CNN   52*

2.3   One-dimensional CNNs for ordered data   56

Format of time-ordered data   57 ▪ *What's special about ordered data?   58* ▪ *Architectures for time-ordered data   59*

3   Principles of curve fitting   62

3.1   "Hello world" in curve fitting   63

Fitting a linear regression model based on a loss function   65

3.2   Gradient descent method   69

Loss with one free model parameter   69 ▪ *Loss with two free model parameters   73*

3.3   Special DL sauce   78

Mini-batch gradient descent   78 ▪ *Using SGD variants to speed up the learning   79* ▪ *Automatic differentiation   79*

3.4   Backpropagation in DL frameworks   80

Static graph frameworks   81 ▪ *Dynamic graph frameworks   88*

PART 2   MAXIMUM LIKELIHOOD APPROACHES FOR PROBABILISTIC DL MODELS 91

4   Building loss functions with the likelihood approach   93

4.1   Introduction to the MaxLike principle: The mother of all loss functions   94

4.2   Deriving a loss function for a classification problem   99

*Binary classification problem   99 ▪ Classification problems with
more than two classes   105 ▪ Relationship between NLL, cross
entropy, and Kullback-Leibler divergence   109*

4.3   Deriving a loss function for regression problems   111

*Using a NN without hidden layers and one output neuron for
modeling a linear relationship between input and output   111
Using a NN with hidden layers to model non-linear relationships
between input and output   119 ▪ Using an NN with additional
output for regression tasks with nonconstant variance   121*

5 *Probabilistic deep learning models with TensorFlow
Probability*   128

5.1   Evaluating and comparing different probabilistic
prediction models   130

5.2   Introducing TensorFlow Probability (TFP)   132

5.3   Modeling continuous data with TFP   135

*Fitting and evaluating a linear regression model with constant
variance   136 ▪ Fitting and evaluating a linear regression model
with a nonconstant standard deviation   140*

5.4   Modeling count data with TensorFlow Probability   145

*The Poisson distribution for count data   148 ▪ Extending the
Poisson distribution to a zero-inflated Poisson (ZIP)
distribution   153*

6 *Probabilistic deep learning models in the wild*   157

6.1   Flexible probability distributions in state-of-the-art
DL models   159

*Multinomial distribution as a flexible distribution   160
Making sense of discretized logistic mixture   162*

6.2   Case study: Bavarian roadkills   165

6.3   Go with the flow: Introduction to normalizing
flows (NFs)   166

*The principle idea of NFs   168 ▪ The change of variable technique
for probabilities   170 ▪ Fitting an NF to data   175 ▪ Going
deeper by chaining flows   177 ▪ Transformation between higher
dimensional spaces*   181 ▪ Using networks to control flows   183
Fun with flows: Sampling faces   188*

PART 3 BAYESIAN APPROACHES FOR PROBABILISTIC DL MODELS 195

7 Bayesian learning   197

7.1   What's wrong with non-Bayesian DL:
      The elephant in the room   198

7.2   The first encounter with a Bayesian approach   201

Bayesian model: The hacker's way   202 ▪ What did we just do?   206

7.3   The Bayesian approach for probabilistic models   207

Training and prediction with a Bayesian model   208 ▪ A coin toss as a Hello World example for Bayesian models   213 ▪ Revisiting the Bayesian linear regression model   224

8 Bayesian neural networks   229

8.1   Bayesian neural networks (BNNs)   230

8.2   Variational inference (VI) as an approximative
      Bayes approach   232

Looking under the hood of VI   233 ▪ Applying VI to the toy problem*   238*

8.3   Variational inference with TensorFlow Probability   243

8.4   MC dropout as an approximate Bayes approach   245

Classical dropout used during training   246 ▪ MC dropout used during train and test times   249

8.5   Case studies   252

Regression case study on extrapolation   252 ▪ Classification case study with novel classes   256

Glossary of terms and abbreviations   264

index   269

preface

Thank you for buying our book. We hope that it provides you with a look under the hood of deep learning (DL) and gives you some inspirations on how to use probabilistic DL methods for your work.

All three of us, the authors, have a background in statistics. We started our journey in DL together in 2014. We got so excited about it that DL is still in the center of our professional lives. DL has a broad range of applications, but we are especially fascinated by the power of combining DL models with probabilistic approaches as used in statistics. In our experience, a deep understanding of the potential of probabilistic DL requires both insight into the underlying methods and practical experience. Therefore, we tried to find a good balance of both ingredients in this book.

In this book, we aimed to give some clear ideas and examples of applications before discussing the methods involved. You also have the chance to make practical use of all discussed methods by working with the accompanying Jupyter notebooks. We hope you learn as much by reading this book as we learned while writing it. Have fun and stay curious!

acknowledgments

We want to thank all the people who helped us in writing this book. A special thanks go out to our development editor, Marina Michaels, who managed to teach a bunch of Swiss and Germans how to write sentences shorter than a few hundred words. Without her, you would have no fun deciphering the text. Also, many thanks to our copyeditor, Frances Buran, who spotted uncountable errors and inconsistencies in the text (and also in the formulas, kudos!). We also got much support on the technical side from Al Krinkler and Hefin Rhys to make the text and code in the notebooks more consistent and easier to understand. Also, thank you to our project editor, Deirdre Hiam; our proofreader, Keri Hales; and our review editor, Aleksandar Dragosavljević. We would also like to thank the reviewers, which at various stages of the book helped with their very valuable feedback: Bartek Krzyszycha, Brynjar Smári Bjarnason, David Jacobs, Diego Casella, Francisco José Lacueva Pérez, Gary Bake, Guillaume Alleon, Howard Bandy, Jon Machtynger, Kim Falk Jorgensen, Kumar Kandasami, Raphael Yan, Richard Vaughan, Richard Ward, and Zalán Somogyváry.

Finally, we would also like to thank Richard Sheppard for the many excellent graphics and drawings making the book less dry and friendlier.

I, Oliver, would like to thank my partner Lena Obendiek for her patience as I worked on the book for many long hours. I also thank my friends from the "Tatort" viewing club for providing food and company each Sunday at 8:15 pm and for keeping me from going crazy while writing this book.

I, Beate, want to thank my friends, not so much for helping me to write the book, but for sharing with me a good time beyond the computer screen—first of all my partner Michael, but also the infamous Limmat BBQ group and my friends and family outside of Zurich who still spend leisure time with me despite the Rösti-Graben, the country border to the big canton, or even the big pond in between.

I, Elvis, want to thank everyone who supported me during the exciting time of writing this book, not only professionally, but also privately during a good glass of wine or a game of football.

We, the Tensor Chiefs, are happy that we made it together to the end of this book. We look forward to new scientific journeys, but also to less stressful times where we not only meet for work, but also for fun.

about this book

In this book, we hope to bring the probabilistic principles underpinning deep learning (DL) to a broader audience. In the end (almost), all neural networks (NNs) in DL are probabilistic models.

There are two powerful probabilistic principles: maximum likelihood and Bayes. Maximum likelihood (fondly referred to as MaxLike) governs all traditional DL. Understanding networks as probabilistic models trained with the maximum likelihood principle helps you to boost the performance of your networks (as Google did when going from WaveNet to WaveNet++) or to generate astounding applications (like OpenAI did with Glow, a net that generates realistic looking faces). Bayesian methods come into play in situations where networks need to say, "I'm not sure." (Strangely, traditional NNs cannot do this.) The subtitle for the book, "with Python, Keras, and TensorFlow Probability," reflects the fact that you really should get your hands dirty and do some coding.

Who should read this book

This book is written for people who like to understand the underlying probabilistic principles of DL. Ideally, you should have some experience with DL or machine learning (ML) and should not be too afraid of a bit of math and Python code. We did not spare the math and always included examples in code. We believe math goes better with code.

How this book is organized: A roadmap

The book has three parts that cover eight chapters. Part 1 explains traditional deep learning (DL) architectures and how the training of neural networks (NNs) is done technically.

- Chapter 1—Sets the stage and introduces you to probabilistic DL.
- Chapter 2—Talks about network architectures. We cover fully connected neural networks (fcNNs), which are kind of all-purpose networks, and convolutional neural networks (CNNs), which are ideal for images.
- Chapter 3—Shows you how NNs manage to fit millions of parameters. We keep it easy and show gradient descent and backpropagation on the simplest network one can think of—linear regression.

Part 2 focuses on using NNs as probabilistic models. In contrast to part 3, we discuss maximum likelihood approaches. These are behind all traditional DL.

- Chapter 4—Explores maximum likelihood (MaxLike), the underlying principle of ML and DL. We start by applying this principle to classification and (simple regression problems).
- Chapter 5—Introduces TensorFlow Probability (TFP), a framework to build deep probabilistic models. We use it for not-so-simple regression problems like count data.
- Chapter 6—Begins with more complex regression models. At the end, we explain how you can use probabilistic models to master complex distributions like describing images of human faces.

Part 3 introduces Bayesian NNs. Bayesian NNs allow you to handle uncertainty.

- Chapter 7—Motivates the need for Bayesian DL and explains its principles. We again look at the simple example of linear regression to explain the Bayesian principle.
- Chapter 8—Shows you how to build Bayesian NNs. Here we cover two approaches called MC (Monte Carlo) dropout and variational inference.

If you already have experience with DL, you can skip the first part. Also, the second part of chapter 6 (starting with section 6.3) describes normalizing flows. You do not need to know these to understand the material in part 3. Section 6.3.5 is a bit heavy on math, so if this is not your cup of tea, you can skip it. The same holds true for sections 8.2.1 and 8.2.2.

About the code

This book contains many examples of source code both in numbered listings and in line with normal text. In both cases, source code is formatted in a `fixed-width font`, `like this` to separate it from ordinary text.

The code samples are taken from Jupyter notebooks. These notebooks include additional explanations and most include little exercises you should do for a better understanding of the concepts introduced in this book. You can find all the code in this directory in GitHub: https://github.com/tensorchiefs/dl_book/. A good place to start is in the directory https://tensorchiefs.github.io/dl_book/, where you'll find links to the notebooks. The notebooks are numbered according to the chapters. So, for example, nb_ch08_02 is the second notebook in chapter 8.

All the examples in this book, except nb_06_05, are tested with the TensorFlow v2.1 and TensorFlow Probability (TFP) v0.8. The notebooks nb_ch03_03 and nb_ch03_04, describing the computation graphs, are easier to understand in TensorFlow v1. For these notebooks, we also include both versions of TensorFlow. The nb_06_05 notebook only works with TensorFlow v1 because we need weights that are only provided in that version of TensorFlow.

You can execute the notebooks in Google's Colab or locally. Colab is great; you can simply click on a link and then play with the code in the cloud. No installation—you just need a browser. We definitely suggest that you go this way.

TensorFlow is still fast-evolving, and we cannot guarantee the code will run in several years' time. We, therefore, provide a Docker container (https://github.com oduerr/dl_book_docker/) that you can use to execute all notebooks except nb_06_05 and the TensorFlow 1.0 versions of nb_ch03_03 and nb_ch03_04. This Docker container is the way to go if you want to use the notebooks locally.

liveBook discussion forum

Purchase of *Probabilistic Deep Learning* includes free access to a private web forum run by Manning Publications where you can make comments about the book, ask technical questions, and receive help from the authors and from other users. To access the forum, go to https://livebook.manning.com/book/probabilistic-deep-learning-with-python/welcome/v-6/. You can also learn more about Manning's forums and the rules of conduct at https://livebook.manning.com/#!/discussion.

Manning's commitment to our readers is to provide a venue where a meaningful dialogue between individual readers and between readers and the authors can take place. It is not a commitment to any specific amount of participation on the part of the authors, whose contribution to the forum remains voluntary (and unpaid). We suggest you try asking the authors some challenging questions lest their interest stray! The forum and the archives of previous discussions will be accessible from the publisher's website as long as the book is in print.

about the authors

Oliver Dürr is professor for data science at the University of Applied Sciences in Konstanz, Germany. **Beate Sick** holds a chair for applied statistics at ZHAW, and works as a researcher and lecturer at the University of Zurich, and as a lecturer at ETH Zurich. **Elvis Murina** is a research scientist, responsible for the extensive exercises that accompany this book.

Dürr and Sick are both experts in machine learning and statistics. They have supervised numerous bachelor's, master's, and PhD theses on the topic of deep learning, and planned and conducted several postgraduate- and master's-level deep learning courses. All three authors have worked with deep learning methods since 2013, and have extensive experience in both teaching the topic and developing probabilistic deep learning models.

about the cover illustration

The figure on the cover of *Probabilistic Deep Learning* is captioned "Danseuse de l'Isle O-tahiti," or A dancer from the island of Tahiti. The illustration is taken from a collection of dress costumes from various countries by Jacques Grasset de Saint-Sauveur (1757–1810), titled *Costumes de Différents Pays,* published in France in 1788. Each illustration is finely drawn and colored by hand. The rich variety of Grasset de Saint-Sauveur's collection reminds us vividly of how culturally apart the world's towns and regions were just 200 years ago. Isolated from each other, people spoke different dialects and languages. In the streets or in the countryside, it was easy to identify where they lived and what their trade or station in life was just by their dress.

The way we dress has changed since then and the diversity by region, so rich at the time, has faded away. It is now hard to tell apart the inhabitants of different continents, let alone different towns, regions, or countries. Perhaps we have traded cultural diversity for a more varied personal life—certainly for a more varied and fast-paced technological life.

At a time when it is hard to tell one computer book from another, Manning celebrates the inventiveness and initiative of the computer business with book covers based on the rich diversity of regional life of two centuries ago, brought back to life by Grasset de Saint-Sauveur's pictures.

Part 1

Basics of deep learning

Part 1 of this book gives you a first high-level understanding of what probabilistic deep learning (DL) is about and which types of tasks you can tackle with it. You'll learn about different neural network architectures for regression (that you can use to predict a number), and about classification (that you can use to predict a class). You'll get practical experiences in setting up DL models, learn how to tune these, and learn how to control the training procedure. If you don't already have substantial experience with DL, you should work through part 1 in full before moving on to the probabilistic DL models in part 2.

Introduction to probabilistic deep learning

This chapter covers

- What is a probabilistic model?
- What is deep learning and when do you use it?
- Comparing traditional machine learning and deep learning approaches for image classification
- The underlying principles of both curve fitting and neural networks
- Comparing non-probabilistic and probabilistic models
- What probabilistic deep learning is and why it's useful

Deep learning (DL) is one of the hottest topics in data science and artificial intelligence today. DL has only been feasible since 2012 with the widespread usage of GPUs, but you're probably already dealing with DL technologies in various areas of your daily life. When you vocally communicate with a digital assistant, when you translate text from one language into another using the free DeepL translator service (DeepL is a company producing translation engines based on DL), or when you use a search engine such as Google, DL is doing its magic behind the scenes. Many state-of-the-art DL applications such as text-to-speech translations boost their performance using probabilistic DL models. Further, safety critical applications like self-driving cars use Bayesian variants of probabilistic DL.

In this chapter, you will get a first high-level introduction to DL and its probabilistic variants. We use simple examples to discuss the differences between non-probabilistic and probabilistic models and then highlight some advantages of probabilistic DL models. We also give you a first impression of what you gain when working with Bayesian variants of probabilistic DL models. In the remaining chapters of the book, you will learn how to implement DL models and how to tweak them to get their more powerful probabilistic variants. You will also learn about the underlying principles that enable you to build your own models and to understand advanced modern models so that you can adapt them for your own purposes.

1.1 *A first look at probabilistic models*

Let's first get an idea of what a probabilistic model can look like and how you can use it. We use an example from daily life to discuss the difference between a non-probabilistic model and a probabilistic model. We then use the same example to highlight some advantages of a probabilistic model.

In our cars, most of us use a satellite navigational system (satnav—a.k.a. GPS) that tells us how to get from A to B. For each suggested route, the satnav also predicts the needed travel time. Such a predicted travel time can be understood as a best guess. You know you'll sometimes need more time and sometimes less time when taking the same route from A to B. But a standard satnav is non-probabilistic: it predicts only a single value for the travel time and does not tell you a possible range of values. For an example, look at the left panel in figure 1.1, where you see two routes going from Croxton, New York, to the Museum of Modern Art (MoMA), also in New York, with a predicted travel time that is the satnav's best guess based on previous data and the current road conditions.

Let's imagine a fancier satnav that uses a probabilistic model. It not only gives you a best guess for the travel time, but also captures the uncertainty of that travel time. The probabilistic prediction of the travel time for a given route is provided as a distribution. For example, look at the right panel of figure 1.1. You see two Gaussian bell curves describing the predicted travel-time distributions for the two routes.

How can you benefit from knowing these distributions of the predicted travel time? Imagine you are a New York cab driver. At Croxton, an art dealer boards your taxi. She wants to participate in a great art auction that starts in 25 minutes and offers you a generous tip ($500) if she arrives there on time. That's quite an incentive!

Your satnav tool proposes two routes (see the left panel of figure 1.1). As a first impulse, you would probably choose the upper route because, for this route, it estimates a travel time of 19 minutes, which is shorter than the 22 minutes for the other route. But, fortunately, you always have the newest gadgets, and your satnav uses a probabilistic model that not only outputs the mean travel time but also a whole distribution of travel times. Even better, you know how to make use of the outputted distribution for the travel times.

You realize that in your current situation, the mean travel time is not very interesting. What really matters to you is the following question: With which route do you

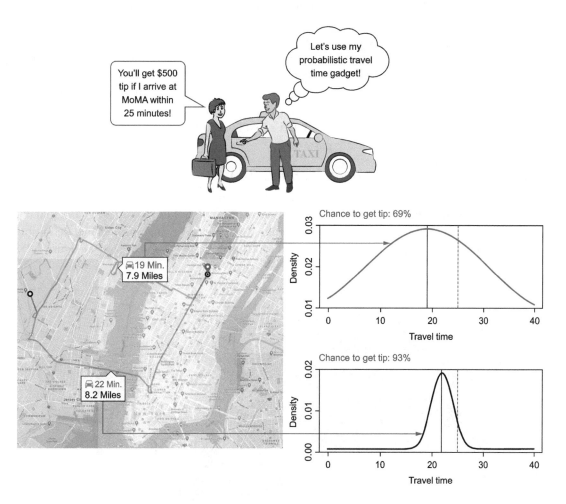

Figure 1.1 Travel time prediction of the satnav. On the left side of the map, you see a deterministic version—just a single number is reported. On the right side, you see the probability distributions for the travel time of the two routes.

have the better chance of getting the $500 tip? To answer this question, you can look at the distributions on the right side of figure 1.1. After a quick eyeball analysis, you conclude that you have a better chance of getting the tip when taking the lower route, even though it has a larger mean travel time. The reason is that the narrow distribution of the lower route has a larger fraction of the distribution corresponding to travel times shorter than 25 minutes. To support your assessment with hard numbers, you can use the satnav tool with the probabilistic model to compute for both distributions the probability of arriving at MoMA in less than 25 minutes. This probability corresponds to the proportion of the area under the curve left of the dashed line in figure 1.1, which indicates a critical value of 25 minutes. Letting the tool compute the probabilities from the distribution, you know that your chance of getting the tip is 93% when taking the lower route and only 69% when taking the upper road.

As discussed in this cab driver example, the main advantages of probabilistic models are that these can capture the uncertainties in most real-world applications and provide essential information for decision making. Other examples of the use of probabilistic models include self-driving cars or digital medicine probabilistic models. You can also use probabilistic DL to generate new data that is similar to your observed data. A famous fun application is to create realistic looking faces of non-existing people. We talk about this in chapter 6. Let's first look at DL from a bird's-eye view before peeking into the curve-fitting part.

1.2   *A first brief look at deep learning (DL)*

What is DL anyway? When asked for a short elevator pitch, we would say that it's a machine learning (ML) technique based on artificial neural networks (NNs) and that it's loosely inspired by the way the human brain works. Before giving our personal definition of DL, we first want to give you an idea of what an artificial NN looks like (see figure 1.2).

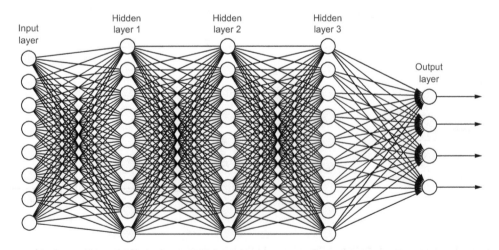

Figure 1.2   An example of an artificial neural network (NN) model with three hidden layers. The input layers hold as many neurons as we have numbers to describe the input.

In figure 1.2, you can see a typical traditional artificial NN with three hidden layers and several neurons in each layer. Each neuron within a layer is connected with each neuron in the next layer.

An artificial NN is inspired by the brain that consists of up to billions of neurons processing, for example, all sensory perceptions such as vision or hearing. Neurons within the brain aren't connected to every other neuron, and a signal is processed through a hierarchical network of neurons. You can see a similar hierarchical network structure in the artificial NN shown in figure 1.2. While a biological neuron is quite complex in how it processes information, a neuron in an artificial NN is a simplification and abstraction of its biological counterpart.

To get a first idea about an artificial NN, you can better imagine a neuron as a container for a number. The neurons in the input layer are correspondingly holding the numbers of the input data. Such input data could, for example, be the age (in years), income (in dollars), and height (in inches) of a customer. All neurons in the following layers get the weighted sum of the values from the connected neurons in the previous layer as their input. In general, the different connections aren't equally important but have *weights*, which determine the influence of the incoming neuron's value on the neuron's value in the next layer. (Here we omit that this input is further transformed within the neuron.) DL models are NNs, but they also have a large number of hidden layers (not just three as in the example from figure 1.2).

The weights (strength of connections between neurons) in an artificial NN need to be learned for the task at hand. For that learning step, you use training data and tune the weights to optimally fit the data. This step is called *fitting*. Only after the fitting step can you use the model to do predictions on new data.

Setting up a DL system is always a two-stage process. In the first step, you choose an architecture. In figure 1.2, we chose a network with three layers in which each neuron from a given layer is connected to each neuron in the next layer. Other types of networks have different connections, but the principle stays the same. In the next step, you tune the weights of the model so that the training data is best described. This fitting step is usually done using a procedure called gradient descent. You'll learn more about gradient descent in chapter 3.

Note that this two-step procedure is nothing special to DL but is also present in standard statistical modeling and ML. The underlying principles of fitting are the same for DL, ML, and statistics. We're convinced that you can profit a lot by using the knowledge that was gained in the field of statistics during the last centuries. This book acknowledges the heritage of traditional statistics and builds on it. Because of this, you can understand much of DL by looking at something as simple as linear regression, which we introduce in this chapter and use throughout the book as an easy example. You'll see in chapter 4 that linear regression already is a probabilistic model providing more information than just one predicted output value for each sample. In that chapter, you'll learn how to pick an appropriate distribution to model the variability of the outcome values. In chapter 5, we'll show you how to use the TensorFlow Probability framework to fit such a probabilistic DL model. You can then transfer this approach to new situations allowing you to design and fit appropriate probabilistic DL models that not only provide high performance predictions but also capture the noise of the data.

1.2.1 A success story

DL has revolutionized areas that so far have been especially hard to master with traditional ML approaches but that are easy to solve by humans, such as the ability to recognize objects in images (*computer vision*) and to process written text (natural language processing) or, more generally, any kind of perception tasks. Image classification is far from being only an academic problem and is used for a variety of applications:

- Face recognition
- Diagnostics of brain tumors in MRI data
- Recognition of road signs for self-driving cars

Although DL reveals its potential in different application areas, probably the easiest to grasp is in the field of computer vision. We therefore use computer vision to motivate DL by one of its biggest success stories.

In 2012, DL made a splash when Alex Krizhevsky from Geoffrey Hinton's lab crushed all competitors in the internationally renowned ImageNet competition with a DL-based model. In this competition, teams from leading computer vision labs trained their models on a big data set of ~1 million images with the goal of teaching these to distinguish 1,000 different classes of image content. Examples for such classes are ships, mushrooms, and leopards. In the competition, all trained models had to list the five most probable classes for a set of new test images. If the right class wasn't among the proposed classes, the test image counted as an error (see figure 1.3, which shows how DL-based approaches took image classification by storm).

Before DL entered the competition, the best programs had an error rate of ~25%. In 2012, Krizhevsky was the first to use DL and achieved a huge drop in the error rate (by 10% to only ~15%). Only a year later, in 2013, almost all competitors used DL, and in 2015, different DL-based models reached the level of human performance, which is about 5%. You might wonder why humans misclassify 1 image in 20 (5%). A fun fact: there are 170 different dog breeds in that data set, which makes it a bit harder for humans to correctly classify the images.

1.3 Classification

Let's look at the differences between non-probabilistic, probabilistic, and Bayesian probabilistic classification. DL is known to outperform traditional methods, especially in image classification tasks. Before going into details, we want to use a face recognition problem to give you a feeling for the differences and the commonalities between a DL approach and a more traditional approach to face recognition. As a side note, face recognition is actually the application that initially brought us into contact with DL.

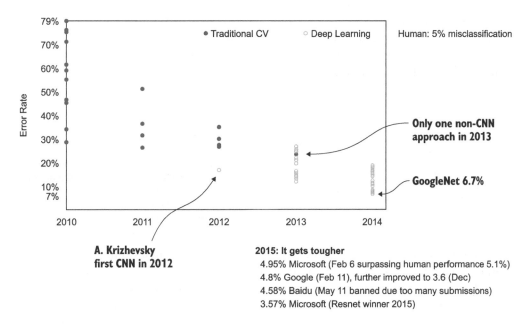

Figure 1.3   The impressive results of DL in the ImageNet competition

As statisticians, we had a collaboration project with some computer science colleagues for doing face recognition on a Raspberry Pi minicomputer. The computer scientists challenged us by kidding about the age of the used statistical methods. We took the challenge and brought them to a surprised silence by proposing DL to tackle our face recognition problem. The success in this first project triggered many other joint DL projects, and our interests grew, looking deeper into the underlying principles of these models.

Let's look at a specific task. Sara and Chantal were together on holidays and took many pictures, each showing at least one of them. The task is to create a program that can look at a photo and determine which of the two women is in the photo. To get a training data set, we labeled 900 pictures, 450 for each woman, with the name of the pictured woman. You can imagine that images can be very different at first sight because the women might be pictured from different angles, laughing or tired, dressed up or casual, or having a bad hair day. Still, for you, the task is quite easy. But for a computer, an image is only an array of pixel values, and programming it to tell the difference between two women is far from trivial.

1.3.1   *Traditional approach to image classification*

A traditional approach to image classification doesn't directly start with the pixel values of the images but tackles the classification task in a two-step process. As a first step, experts in the field define features that are useful to classify the images. A simple example of such a feature would be the mean intensity value of all pixels, which can be useful to distinguish night shots from pictures taken during the day. Usually these features are more complex and tailored to a specific task. In the face recognition problem, you can think about easily understandable features like the length of the nose, width of the mouth, or the distance between the eyes (figure 1.4).

Figure 1.4   Chantal (left) has a large distance between the eyes and a rather small mouth. Sara (right) has a small distance between the eyes and a rather large mouth.

But these kinds of high-level features often are difficult to determine because many aspects need to be taken into account, such as mimics, scale, receptive angle, or light conditions. Therefore, non-DL approaches often use less interpretable, low-level features like SIFT features (Scale-Invariant Feature Transform), capturing local image properties such as magnification or rotation that are invariant to transformations. You can, for example, think about an edge detector: an edge won't disappear if the image is rotated or scaled.

Already this simple example makes clear that feature engineering, meaning defining and extracting those properties from the image that are important for the classification, is a complicated and time-consuming task. It usually requires a high level of expertise. The (slow) progress in many applications of computer vision like face recognition was mainly driven by the construction of new and better features.

NOTE   You need to extract all these features from all images before you can tackle the actual classification task.

After the features-extraction step, the values of these features represent each image. In order to identify Sara or Chantal from this feature representation of the image, you need to choose and fit a classification.

What is the task of such a classification model? It should discriminate between the different class labels. To visualize this idea, let's imagine that an image is described by only two features: say, distance of the eyes and width of the mouth. (We are aware that in most real cases, a good characterization of an image requires many more features.)

Because the women aren't always pictured head on but from different viewpoints, the apparent distance between the eyes isn't always the same for the same women. The apparent width of the mouth can vary even more, depending if the woman laughs or makes an air-kiss. When representing each image of the pictured woman by these two features, the feature space can be visualized by a 2D plot. One axis indicates the eye distance and the other axis shows the mouth width (see figure 1.5). Each image is represented by a point; images of Sara are labeled with an *S* and images of Chantal with a *C.*

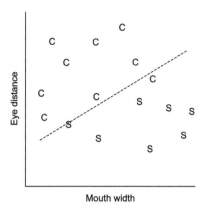

Figure 1.5 A 2D space spanned by the features mouth width and eye distance. Each point represents an image described by these two features (S for Sara and C for Chantal). The dashed line is a decision boundary separating the two classes.

One way you can think about a non-probabilistic classification model is that the model defines decision boundaries (see the dashed line in figure 1.5) that split the feature space into different regions. Each resulting region corresponds to one class label. In our example, we've determined a *Sara region* and a *Chantal region*. You can now use this decision boundary to classify new images from which you only know the values for the two features: if the corresponding point in the 2D feature space ends up in the Sara region, you classify it as Sara; otherwise, as Chantal.

You might know from your data analysis experiences some methods like the following, which you can use for classification. (Don't worry if you aren't familiar with these methods.)

- Logistic or multinomial regression
- Random forest
- Support vector machines
- Linear discriminant analysis

Most classification models, including the listed methods and also DL, are *parametric models*, meaning the model has some parameters that determine the course of the boundaries. The model is only ready to actually perform a classification or class probability prediction after replacing the parameters by certain numbers. *Fitting* is about how to find these numbers and how to quantify the certainty of these numbers.

Fitting the model to a set of training data with known class labels determines the values of the parameter and fixes the decision boundaries in the feature space. Depending on the classification method and the number of parameters, these decision boundaries could be simple straight lines or a complex boundary with wiggles. You can summarize the traditional workflow to set up a classification method in three steps:

1 Defining and extracting features from the raw data
2 Choosing a parametric model
3 Fitting the classification model to the data by tuning its parameter

To evaluate the performance of the models, you use a validation data set that is not used during the training. A validation data set in the face recognition example would consist of new images of Chantal and Sara that were not part of the training data set. You then can use the trained model to predict the class label and use the percentage of correct classifications as a (non-probabilistic) performance measure.

Depending on the situation, one or another classification method will achieve better results on the validation data set. However, in classical image classification, the most important ingredient for success isn't the choice of the classification algorithm but the quality of the extracted image features. If the extracted features take different values for images from different classes, you'll see a clear separation of the respective points in the feature space. In such a situation, many classification models show a high classification performance.

With the example of discriminating Sara from Chantal, you went through the traditional image classification workflow. For getting good features, you first had to recognize that these two women differ in their mouth width and their eye distance. With these specific features, you saw that it is easy to build a good classifier. However, for discriminating between two other women, these features might not do the trick, and you would need to start over with the feature developing process again. This is a common drawback when working with customized features.

1.3.2 Deep learning approach to image classification

In contrast to the traditional approach to image classification, the DL approach starts directly from the raw image data and uses only the pixel values as the input features to the model. In this *feature representation* of an image, the numbers of pixels define the dimension of the feature space. For a low-resolution picture with 100×100 pixels, this already amounts to 10,000.

Besides such a high dimension, the main challenge is that pixel similarity of two pictures doesn't imply that the two images correspond to the same class label. Figure 1.6 illustrates where the images in the same column obviously correspond to the same class but are different on the pixel level. Simultaneously, images in the same row of figure 1.6 show high pixel similarity but don't correspond to the same class.

The core idea of DL is to replace the challenging and time-consuming task of feature engineering by incorporating the construction of appropriate features into the fitting process. Also, DL can't do any magic so, similar to traditional image analysis, the features have to be constructed from the pixel values at hand. This is done via the hidden layers of the DL model.

Each neuron combines its inputs to yield a new value, and in this manner, each layer yields a new feature representation of the input. Using many hidden layers allows the NN to decompose a complicated transformation from the raw data to the outcome in a hierarchy of simple transformations. When going from layer to layer, you get a more and more abstract representation of the image that becomes better suited for discriminating between the classes. You'll learn more about this in chap-

Figure 1.6 The left column shows two images of the class *dog*. The right column shows two images of the class *table*. When comparing the pictures on the pixel level, the two images in the same column are less similar than the two images in the same row, even if one image in a row shows a dog and the other image displays a table.

ter 2, where you'll see that during the fitting process of a DL model, a hierarchy of successively more complex features is learned. This then allows you to discriminate between the different classes without the need of manually specifying the appropriate features.

Branding DL (deep learning)

In the earlier days of machine learning (ML), neural networks (NNs) were already around, but it was technically impossible to train deep NNs with many layers, mainly because of a lack of computer power and training data. With the technical obstacles resolved, some tricks have been discovered that made it possible to train NNs with several hundred layers.

Why do we talk about DL instead of artificial NNs? DL sells better than artificial NNs. This might sound disrespectful, but such rebranding was probably a smart move, especially because NNs haven't delivered what was promised during the last decades and, therefore, gained a somewhat bad reputation. We work with "deep" NNs with many hidden layers. This leads to a deep hierarchy in the construction of features, allowing these to become more abstract with every step up in the hierarchy.

After defining the architectures, the network can be understood as a parametric model that often contains millions of parameters. The model takes an input x and produces an output *y*. This is true for every DL model (including reinforcement learning). The DL modeling workflow can be summarized in two steps:

1 Defining the DL model architecture
2 Fitting the DL model to the raw data

The next sections discuss what is meant by non-probabilistic and probabilistic classification models and what benefits you can get from a Bayesian variant of a probabilistic classification model.

1.3.3   *Non-probabilistic classification*

Let's first look at non-probabilistic classification. To make it easy and illustrative, we use the image classification example again. The goal in image classification is to predict for a given image which class it corresponds to. In the ImageNet competition in section 1.2, there were 1,000 different classes. In the face recognition example, there were only two classes: Chantal and Sara.

In non-probabilistic image classification, you only get the predicted class label for each image. More precisely, a non-probabilistic image classifier takes an image as input and then predicts only the best guess for the class as output. In the face recognition example, it would either output Chantal or Sara. You can also think about a non-probabilistic model as a deterministic model without any uncertainty. When looking with probabilistic glasses at a non-probabilistic model, it seems that a non-probabilistic model is always certain. The non-probabilistic model predicts with a probability of one that the image belongs to one specific class.

Imagine a situation where the image shows Chantal where she dyes her hair the same color as that of Sara and the hair covers Chantal's face. For a human being, it's quite hard to tell if the image shows Chantal or Sara. But the non-probabilistic classifier still provides a predicted class label (for example, Sara) without indicating any uncertainty. Or imagine an even more extreme situation where you provide an image that shows neither Chantal nor Sara (see figure 1.7). Which prediction will you get from the classifier? You would like the classifier to tell you that it is not able to make a reliable prediction. But a non-probabilistic classifier still yields either Chantal or Sara as a prediction without giving a hint of any uncertainty. To tackle such challenges of handling difficult or novel situations, we turn to probabilistic models and their Bayesian variants. These can express their uncertainty and indicate potentially unreliable predictions.

1.3.4   *Probabilistic classification*

The special thing in probabilistic classification is that you not only get the best guess for the class label but also a measure for the uncertainty of the classification. The uncertainty is expressed by a probability distribution. In the face recognition example, a probabilistic classifier would take a face image and then output a certain probability for Chantal and for Sara. Both probabilities add up to 1 (see figure 1.8).

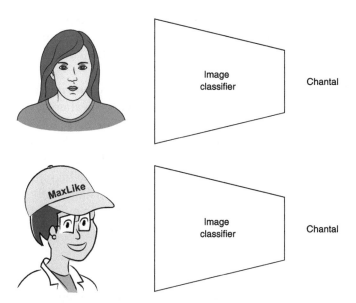

Figure 1.7 A non-probabilistic image classifier for face recognition takes as input an image and yields as outcome a class label. Here the predicted class label is *Chantal*, but only the upper image really shows Chantal. The lower image shows a woman who is neither Chantal nor Sara.

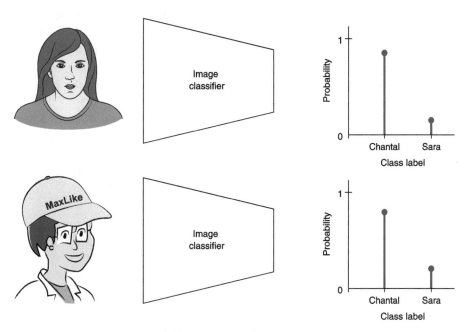

Figure 1.8 A probabilistic image classifier for face recognition takes as input an image and yields as outcome a probability for each class label. In the upper panel, the image shows Chantal, and the classifier predicts a probability of 0.85 for the class *Chantal* and a probability of 0.15 for the class *Sara*. In the lower panel, the image shows neither Chantal nor Sara, and the classifier predicts a probability of 0.8 for the class *Chantal* and a probability of 0.2 for the class *Sara*.

To give a best single guess, you would pick the class with the highest probability. It is common to think about the probability of the predicted class as an uncertainty of the prediction. This is the case when all the images are sufficiently similar to the training data.

But in reality, this is not always the case. Imagine that you provide the classifier with an image that shows neither Chantal nor Sara. The classifier has no other choice than to assign probabilities to the classes *Chantal* or *Sara*. But you would hope that the classifier shows its uncertainty by assigning more or less equal probabilities to the two possible but wrong classes. Unfortunately, this is often not the case when working with probabilistic NN models. Instead, often quite high probabilities are still assigned to one of the possible but wrong classes (see figure 1.8). To tackle this problem, in part 3 of our book, we extend the probabilistic models by taking a Bayesian approach, which can add an additional uncertainty that you can use to detect novel classes.

1.3.5   *Bayesian probabilistic classification*

The nice thing about Bayesian models is that these can express uncertainty about their predictions. In our face recognition example, the non-Bayesian probabilistic model predicts an outcome distribution that consists of the probability for Chantal and the probability for Sara, which add up to 1. But how certain is the model about the assigned probabilities? Bayesian models can give an answer to this question. In part 3 of this book, you will learn how this is done in detail. At this point, let's just note that you can ask a Bayesian model several times and get different answers when you ask it. This reflects the uncertainty inherent in the model (see figure 1.9). Don't worry if you do not see how you get these different model outputs for the same input. You will learn about that in the third part of the book.

The main advantage of Bayesian models is that these can indicate a non-reliable prediction by a large spread of the different sets of predictions (see lower panel of figure 1.9). In this way, you have a better chance to identify novel classes like the young lady in the lower panel of figure 1.9 who is neither Chantal nor Sara.

1.4   *Curve fitting*

We want to finish this introductory chapter talking about the differences in probabilistic and non-probabilistic DL methods on regression tasks. Regression is sometimes also referred to as *curve fitting*. This reminds one of the following:

> *All the impressive achievements of deep learning amount to just curve fitting.*
>
> —Judea Pearl, 2018

When we heard that Judea Pearl, the winner of the prestigious Turing Award in 2011 (the computer science equivalent of the Nobel prize), claimed DL to be just curve fitting (the same curve fitting done in simple analysis like linear regression for centuries), at first we were surprised and even felt a bit offended. How could he be so

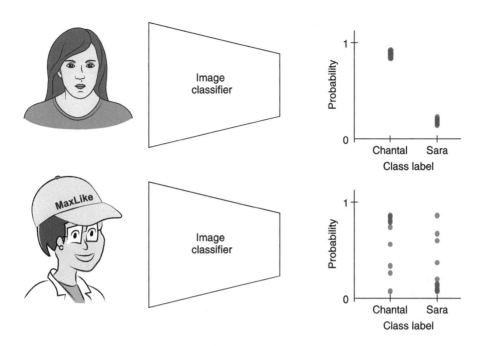

Figure 1.9 A Bayesian probabilistic image classifier for face recognition takes as input an image and yields as outcome a distribution of probability sets for the two class labels. In the upper panel, the image is showing Chantal, and the predicted sets of probabilities all predict a large probability for Chantal and an accordingly low probability for Sara. In the lower panel, the image shows a lady who is neither Chantal nor Sara, so the classifier predicts different sets of probabilities indicating a high uncertainty.

disrespectful about our research subject, which, moreover, showed such impressive results in practice? Our relative calmness is probably due to the fact that we aren't computer scientists but have a background in physics and statistical data analysis. Curve fitting isn't *just* curve fitting for us. However, giving his statement a second thought, we can see his point: the underlying principles of DL and curve fitting are identical in many respects.

1.4.1 *Non-probabilistic curve fitting*

Let's first take a closer look at the non-probabilistic aspects of traditional curve-fitting methods. Loosely speaking, *non-probabilistic curve fitting* is the science of putting lines through data points. With linear regression in its most simple form, you put a straight line through the data points (see figure 1.10). In that figure, we assume that we have only one feature, x, to predict a continuous variable, y. In this simple case, the linear regression model has only two parameters, a and b:

$$y = a \cdot x + b$$

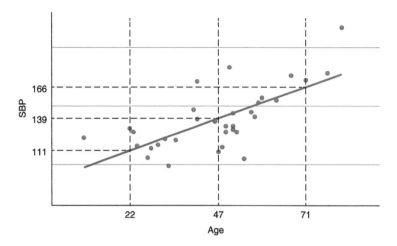

Figure 1.10 Scatter plot and regression model for the systolic blood pressure (SBP) example. The dots are the measured data points; the straight line is the linear model. For three age values (22, 47, 71), the positions of the horizontal lines indicate the predicted best guesses for the SBP (11, 139, 166).

After the definition of the model, the parameters a and b need to be determined so that the model can be actually used to predict a single best guess for the value of y when given x. In the context of ML and DL, this step of finding good parameter values is called *training*. But how are networks trained? The training of the simple linear regression and DL models is done by fitting the model's parameters to the training data—a.k.a. curve fitting.

Note that the number of parameters can be vastly different, ranging from 2 in the 1D linear regression case to 500 million for advanced DL models. The whole procedure is the same as in linear regression. You'll learn in chapter 3 how to fit the parameter of a non-probabilistic linear regression model.

So, what do we mean when we say a non-probabilistic model is fit to data? Let's look at the model $y = a \cdot x + b$ for a concrete example of predicting the blood pressure y based on the age x. Figure 1.10 is a plot of the systolic blood pressure (SBP) against the age for 33 American women. Figure 1.10 shows concrete realizations with $a = 1.70$ and $b = 87.7$ (the solid line). In a non-probabilistic model, for each age value you get only one best guess for the SBP for women of this age. In figure 1.10, this is demonstrated for three age values (22, 47, and 71), where the predicted best guesses for the SBP (111, 139, and 166) are indicated by the positions of the dashed horizontal lines.

1.4.2 *Probabilistic curve fitting*

What do you get when you fit a probabilistic model to the same data? Instead of only a single best guess for the blood pressure, you get a whole probability distribution. This tells you that women with the same age might well have different SBPs (see figure 1.11).

In the non-probabilistic linear regression, an SBP of 111 is predicted for 22-year-old women (see figure 1.10). Now, when looking at the predicted distribution for 22-year-old women, SBP values close to 111 (the peak of the distribution) are expected with higher probability than values further away from 111.

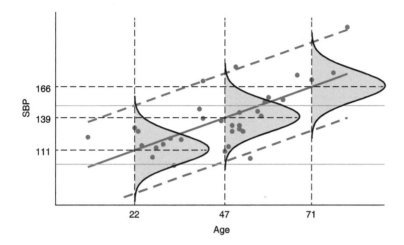

Figure 1.11 Scatter plot and regression model for the systolic blood pressure (SBP) example. The dots are the measured data points. At each age value (22, 47, 71), a Gaussian distribution is fitted that describes the probability distribution of possible SBP values of women in these age groups. For the three age values, the predicted probability distributions are shown. The solid line indicates the positions of the mean values of all distributions corresponding to the ages between 16 and 90 years. The upper and lower dashed lines indicate an interval in which 95% of all values are expected by the model.

The solid line in figure 1.10 indicates the positions of the mean values of all distributions corresponding to the age values between 16 and 90 years. The solid line in figure 1.11 exactly matches the regression line in figure 1.10, which is predicted from a non-probabilistic model. The dashed lines that are parallel to the mean indicate an interval in which 95% of all individual SBP values are expected by the model.

How do you find the optimal values for the parameters in a non-probabilistic and a probabilistic model? Technically, you use a loss function that describes how poorly the model fits the (training) data and then minimizes it by tuning the weights of the model. You'll learn about loss functions and how to use these for fitting non-probabilistic or probabilistic models in chapters 3, 4, and 5. You'll then see the difference between the loss function of a non-probabilistic and a probabilistic model.

The discussed linear regression model is, of course, simple. We use it mainly to explain the underlying principles that stay the same when turning to complex DL models. In real world applications, you would often not assume a linear dependency, and you would also not always want to assume that the variation of the data stays constant. You'll see in chapter 2 that it's easy to set up a NN that can model non-linear relationships. In chapters 4 and 5, you'll see that it is also not hard to build a probabilistic model for regression tasks that can model data with non-linear behavior and changing variations (see figure 1.12). To evaluate the performance of a trained regression model, you should always use a validation data set that is not used during training. In figure 1.12, you can see the predictions of a probabilistic DL model on a new validation set that shows that the model is able to capture the non-linear behavior of the data and also the changing data variation.

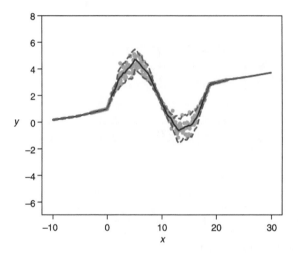

Figure 1.12   Scatter plot and validation data predictions from a (non-Bayesian) probabilistic regression model. The model is fitted on some simulated data with a non-linear dependency between *x* and *y* and with non-constant data variation. The solid line indicates the positions of the mean values of all predicted distributions. The upper and lower dashed lines indicate an interval in which 95% of all values are expected by the model.

What happens if we use the model to predict the outcome of *x* values outside the range of the training data? You can get a first glimpse when looking at figure 1.12, where we only have data between –5 and 25 but show the predictions in a wider range between –10 and 30. It seems that the model is especially certain about its predictions in the ranges where it has never seen the data. That is strange and not a desirable property of a model! The reason for the model's shortcoming is that it only captures the data variation—it does not capture the uncertainty about the fitted parameters. In statistics, there are different approaches known to capture this uncertainty; the Bayesian approach is among these. When working with DL models, the Bayesian approach is the most feasible and appropriate. You will learn about that in the last two chapters of this book.

1.4.3   *Bayesian probabilistic curve fitting*

The main selling point of a Bayesian DL model is its potential to sound the alarm in case of novel situations for which the model was not trained. For a regression model, this corresponds to extrapolation, meaning you use your model in a data range that is outside the range of the training data. In figure 1.13, you can see the result of a Bayesian variant of the NN that produces the fit shown in figure 1.12. It is striking that only the Bayesian variant of the NN raises the uncertainty when leaving the range of the training data. This is a nice property because it can indicate that your model might yield unreliable predictions.

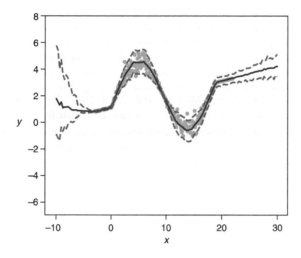

Figure 1.13   Scatter plot and validation data predictions from a Bayesian probabilistic regression model. The model was fitted on some simulated data with non-linear dependency between x and y and non-constant data variation. The solid line indicates the positions of the mean values of all predicted distributions. The upper and lower dashed lines indicate an interval in which 95% of all values are expected by the model.

1.5   When to use and when not to use DL?

Recently, DL has had several extraordinary success stories. You therefore might ask yourself whether you should forget about traditional ML approaches and use DL instead. The answer depends on the situation and the task at hand. In this section, we cover when not to use DL as well as what problems DL is useful for.

1.5.1   When not to use DL

DL typically has millions of parameters and, therefore, usually needs a lot of data to be trained. If you only have access to a limited number of features that describe each instance, then DL isn't the way to go. This includes the following applications:

- Predict the scores of a student in their first university year based on only their scores in high school
- Predict the risk for a heart attack within the next year based on the sex, age, BMI (body mass index), blood pressure, and blood cholesterol concentration of a person
- Classify the sex of a turtle based on its weight, its height, and the length of its feet

Also, in situations where you have only few training data and you know exactly which features determine the outcome of interest (and it's easy for you to extract these features from your raw data), then you should go for these features and use those as a basis for a traditional ML model. Imagine, for example, you get images from a soccer player collection of different individual French and Dutch soccer players. You know that the jerseys of the French team are always blue, and those of the Dutch team are always orange. If your task is to develop a classifier that discriminates between players of these two teams, it's probably best to decide if the number of blue pixels (the French team) in the image is larger than the number of orange pixels (the Dutch team). All other features (such as hair color, for example) that seem to discriminate between the two teams would add noise rather than help with the classification of new images. It's therefore probably not a good idea to extract and use additional features for your classifier.

1.5.2 *When to use DL*

DL is the method of choice in situations where each instance is described by complex raw data (like images, text, or sound) and where it isn't easy to formulate the critical features that characterize the different classes. DL models are then able to extract features from the raw data that often outperform models that rely on handcrafted features. Figure 1.14 displays various tasks in which DL recently changed the game.

Input x to DL model		Output y of DL model		Application
Type	Example	Type	Example	
Images		Label	"Tiger"	Image classification
Audio	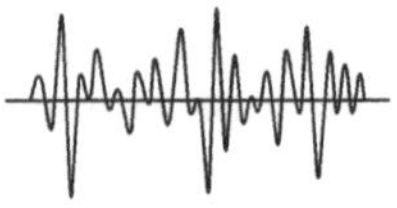	Sequence/Text	"See you tomorrow."	Voice recognition
ASCII sequences	"Hallo, wie gehts?"	Unicode sequences	你好，你好嗎？	Translation
Environment	The input is twofold. The first is the state of the world. The second part of the input is the reward for the last action (whether it was good or bad).	The output of the neural network is an action the agent does next.	Walk left/place stone at certain position on the Go board	Deep reinforcement learning; for example, Go

Figure 1.14 **The various tasks recently solved by DL that were out-of-reach for traditional ML for a long time**

1.5.3 *When to use and when not to use probabilistic models?*

You will see in this book that for most DL models, it is possible to set up a probabilistic version of the model. You get the probabilistic version basically for free. In these cases, you can only gain when using the probabilistic variant because it provides not only the information that you get from the non-probabilistic version of the model, but also additional information that can be essential for decision making. If you use a Bayesian variant of a probabilistic model, you have the additional advantage of getting a measure that includes the model's parameter uncertainty. Having an uncertainty measure is especially important to identify situations in which your model might yield unreliable predictions.

1.6   *What you'll learn in this book*

This book gives you a hands-on introduction to probabilistic DL. We'll provide exercises and code demos as Jupyter notebooks, which allow you to get experiences and so gain a deeper understanding of the concepts. To benefit from this book, you should already know how to run simple Python programs and how to fit a model to data (a simple model such as a linear regression is fine). For a deep understanding of the more advanced sections (indicated by an asterisk after the end of the heading), you should be fluent with intermediate math such as matrix algebra and differential calculus, as well as with intermediate statistics such as interpreting probability distributions. You will learn how to

- Implement DL models with different architectures by using the Keras framework
- Implement a probabilistic DL model, predicting from a given input a whole distribution for the outcome
- For a given task, choose an appropriate outcome distribution and loss function by using the maximum likelihood principle and the TensorFlow Probability framework
- Set up flexible probabilistic DL models such as currently used state-of-the-art models for image generation of text to speech translations
- Build Bayesian variants of DL models that can express uncertainties, letting you identify non-reliable predictions

We'll introduce you to the different DL architectures in the next chapter.

Summary

- Machine learning (ML) methods were invented to allow a computer to learn from data.
- Artificial neural networks (NNs) are ML methods that start from raw data and include the feature extraction process as part of the model.
- Deep learning (DL) methods are NNs that are called deep because they have a large number of layers.
- DL outperforms traditional ML methods in perceptual tasks such as grasping the content of an image or translating text to speech.
- Curve fitting is a technique that fits a model (the curve or a distribution) to data.

- DL and curve fitting are similar and rely on the same principles. These principles are at the heart of this book. Understanding these lets you build better-performing DL models in terms of accuracy, calibration, and the ability to quantify uncertainty measures for the predictions.

- Probabilistic models go beyond single value predictions and capture the variation of real data and the uncertainty of the model fit, which allows for better decision making.

- Bayesian variants of probabilistic models can help to identify unreliable predictions.

Neural network architectures

This chapter covers

- Needing different network types for different data types
- Using fully connected neural networks for tabular-like data
- Using 2D convolutional neural networks for image-like data
- Using 1D convolutional neural networks for ordered data

The vast majority of DL models are based on one or a combination of three types of layers: fully connected, convolutional, and recurrent. The success of a DL model depends in great part on choosing the right architecture for the problem at hand.

If you want to analyze data that has no structure, like tabular data in Excel sheets, then you should consider fully connected networks. If the data has a special local structure like images, then convolutional neural networks (NNs) are your friends. Finally, if the data is sequential like text, then the easiest option is to use 1D convolutional networks. This chapter gives you an overview of the different architectures used in DL and provides hints as to when to use which architectural type.

2.1 Fully connected neural networks (fcNNs)

Before diving into the details of the different DL architectures, let's look at figure 2.1. Recall the architecture of a typical traditional artificial NN that we discussed in chapter 1. The visualized NN has three hidden layers, each holding nine neurons. Each neuron within a layer connects with each neuron in the next layer. This is why this architecture is called a *densely connected NN* or a *fully connected neural network* (fcNN).

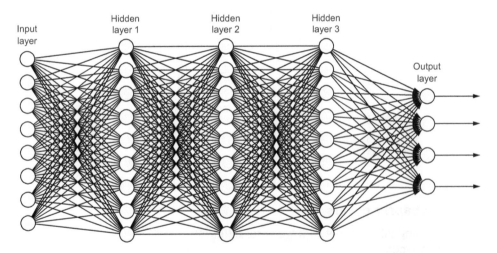

Figure 2.1   An example of a fully connected neural network (fcNN) model with three hidden layers

2.1.1   The biology that inspired the design of artificial NNs

The design of NNs is inspired by the way the brain works. You shouldn't overstretch this point; it's just a loose inspiration. The brain is a network of neurons. The human brain has about 100 billion neurons, and each neuron, on average, connects with 10,000 other neurons. Let's take a look at the brain's basic unit—the neuron (see figure 2.2).

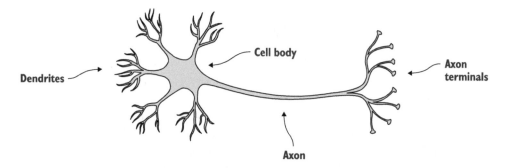

Figure 2.2 A single biological brain cell. The neuron receives the signal from other neurons via its dendrites (shown on the left). If the accumulated signal exceeds a certain value, an impulse is sent via the axon to the axon terminals (on the right), which, in turn, couple to other neurons.

Figure 2.2 shows a very simplified sketch of a neuron. It receives signals from other neurons via its dendrites. Some inputs have an activating impact, and some inputs have an inhibiting impact. The received signal accumulates and is processed within the cell body of the neuron. If the signal is strong enough, the neuron fires. That means it produces a signal that's transported to the axon terminals. Each axon terminal connects to another neuron. Some connections can be stronger than others, which makes it easier to transduce the signal to the next neuron. Experiences and learning can change the strength of these connections. Computer scientists have derived a mathematical abstraction from the biological brain cell: the artificial neuron shown in figure 2.3.

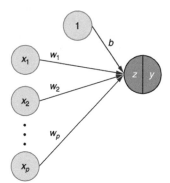

Figure 2.3 The mathematical abstraction of a brain cell (an artificial neuron). The value z is computed as the weighted sum of the input values p, x_1 to x_p, and a bias term b that shifts up or down the resulting weighted sum of the inputs. The value y is computed from z by applying an activation function.

An artificial neuron receives some numeric input values, x_i, which are multiplied with some corresponding numeric weights, w_i. To accumulate the inputs, determine the weighted sum of the inputs plus a bias term b (that gets 1 as input) as $z = x_1 \cdot w_1 + x_2 \cdot w_2 + \ldots + x_p \cdot w_p + 1 \cdot b$. Note that this formula is the same as that used in linear regression. You can then further transform the resulting z value by a non-linear activation function, the so-called sigmoid function, which transfers z to a number between 0 and 1 (see figure 2.4). This function is given by:

$$y = \sigma(z) = \frac{1}{1+e^{-z}} = \frac{e^z}{1+e^z}$$

As you can see in figure 2.4, large positive values of z result in values close to 1, and negative values with large absolute values result in values close to 0. In this sense, the resulting value y can be interpreted as the probability that the neuron fires. Or, in the context of classification, as a probability for a certain class. If you want to build a binary classifier (with 0 and 1 as possible classes), which takes several numeric features, x_i, and generates the probability for class 1, then you can use a single neuron. If you have a background in statistics, this might look familiar, and indeed, a network with a single neuron is known in statistics also as *logistic regression*. But no need to worry if you've never heard of logistic regression.

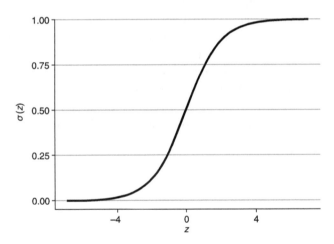

Figure 2.4   The sigmoid function *f* translating (squeezing) an arbitrary number *z* to a number between 0 and 1.

2.1.2   *Getting started with implementing an NN*

To get started working with DL, you need to know the basic data structures, the tensors, and the software packages manipulating those entities.

TENSORS: THE BASIC ENTITIES IN DL

Looking at figure 2.3, the mathematical abstraction of a neuron, you might ask the question, "What goes in and what comes out?" Assuming that $p = 3$ in figure 2.3, then you see three numbers (x_1, x_2, and x_3) entering the neuron and a single number leaving the neuron. These three numbers can be treated as an array with one index. More complex neural networks can take a grayscale image, say of size 64 × 32 as input, which can be also expressed as an array. But this time the array has two indices. The first index, i, ranges from 0 to 63 and the second, j, from 0 to 31.

Going further, say you have a color image with the colors red, green, and blue. For such an image, each pixel has x,y coordinates and three additional values. The image can be stored in an array with three indices (i, j, c). Taking it to the extreme, say you input a whole stack of 128 color images into the network. These could be stored in an array of (b, x, y, c) with b ranging from 0 to 127. Also, you can view the three weights in figure 2.3 as an array with one index, going from 0 to 2.

As it turns out, all quantities in DL can be put into arrays. In the context of DL, these arrays are called *tensors*, and from an abstract standpoint, all that happens in DL is the manipulation of tensors. The number of indices tensors have is the so-called dimension, order, or sometimes rank (so don't get confused). Tensors of order 0, like the output of the neuron in figure 2.3, have no indices. Tensors with low orders also have special names:

- Tensors of order 0 are called scalars.
- Tensors of order 1 are called vectors.
- Tensors of order 2 are called matrices.

The shape of a tensor defines how many values each index can have. For example, if you have a gray-valued image of 64×32 pixels, the shape of the tensor is (64, 32). That's all you need to know about tensors when you use DL. But be aware when you google tensors, you might find frightening stuff, like the mathematical definition by its transformation properties. Don't worry. In the context of DL, a tensor is only a data container with a special structure like, for example, a vector or a matrix. If you feel insecure with vectors and matrices, it's worth taking a look at chapter 2 of François Chollet's book, *Deep Learning with Python*, 2nd ed., (Manning, 2017), at http://mng.bz/EdPo for an in-depth explanation.

SOFTWARE TOOLS

DL has gained enormous popularity with the availability of software frameworks built to manipulate tensors. In this book, we mainly use Keras (https://keras.io/) and TensorFlow (https://www.tensorflow.org/). Currently, these two frameworks are most often used by DL practitioners. TensorFlow is an open source framework developed by Google that comes with strong support for DL. Keras is a user-friendly, high-level neural networks API written in Python and capable of running on top of TensorFlow, allowing for fast prototyping.

To work through the exercises in this book, we recommend that you use the Google Colab environment (https://colab.research.google.com) as a cloud solution that runs in your browser. The most important frameworks, packages, and tools for DL are already installed, and you can immediately start coding. If you want to install a DL framework on your own computer, we recommend you follow the description given in chapter 3 of Chollet's book at http://mng.bz/NKPN.

- To dig deeper into TensorFlow, Martin Görner's tutorial is a good starting point: https://www.youtube.com/watch?v=vq2nnJ4g6N0.
- To learn more about Keras, we recommend the website https://keras.io/.

We use Jupyter notebooks (https://jupyter.org/) to provide you with some hands-on exercises and code examples. Jupyter notebooks offer the ability to mix Python, Tensor-Flow, and Keras code with text and Markdown. The notebooks are organized in cells containing either text or code. This lets you play around with the code by changing only the code in one cell. In many exercises, we provide large parts of the code, and you can experiment in individual cells with your own code. Feel free to also change the code at any location; you can't break anything. While DL often involves huge data sets and needs enormous computing power, we distilled simple examples so that you can interactively work with the notebooks. We use the following icon to indicate the positions in the book where you should open a Jupyter notebook and work through the related code:

You can open these notebooks directly in Google Colab, where you can edit and run these in your browser. Colab is great, but you need to be online to use it. Another option (good for working offline) is to use the provided Docker container. For details on how to install Docker, see https://tensorchiefs.github.io/dl_book/. Within the Jupyter note-books, we use the following icon to indicate where you should return to this book:

SETTING UP A FIRST NN MODEL TO IDENTIFY FAKE BANKNOTES
Let's get started and do a first DL experiment. In this experiment, you use a single artificial neuron to discriminate real from fake banknotes.

 HANDS-ON TIME   Open http://mng.bz/lGd6, where you'll find a data set describing 1,372 banknotes by two features and a class label *y*.

The two image features are based on *wavelet analysis,* a frequently used method in tra-ditional image analysis. It's common to store the input values and the target values in two separate tensors. The input data set contains 1,372 instances described by two fea-tures that you can organize in one 2D tensor. The first dimension usually describes the samples. This axis is referred to as axis 0. For the example, you have a 2D tensor with a shape (1372, 2). The target values are the true class labels that can be stored in a sec-ond 1D tensor with a shape (1372).

DL models typically run on graphic cards, also called *graphic processing units* (GPUs). These GPUs have limited memory. You therefore can't process an entire data set at once. The data is split into smaller batches containing only a subset of the entire data set. These batches are called *mini-batches,* and a typical number of instances contained in a mini-batch is either 32, 64, or 128. In our banknote example, we use mini-batches with a size shape of 128.

Because the banknotes are described by only two features, you can easily see the positions of real and fake banknotes in the 2D feature space (see figure 2.5). Also, the boundary between the two classes isn't separated by a straight line.

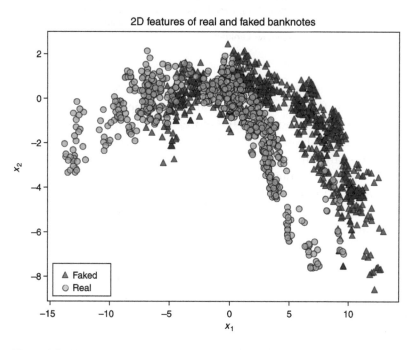

Figure 2.5   The (training) data points for the real and fake banknotes

Let's use a single neuron with a sigmoid activation function (also known as logistic regression) as a classification model (see figure 2.6). We'll separate the fake banknotes from the real banknotes for the data shown in figure 2.5.

Before we define the Keras code, let's think of the tensor structure needed. What goes into the network? If you use a single training data point, it's a vector with two entries (the next section discusses how the bias is handled). If you take a batch of size 128 of those vectors, you have a tensor of order 2 (a matrix) with the shape (128, 2). Usually one doesn't specify the batch size when defining the network. In that case, you use None as the batch size. As in figure 2.6, the input is processed by a single neuron with sigmoid activation.

NOTE   Here we only briefly discuss the main building blocks needed for our DL experiment. To learn about Keras, refer to the Keras website at https:// keras.io/, and the book, *Deep Learning With Python*, written by the creator of Keras, François Chollet.

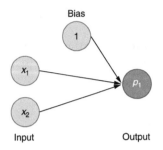

Figure 2.6   An fcNN with one single neuron. The two nodes in the input layer correspond to the two features describing each banknote. The output layer has one node that corresponds to the probability of class 1 (a fake banknote).

In listing 2.1, we use the sequential mode to define the NN model. In the sequential model definition, the layers are added one after the other. The output of one layer is the input to the next layer and so on; therefore, you usually don't need to specify the shape of the inputs to a layer. The first layer is an exception, and here you need to specify the shape of the input.

Under the hood, Keras translates the model into tensor operations. In our simple model in listing 2.1, the dense layer, Dense(1), takes the input tensor X with the dimension (batch_size, 2), multiplies it with a 2×2 matrix W, and adds a bias term b. This gives a vector of length batch_size. If this sounds strange to you, take a look at chapter 2 of Chollet's book, *Deep Learning with Python*, at http://mng.bz/EdPo to learn more about matrix multiplication.

After defining the model, it's compiled, and the used loss and an optimization function need to be specified. Here we use the loss function crossentropy, which is commonly used for classification and which quantifies how well the correct class is predicted. You'll learn more about loss functions in chapter 4. Last but not least, we optimize the weights of the model by an iterative training process, which is called *stochastic gradient descent* (SGD), discussed in chapter 3. The goal of the fitting process is to adapt the model weights so that the loss is minimized. The model weights are updated after each mini-batch, here containing 128 instances. One iteration over the complete training set is called an *epoch*; here we train for 400 epochs.

Listing 2.1   Definition of an NN with only one neuron after the input

```
model = Sequential()                          Adds a new layer to the network with a
                                              single neuron; hence, 1 in Dense(1)
model.add( Dense(1,
               batch_input_shape=(None, 2),      The input is a tensor of size (Batch
               activation='sigmoid')             Size, 2). Using None, we don't need
)                                                 to specify the batch size now.
sgd = optimizers.SGD(lr=0.15)
                                              Chooses the activation function
                                              sigmoid as in figure 2.4
Sequential starts
the definition of
the network.                                  Compiles the model, which ends
                                              the definition of the model
```

```
model.compile(
        loss='binary_crossentropy',
        optimizer=sgd
)
```

Defines and uses the stochastic gradient descent optimizer

```
history = model.fit(X, Y, epochs=400,
                    batch_size=128)
```

Fixes the batch size to 128 examples

Trains the model using the data stored in X and Y for 400 epochs

HANDS-ON TIME When running the code in the http://mng.bz/lGd6 notebook, you'll observe a decreasing loss and an increasing accuracy. This indicates that the training works fine.

Let's take the trained network, use it for a prediction, and look at the output. In figure 2.7, you see a systematic evaluation of the probability that a banknote is fake, given the features x_1 and x_2.

The shading of the background in figure 2.7 indicates the predicted probability for an instance with the corresponding values of the two features. The white color indicates positions in the feature space where the probability for both classes is 0.5. Points on the one side are classified to one class and points on the other side, to the other class. This boundary is called the *decision boundary*. As you can see, it's a line. This isn't a coincidence but a general property of a single artificial neuron with a sigmoid as an activation function. In a 2D features space, the decision boundary is a straight line. It isn't curved and has no wiggles. If you have three features, the boundary is a plane (no wiggles), and it stays as an object with no wiggles for a feature space with more than three dimensions, which is called *hyperplane*.

But in the banknote example, the true boundary between the two classes is curved. Therefore, a single neuron isn't appropriate to model the probability for a fake banknote based on its two features. To get a more flexible model, we introduce an additional layer between the input and output layers (see figure 2.8). This layer is called the *hidden layer* because its values aren't directly observed but are constructed from the values in the input layer.

In this example, the hidden layer holds eight neurons; each gets as input a weighted sum of the same input features but with different weights. The weighted sum is then transformed by the activation function. You can think about these neurons in the hidden layer as a new representation of the input. Originally, it was represented by two values (features), now it's represented by eight values (features): the output of the eight neurons. This is sometimes called *feature expansion*. You can use different numbers of neurons in the hidden layer, which is part of the design of the NN.

The output layer gives the probability for the instance to be a real or fake banknote. You have seen that one neuron is sufficient in a binary classification problem because knowing the probability p of one class fixes the probability of the other class to $1 - p$. You can also use two neurons in the output layer: one neuron modeling the probability

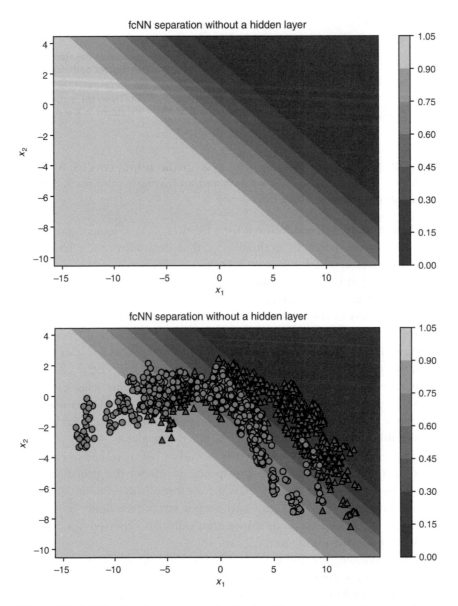

Figure 2.7   **An NN with only one neuron after the input layer produces a linear decision boundary. The shading of the background in the 2D feature space shows the probability for a fake banknote. The right side overlays the training data, showing that the linear decision curve doesn't fit nicely in the boundary between the real and fake banknotes.**

for the first class and the other neuron modeling the probability for the second class. This output layer design generalizes to classification tasks with more than two classes. In this case, the output layer has as many neurons as you have classes in the classification

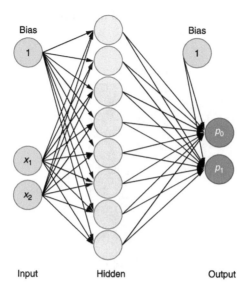

Figure 2.8 An fcNN with one hidden layer consisting of eight nodes. The input layer has two nodes corresponding to two features in the banknote data set, and the output layer has two nodes corresponding to two classes (real and fake banknotes).

problem. Each neuron stands for a class, and you want to interpret the output of the neuron as the probability for the class. This can be done using the softmax function. The softmax function takes the weighted sum z_i and transforms it into a probability p_i by setting $p_i = e^{z_i} / \sum_j e^{z_j}$.

This ensures that the values are between 0 and 1 and, further, add up to 1. You can therefore interpret p_i as the probability for the class i. The "soft" in softmax indicates that, rather than giving a hard call to one of the possible classes, the network can assign smaller probabilities to the other classes.

The y vector of the training data also has to be changed to be compatible with the two outputs. It was $y = 1$ if the example belonged to the class fake and $y = 0$ for the class real. Now you want the label to describe the two possible outputs. A real banknote should have the output values $p_0 = 1$ and $p_1 = 0$, and a fake banknote, the values $p_0 = 0$ and $p_1 = 1$. This can be achieved by a one-hot encoding of y. You start with a vector with as many zeros as you have classes (here two). Then you set one entry to 1. For $y = 0$, you set the 0th entry to 1 so that you have the vector $(1, 0)$, and for $y = 1$, you have the vector $(0, 1)$. For the architecture of the fcNN, see figure 2.8, and for the corresponding Keras code, see listing 2.2.

Listing 2.2 Definition of the network with one hidden layer

```
model = Sequential()
model.add(Dense(8, batch_input_shape=(None, 2),
                activation='sigmoid'))
model.add(Dense(2, activation='softmax'))
# compile model
model.compile(loss='categorical_crossentropy',
              optimizer=sgd)
```

Definition of the hidden layer with eight neurons

The output layer with two output neurons

As you can see in figure 2.9, the network now yields a curved decision surface, and it's better able to separate the two classes in the training data.

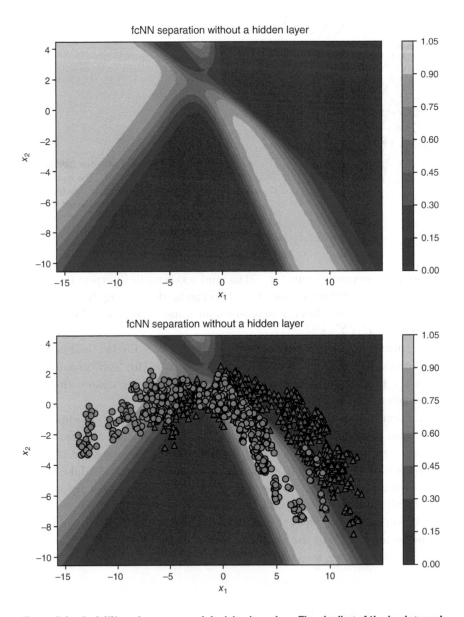

Figure 2.9   An fcNN produces a curved decision boundary. The shading of the background in the 2D feature space shows the probability for a fake banknote predicted by an fcNN with one hidden layer that contains eight neurons and uses the features x_1 and x_2 as input. The right side overlays the training data, showing that the curved decision boundary better fits the boundary between the real and fake banknotes.

HANDS-ON TIME Become a member of the DL club by just adding more hidden layers in the banknote notebook at http://mng.bz/lGd6. It's much easier than machine learning (see figure 2.10).

Figure 2.10   A DL expert at work. Inspired by http://mng.bz/VgJP.

But what's going on when adding an additional layer? In principle, the same thing as we discussed for the first hidden layer. You can see the neuron values in the added hidden layer as a new feature representation of the input. But there's one difference: the features in deeper layers aren't directly constructed from the input but from the previous layer. For example, in the second hidden layer, the features are constructed from the features in the first hidden layer (see figure 2.12). This hierarchical construction of the features is often efficient because it allows you to learn from the first layer basic features that can be used as components in several more complex features of the next layer.

By stacking many layers together, you allow the NN to construct hierarchical and complex features that get more and more abstract and task-specific when going from layer to layer. As the number of neurons per layer (and also the number of hidden layers) is part of the design, you need to decide if this number, for example, is based on the complexity of your problem and your experience, or if it's what's reported by other successful deep learners.

The good news in DL is that you don't need to predefine weights that determine how to construct the features in one layer from the features in the previous layer. The NN learns this during the training. You also don't need to train each layer separately, but you usually train the NN as a whole, which is called *end-to-end training*. This has the advantage that changes in one layer automatically trigger adaptations in all other layers. In chapter 3, you'll learn how this training process works.

2.1.3   *Using a fully connected NN (fcNN) to classify images*

Let's now use your new skills to build a larger network and see how it performs on the task of classifying handwritten digits. Different scientific disciplines have different model systems that benchmark their methods: molecular biologists use a worm called C. Elegance; people performing social network analysis use the Zachary Karate Club, and finally, people working with DL use the famous MNIST digit data set. This benchmark data set consists of 70,000 handwritten digits and is available from http://mng .bz/xW8W. The images all have 28 × 28 pixels and are grayscaled with values between 0 and 255. Figure 2.11 displays the first four images of the data set.

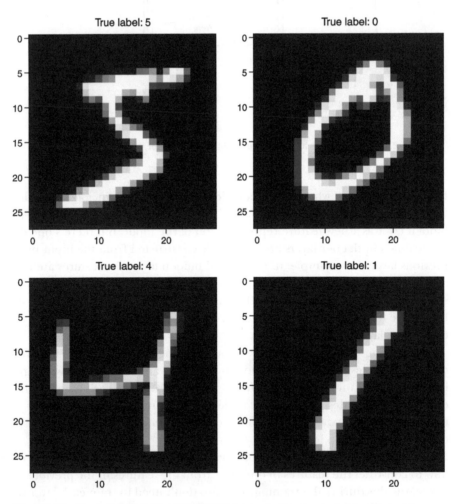

Figure 2.11   The first four digits of the MNIST data set—the standard data set used for benchmarking an NN for image classification.

This data set is well known in the machine learning community. If you develop a novel algorithm for image classification, you usually also report its performance on the MNIST data set. The MNIST images are grayscale images, and the gray value of each pixel is defined by an integer in the range from 0 to 255. For a fair comparison, there's a standard split of the data: 60,000 of the images are used for training the network and 10,000 are used for testing. In Keras, you can download the whole data set with a single line (see listing 2.3). You can also download the companion MNIST notebook for this section (on which you can work later) at http://mng.bz/AAJz.

Simple neural networks can't deal with 2D images but need a 1D input vector. Hence, instead of feeding the 28 × 28 images directly, you first flatten the image into a vector of size $28 \cdot 28 = 784$. The output should indicate whether the input image is one of the digits 0–9. More precisely, you want to model the probability that the network *thinks* that a given input image is a certain digit. For this, the output layer has ten neurons (one for each digit). You again use the activation function softmax to ensure that the computed outputs can be interpreted as probabilities (numbers between 0 and 1), adding up to 1. For this example, we also include hidden layers. Figure 2.12 shows a simplified version of the network and the definition of the corresponding model in Keras is shown in listing 2.4.

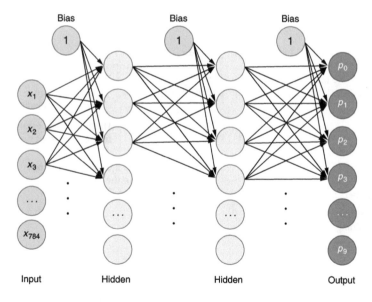

Figure 2.12 An fcNN with two hidden layers. In the MNIST example, the input layer has 784 values for the 28 × 28 pixels and the output layer has 10 nodes for the 10 classes.

Listing 2.3   Loading the MNIST data

```
from tensorflow.keras.datasets import mnist
(x_train, y_train), (x_test, y_test) = \
mnist.load_data()

X_train = x_train[0:50000] / 255
Y_train = y_train[0:50000]
Y_train = to_categorical(Y_train,10)
X_val=x_train[50000:60000] / 255
...
```

Loads the MNIST training
(60,000 images) and test set

Uses 50,000 images for training,
dividing by 255 so that the pixel
values are in the range 0 to 1

Stores the labels given as integers from
0 to 9 as one-hot encoded vectors

We do the same with
the validation set.

NOTE We don't use the test set for this listing.

Also, where we store the labels for the y_train for the network, we transform those to
categorical data of length 10 to match the output. A 1 is translated as (0,1,0,0,0,0,0,0,0,0).
This is called *one-hot encoding*. In the next listing, you can see a small fcNN using the
one-hot encoded labels Y_train.

Listing 2.4   Definition of an fcNN for the MNIST data

```
model = Sequential()

model.add(Dense(100, batch_input_shape=(None, 784),
                        activation='sigmoid'))
model.add(Dense(50, activation='sigmoid'))
model.add(Dense(10, activation='softmax'))

model.compile(loss='categorical_crossentropy',
              optimizer='adam',
        metrics=['accuracy'])

history=model.fit(X_train_flat, Y_train,
                  batch_size=128,
                  epochs=10,
                  validation_data=(X_val_flat, Y_val)
        )
```

The first hidden layer
with 100 neurons,
connected to the input
size 28 × 28 pixels

A second dense layer
with 50 neurons

The third layer connecting
to the 10 output neurons

Uses a different optimizer
than the SGD, which is
faster (see chapter 3)

Tracks the accuracy (fraction
of correctly classified training
and validation examples)
during the training

HANDS-ON TIME Now open the MNIST notebook http://mng.bz/AAJz, run it,
and try to understand the code.

When looking at the course of the loss curves over the number of iterations (figure 2.13), you can observe that the model fits the data. The performance of the
trained fcNN on the validation set is around 97%, which isn't bad, but the state of
the art is about 99%.

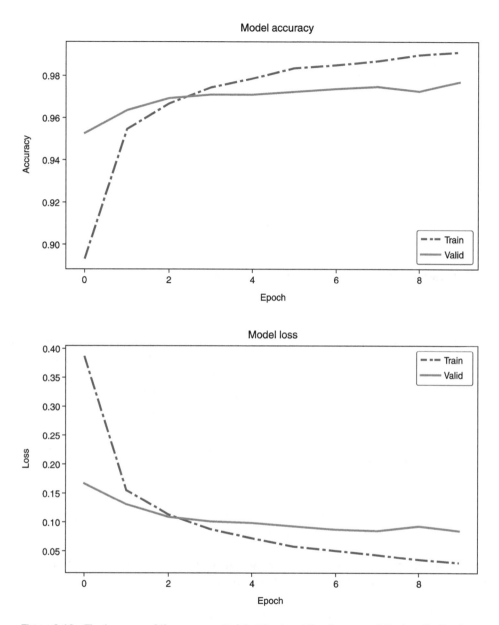

Figure 2.13   The increase of the accuracy training (top) and the decrease of the loss (bottom) during the different training steps

Play the DL game and stack more layers. Another trick that's often used is to replace the sigmoid activation function in the hidden layers with something easier: ReLU. ReLU stands for Rectified Linear Unit and is quite a mouthful for what it really does. It simply clamps values smaller than zero to zero and leaves values larger than zero as they are (see figure 2.14). It is essential to use non-linear activation functions in

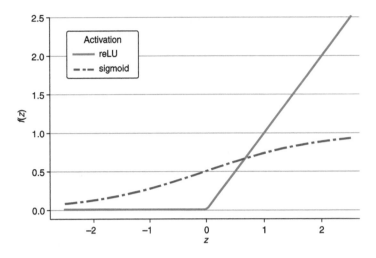

Figure 2.14   A comparison between the ReLU and the sigmoid activation functions

hidden layers, because when using a linear activation function, you can replace a stack of layers by only one layer. (This is because going through a linear layer corresponds to a matrix multiplication, and you can replace a series of matrix multiplications by one matrix multiplication.) To change the activation in Keras, simply exchange sigmoid with relu. If you like, you can change the activation function in the notebook http://mng.bz/AAJz.

Let's do a small experiment and investigate what happens if you shuffle the pixel values before you feed those into the network. Figure 2.15 shows the same digits as in figure 2.11, but this time randomly shuffled.

For each image, the pixels have been shuffled the same way. You'd have a hard time telling the right digit even after seeing thousands of training examples. Can a network still learn to recognize the digits?

HANDS-ON TIME   Try it out and play with the code in the MNIST notebook http://mng.bz/2XN0. What do you observe?

NOTE   Only follow the notebook until you reach the section "CNN as a classification model for MNIST data." We'll look at CNNs later and then revisit the notebook.

You'll probably reach the same accuracy (within statistical fluctuations) as with the original images. This might come as a surprise at first. But looking at the network architecture of an fcNN, the order of the input doesn't matter whatsoever. Because the network has no concept of nearby pixels, there's nothing like a neighborhood. People, therefore, also call fcNN *permutation invariant NN* because its performance

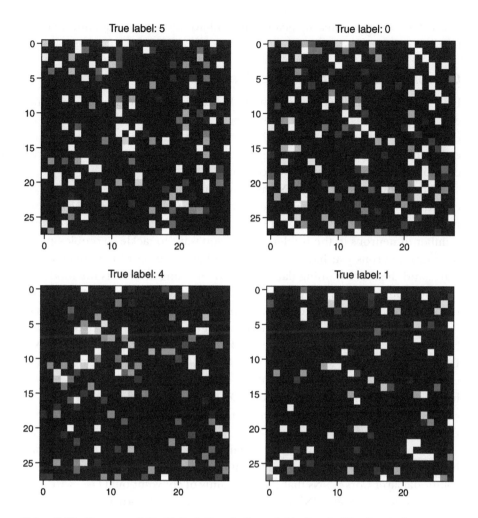

Figure 2.15 The same digits (5, 0, 4, 1) as in figure 2.11 after shuffling the pixels

doesn't depend on whether the data is permuted (shuffled). However, real image data isn't permutation invariant, and nearby pixels tend to have similar values. If you shuffle images, people will have a problem recognizing those. Moreover, two images showing the same digit don't need to show the same pixel values. You can move (translate) the image a bit, and it still shows the same object.

The fact that humans are great in visual tasks but have problems with shuffled images indicates that the evolution has found ways to take advantage of the special properties of image data. While fcNNs are good for spreadsheet-like data where the order of the columns doesn't matter, there are better architectures when the order or the spatial alignment does matter, like convolutional NNs. In principle, fcNN can be used for images, but you need many layers and huge training data sets that allow the network to learn that nearby pixels tend to have the same values and that images are translation invariant.

2.2   *Convolutional NNs for image-like data*

Fully connected NNs with even a single hidden layer can represent any function, but quickly get too big and contain so many parameters that you usually don't have enough data to fit them. Much of the progress in DL has been around creating different architectures that more efficiently exploit the structure of the data. For image data, one such architecture is convolutional NNs.

For the example of an fcNN with only one hidden layer (see figure 2.8), we discussed that you can view the number of neurons in the hidden layer as the number of new features that are constructed from the input. This implies that you need a large number of neurons in the hidden layer if you want to tackle a complex problem. But the more neurons you have in the hidden layer, the more parameters you need to learn, and the more training data you need. Stacking layers lets the model learn task-specific features in a hierarchical manner. This approach needs fewer parameters than an fcNN to construct complex features and, therefore, is less data hungry.

You learned in the last section that you get more out of an fcNN if you add more hidden layers. Going deep is a great trick to enhance the performance of NNs, giving DL its name. You also learned that an fcNN ignores the neighboring structure of pixels in an image. This suggests that there might be a better NN architecture to analyze image data. And indeed, the success of DL in the field of computer vision was not possible without some additional architectural tricks that exploit the knowledge about the local structure of image data.

The most important ingredient to tailor an NN for locally correlated data such as image data is the so-called convolutional layers. In this section, we explain how a convolutional layer works. NNs that consist mainly of convolutional layers are called *convolutional neural networks* (CNNs) and have an extremely broad range of applications including:

- Image classification, such as discriminating a truck from a road sign
- Video data prediction, such as generating future radar images for weather forecasting
- Quality control in production lines based on image or video data
- Classification and detection of different tumors in histopathological slices
- Segmentation of different objects in an image

2.2.1   *Main ideas in a CNN architecture*

Let's focus on image data and discuss a specialized NN architecture that takes into account the highly local structure within an image (see figure 2.16). In 2012, Alex Krizhevsky used this architecture in the internationally renowned ImageNet competition, which brought with it a breakthrough for DL into the field of computer vision.

Figure 2.16 An image can be broken into local patterns such as edges, textures, and so on.

We'll now dive into the architecture of CNNs and discuss how they got their name. Let's look at the main idea of a CNN: instead of connecting all neurons between two successive layers, only a small patch of neighboring pixels connects to a neuron in the next layer (see figure 2.17). With this simple trick, the network architecture has the local structure of images built in. This trick also reduces the number of weights in the NN. If you only consider small patches of, for example, 3×3 pixels as a local pattern (see figure 2.18) that's connected to a neuron in the next layer, then you have only $3 \cdot 3 + 1 = 10$ weights to learn for the weighted sum $z = x_1 \cdot w_1 + x_2 \cdot w_2 + \ldots + x_9 \cdot w_9 + b$, which is the input to the next neuron.

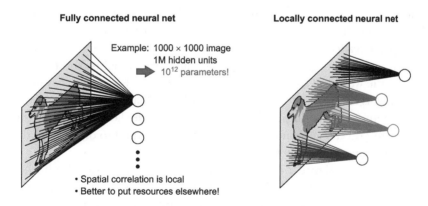

Figure 2.17 Connectivity between the input image and a neuron in the first hidden layer for an fcNN (on the left) or for a CNN (on the right). This representation ignores the bias term.

If you have experience with classical image analysis, then you know that this idea isn't new at all. What you're doing here is called *convolution*.

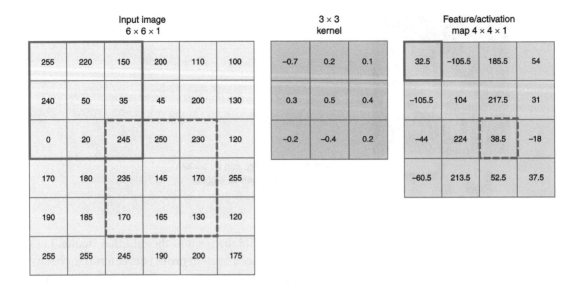

Figure 2.18 Convolution of a 6 × 6 grayscale image with a 3 × 3 kernel and a stride of 1 without padding yields as output a 4 × 4 feature map. The kernel is applied at all 16 possible positions to determine the 16 values of the activation map. Two possible kernel positions are marked in the input with thick solid and dashed borders. The respective positions of the resulting pixels in the activation map are also marked with thick solid and dashed borders. The CNN computes the resulting values by multiplying the pixel values with the overlaid kernel values and adding all terms (bias is assumed to be 0).

Have a look at figure 2.18, where you see a small image with 6 × 6 pixels and a 3 × 3 kernel[1] with predefined weights. You can slide the kernel over the image by taking steps of 1 pixel (called `stride=1`). At each position, you compute the element-wise multiplication of the image pixel and the overlaid kernel weights. You then add these values to get the weighted sum $z = x_1 \cdot w_1 + x_2 \cdot w_2 + \ldots + x_k \cdot w_k + b$, where k is the number of pixels connected to each neuron and b is a bias term. The computed value z is a single element of the output matrix. After shifting the kernel to the next position over the image, you can compute the next output value z and so on. We call the resulting output an *activation map* or *feature map*.

In the example in figure 2.18, we start with a 6 × 6 image, convolve it with a 3 × 3 kernel, and receive a 4 × 4 activation map. Sliding a kernel over an image and requiring that the whole kernel is at each position completely within the image yields an activation map with reduced dimensions. For example, if you have a 3 × 3 kernel on all sides, one pixel is knocked off in the resulting activation map; in case of a 5 × 5 kernel, 2 pixels would be knocked off. If you want to have the same dimension after applying the convolution, you can use a zero padding of the input image (called

---

[1] People in the field of DL and computer vision use the word *kernel*, but sometimes you also see the term *filter*, which can be used as a synonym.

padding='same', the argument of the convolution layer in listing 2.5; if you don't want zero padding, the argument would be padding='valid').

In CNNs, the kernel weights are learned (see chapter 3). Because you use the same kernel at each position, you have *shared weights*, and in our example, you only need to learn $3 \cdot 3 = 9$ weights to compute a whole activation map. Usually a bias term is also included in case there are 10 weights to learn. To interactively apply different kernels to a real image, see http://setosa.io/ev/image-kernels/.

What can the values in an activation map tell you? If you apply a kernel to all possible positions within the image, you get only a high signal where the underlying image shows the pattern of the kernel. Assembling the outputs to an image yields a map that shows at which positions in the image the kernel pattern appears. This is the reason why the resulting image is often called a feature map or an activation map.

Each neuron in the same activation map has the same number of input connections, and the connecting weights are also the same. (You'll soon see that real applications use more than one kernel.) Each neuron is connected to a different patch of the input (previous layer), meaning that each neuron within the same feature map looks for the same pattern but at different positions of the input. Figure 2.19 demonstrates this concept for an abstract image that consists of rectangular areas where a kernel with a vertical edge pattern is applied. We use this technique in image manipulation, for example, to enhance the edges of an image or to blur it. Visit http://setosa.io/ev/image-kernels/ to get a feel for the effect of different kernels on more complex images.

In figure 2.19, you see the vertical-edge kernel (going from bright to dark) in three positions of the image. At an image position with a vertical edge that goes from bright to dark, you get a high value (shown as dark gray pixels in the activation map). At an image position with a vertical edge that goes from dark to bright, you get a low value (shown as light gray pixels in the activation map). At positions where there's no vertical edge in the image, the resulting values are neither high nor low (shown as mid-gray pixels in the activation map). In case of the displayed filter where the weights add up to one, the values in the activation maps are zero if the input is an image patch with a constant gray value.

2.2.2 *A minimal CNN for edge lovers*

Let's imagine an art lover who gets excited if an image contains vertical edges. Your task is to predict for a set of striped images if the art lover will like those. Some of the images in the set have horizontal edges and some vertical edges. To identify the images with vertical stripes, a vertical-edge detection model would be great. For this purpose, you might want to do something similar to that depicted in figure 2.19 and perform a convolution of a predefined vertical-edge filter, using the maximal value in the resulting feature map as a score that indicates if the art lover will like the image.

Using a predefined kernel for convolution is often done in traditional image analysis when the feature of interest is known and can be described as a local pattern. In

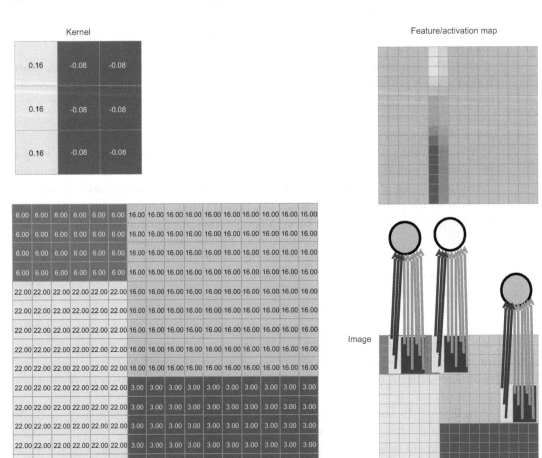

Figure 2.19   Convolution of a 3 × 3 kernel with a weight pattern that resembles a vertical edge (upper left panel) with an image consisting of squared areas (lower left and right panel) results in a feature map that highlights the positions of vertical edges in the input image (upper right panel). In the left panel, the numbers indicate the weighted values for the kernel (upper left) and the pixel values for the image (lower left).

such a situation, it'd be rather silly not to use this traditional image analysis approach. But let's pretend you don't know that the art lover likes vertical edges, and you only have a list of images that they like and dislike. You want to learn the values for the weights within the kernel that you can use for convolution. Figure 2.20 shows the corresponding network architecture, where the size of the kernel is 5 × 5. The resulting hidden layer is a feature map.

To check if this feature map indicates that the image contains the kernel pattern, you take the maximum value of the feature map. From this value, you want to predict

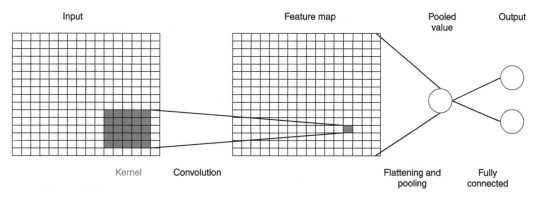

Figure 2.20   A CNN with only one hidden layer consisting of one feature map. As a pooled value, you take a maximum of all values within the feature map. You add a dense layer to determine the probability for two possible class labels in the output.

the probability that the art lover likes the image. You already saw how to do that: you add a single, fully connected layer with two output nodes and use softmax activation to ensure that the two output values can be taken as probabilities for the two classes (art lover likes the image; art lover doesn't like the image). This adds up to 1. This small CNN network (the feature map in the first hidden layer) results from the convolution of the image with a kernel. The classification is done in the fully connected part shown on the right side in figure 2.20. This architecture is probably one of the smallest possible CNNs one can think of. To model image data with TensorFlow and Keras, you need to create 4D tensors with the form:

```
(batch, height, width, channels)
```

The batch dimension corresponds to the number of images in one batch. The next two elements define the height and width of the image in units of pixels. The last dimension defines the number of channels. (A typical RGB color image has 3 channels. This means that a batch of 128 color images, each having 256 rows and columns, could be stored in a tensor of shape (128, 256, 256, 3.)

You can set up, train, and evaluate the CNN model with a few lines of Keras code (see listing 2.5). The only thing you need is a data set of images with horizontal or vertical stripes and a corresponding class label. This can be easily simulated.

HANDS-ON TIME   Open the edge lovers' notebook at http://mng.bz/1zEj and follow the instructions there to simulate the image data and fit the model. Check out which kernel weights are learned and if these form a vertical edge. If you can't reproduce the result, don't worry; just do the training again until you get the result. Investigate the impact of the activation function and the pooling method.

Listing 2.5   Edge lovers' CNN

```
model = Sequential()

model.add(Convolution2D(1,(5,5),padding='same',\          ◁──   Uses a convolutional layer
                        input_shape=(pixel,pixel,1)))            with one kernel of the size
                                                                 5 × 5 with the same padding

model.add(Activation('linear'))                          ◁──   Adds a linear
# take the max over all values in the activation map           activation function
model.add(MaxPooling2D(pool_size=(pixel,pixel)))         ◁──   (passes all values
model.add(Flatten())                                     ◁──   through)
model.add(Dense(2))                                      ◁──
model.add(Activation('softmax'))                               The MaxPooling layer
                                                               extracts the maximal
                                                               value of the feature map.
# compile model and initialize weights
model.compile(loss='categorical_crossentropy',
              optimizer='adam',                                Flattens the output of
              metrics=['accuracy'])                            the previous layer to
                                                               make it a vector

# train the model
history=model.fit(X_train, Y_train,
                  validation_data=(X_val,Y_val),               A dense layer with two
                  batch_size=64,                               neurons predicts the
                  epochs=15,                                   probabilities of two labels.
                  verbose=1,
                  shuffle=True)
```

Adds a softmax activation function to compute the probability for the two classes

NOTE   In the listing, using a convolutional layer with padding='same' means that the output feature map has the same size as the input image.

In your experiments with the edge lovers' notebook at http://mng.bz/1zEj, you've probably seen that a vertical edge kernel isn't always learned; sometimes a horizontal edge kernel is learned instead. This is perfectly fine because the data set consists of images with either horizontal or vertical edges, and the task is only to discriminate between horizontal and vertical edges. Finding no horizontal edges indicates that the image contains only vertical edges.

   In this edge lovers' example, it probably makes no difference if you use a predefined kernel or learn the weights of the kernel. But in a more realistic application, the best discriminating pattern is sometimes hard to predefine, and learning the optimal kernel weights is a great advantage of CNNs. In chapter 3, you'll learn how the weights of a model are trained.

2.2.3   *Biological inspiration for a CNN architecture*

The edge lovers' example was only a toy, and you might think that there's certainly no edge-loving neuron in a real brain. The opposite is true! The so-called visual cortex in the brains of humans and animals, indeed, have such edge-loving neurons. Two biologists, Hubel and Wiesel, received the Nobel prize in Physiology or Medicine for discovering this in 1981. The way they found this is quite interesting. And, as is often in research, there is a great deal of luck involved.

In the late 1950s, Hubel and Wiesel wanted to investigate the correlation of the neuronal activity due to stimuli in the visual cortex of a cat. For this purpose, they anesthetized a cat and projected some images on a screen in front of it. They picked a single neuron to measure the electrical signal (see figure 2.21). The experiment, however, seemed not to work because they couldn't observe the neuron firing while presenting different images to the cat. They changed the slides in the projector to those of an increasingly higher frequency. Finally, they shook the projector because a slide got stuck and then the neuron started to fire. In this manner, they discovered that neurons in different positions in the visual cortex are activated if edges with different orientations slide over the retina of the cat's eye.

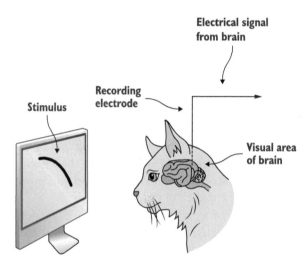

Figure 2.21 Setup of the experiment of Hubel and Wiesel in which they discovered neurons in the visual cortex that responded when they showed moving edges to a cat.

Brain research continued to develop, and now it's widely known that in the area of the brain where Hubel and Wiesel did their experiments (called the V1 region), all neurons respond to rather simple forms of stimuli on different areas of the retina. This isn't only true for cats but also for other animals and humans. It's also known that neurons in other regions of the brain (called V2, V4, and IT) respond to increasingly complex visual stimuli like, for example, a whole face (see figure 2.22). Research shows that a neuron's signal is transmitted from region to region. Also, only parts of the neurons in one region of the brain connect to the neurons in the next region. Via the connections of the neurons, the activation of different neurons is combined in a hierarchical way that allows the neurons to respond on increasingly larger regions in the retina and to more and more complex visual stimuli.

NOTE You'll see soon that the architecture of deeper CNNs are loosely inspired by this hierarchical detection of complex structures from simple

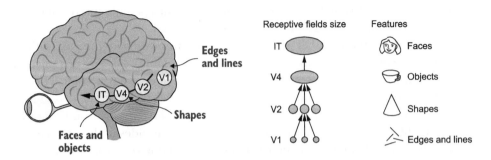

Figure 2.22   Organization of the visual cortex in a brain. Neurons in different regions respond to an increasingly larger receptive field and more and more complex stimuli.

structures. However, the analogy shouldn't be overstressed; the brain isn't wired up to form a CNN.

2.2.4   *Building and understanding a CNN*

More realistic image classification tasks can't be tackled by such a simple CNN architecture such as that depicted in figure 2.20, which only learns to detect one local image pattern like an edge. Even simple image classification tasks like discriminating between the 10 digits in the MNIST data set require learning lots of more complex image features. You can probably already guess how to do that: going deep is the main secret. But before going deep, you need to go broad and add more kernels to the first layer.

Each kernel can learn another set of weights, and so for each kernel, you get another activation map in the hidden layer (see figure 2.23). If the input has not only 1 but d channels, then the kernel also needs to have d channels to compute an activation map. For color images, $d = 3$ for (red, green, blue), and a valid kernel can be one that is active for a vertical edge in the green channel and for horizontal edges in the blue and red channels. The kernel matrix again defines the weights for the weighted sum, which determines the input to the neuron in the respective position of the activation map.

Now let's talk about analogies between fcNNs and CNNs. An fcNN learns a new set of weights for each neuron (the learning process is discussed in chapter 3) that combines the input of the former layer to a new value that can be seen as a feature of the image (see, for example, figure 2.8). In an fcNN, you can go deep by adding layers where all neurons of one layer are connected to all neurons in the next layer. In this sense, the number of kernel sets or activation maps in a CNN correspond to the number of neurons in one layer of an fcNN. If you want to go deep in a CNN, you need to add more convolutional layers. This means that you learn kernels that are again applied to the stack of activation maps of the previous layers.

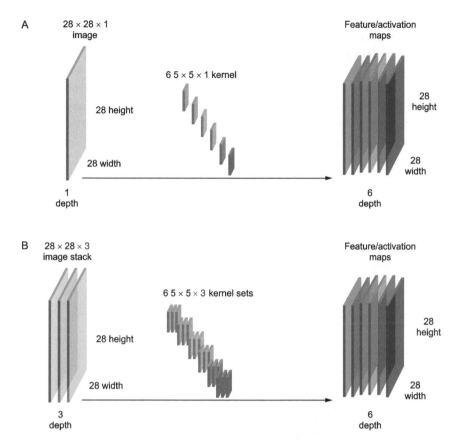

Figure 2.23 Convolution of the input image with six different kernels results in six activation maps. If the input image has only one channel (a), then each kernel has also only one channel. If the input image has three channels (b), then each filter has also three channels.

Figure 2.25 illustrates this principle. In that figure, you see a CNN with 3 convolutional layers. The convolution over a stack of activation maps isn't different than the convolution with an input of several channels. In figure 2.23, only 6 activation maps are generated from a 3-channel input image. However, learning only 6 kernels isn't common. A typical number to learn is 32 kernels in the first layer or even more kernels. (Often the number of kernels doubles when moving from layer to layer.) To reduce the number of weights in a CNN, it's also common to downsample the activation maps before doing the next round of convolution. This is often done by replacing a 2 × 2 patch of neurons in an activation map with the maximal activation. We call this step *max pooling*.

When adding more layers to a CNN, the area that a neuron sees in the original image gets larger. We call this a *receptive field*, and it's composed of all the pixels in the original image to which the neuron is connected, through all intermediate layers.

Depending on the image size and the kernel size (often after around four to ten layers), all neurons connect to the whole input image. Still, the complexity of image patterns that activate the neurons in different layers of the CNN gets higher with each layer.

When checking which images or image parts can activate a neuron in the different layers of a CNN, layers close to the input respond to simple image patterns (like edges) and layers close to the output combine these simple patterns into more complex patterns (see figure 2.24).

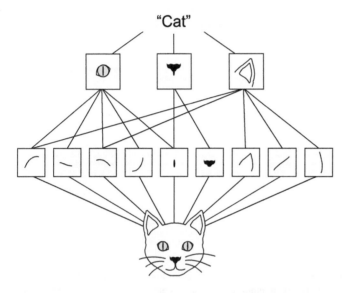

Figure 2.24   Image patterns that activate neurons in different convolutional layers of a CNN show a hierarchy of increasing complexity: simple patterns (like edges) combine into local objects (like eyes or ears) that further combine into higher-level concepts (such as a cat). Figure used with permission from François Chollet's book, *Deep Learning with Python* (Manning, 2017).

The number of convolutional layers and the numbers of kernels within each layer are *tuning parameters* in a CNN. When the complexity of the problem increases, you usually need more convolutional layers and more kernels per layer. In the last convolutional layer of the CNN, we have a new representation of the input. Flattening all neurons of this layer into a vector results in a new feature representation of the image with as many features as there were neurons in the last convolutional layer (see figure 2.25). We end up with the same situation as before: the input is described by a vector of image features. But this time, the features are results from trained kernels. Now you can add a couple of densely connected layers to construct the prediction.

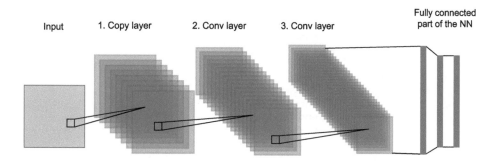

Figure 2.25　A CNN with three convolutional layers followed by three fully connected layers. The number of feature maps in each convolutional layer indicate the number of kernel sets learned. The number of elements in each layer of the fully connected part indicate the number of weighted sets learned.

Let's try a CNN on the MNIST data. In listing 2.6, you see the definition of a CNN with convolutional layers followed by fully connected layers.

 HANDS-ON TIME　Open the MNIST notebook again http://mng.bz/AAJz and fit a CNN with two convolutional layers to the MNIST data (see the second part of the notebook). Then compare the performance to what you achieved with an fcNN. Play with the code and perform a permutation experiment to check that the order of the pixels within the images matter for the performance of the CNN.

Listing 2.6　A CNN for MNIST classification

```
# define CNN with 2 convolution blocks and 2 fully connected layers
model = Sequential()

model.add(Convolution2D(8,kernel_size,\
padding='same',input_shape=input_shape))
model.add(Activation('relu'))
model.add(Convolution2D(8, kernel_size,padding='same'))
model.add(Activation('relu'))
model.add(MaxPooling2D(pool_size=pool_size))

model.add(Convolution2D(16, kernel_size,padding='same'))
model.add(Activation('relu'))
model.add(Convolution2D(16,kernel_size,padding='same'))
model.add(Activation('relu'))
model.add(MaxPooling2D(pool_size=pool_size))

model.add(Flatten())
model.add(Dense(40))
model.add(Activation('relu'))
model.add(Dense(nb_classes))
model.add(Activation('softmax'))
```

Applies the relu activation function to the feature maps

Outputs nb_classes (here 10)

Uses a convolutional layer with eight kernels of the size 3 × 3

This max pooling layer has a pooling size of 2 × 2 and a stride of 2.

Uses a convolutional layer with 16 kernels of the size 3 × 3

This max pooling layer transforms the 14 × 14 × 16 input tensor into a 7 × 7 × 16 output tensor.

Flattens the output of the previous layer resulting in a vector of length 784 (7 × 7 × 16)

Uses softmax to transform the 10 outputs to 10 prediction probabilities

```
        # compile model and initialize weights
        model.compile(loss='categorical_crossentropy',
                      optimizer='adam',
                      metrics=['accuracy'])

    # train the model
        history=model.fit(X_train, Y_train,
                          batch_size=128,
                          epochs=10,
                          verbose=2,
                          validation_data=(X_val, Y_val)
                          )
```

The first convolutional layer with eight kernels with the same padding results in an output feature map that has the same size as the input image. In the MNIST case, the input image has a size $28 \times 28 \times 1$ pixels. The resulting eight feature maps each have a size of 28×28. After the first pooling, the input has a shape of $28 \times 28 \times 8$, and the output has a shape of $14 \times 14 \times 8$.

From your experiments with the MNIST notebook at http://mng.bz/AAJz, you've learned that with this image classification task, it's easy to achieve a higher performance with a CNN (around 99%) than with an fcNN (around 96%). The permutation experiment shows that the arrangement of the pixels within the image *does* matter: the CNN performs much better when trained on the original image data (99%) than when trained on a shuffled version of the image data (95%). This supports the idea that the secret of the high performance of a CNN in image-related tasks lies in the architecture that takes the local order of an image into account. Before moving on, let us look back and emphasize some advantages of CNNs when working with image data:

- Local connectivity makes use of the local information of image data.
- You need less weight parameters in a CNN than in an fcNN.
- A CNN is to a large extent invariant to translations within the images.
- The convolutional part of a CNN allows the network to learn hierarchically task-specific abstract image features.

The next special case of data that's successfully analyzed with DL is data that shows an ordering. Let's look at that next.

2.3 *One-dimensional CNNs for ordered data*

Ordered data can be text (understood as sequences of words or characters), time series (like the daily maximum temperature in Zürich), sound, or any other data that's ordered. Applications of these algorithms include the following:

- Document and time series classification, such as identifying the topic of an article or the author of a book
- Sequence comparisons, such as estimating how closely related two documents or two stock tickers are

- Sequence-to-sequence learning, such as decoding an English sentence into French
- Sentiment analysis, such as classifying the sentiment of tweets or movie reviews as positive or negative
- Time series forecasting, such as predicting the future weather at a certain location given recent weather data

2.3.1 Format of time-ordered data

To model sequential data with TensorFlow and Keras, you need to provide that data as 3D tensors:

```
(batch, timestep, input_feature)
```

The `batch` dimension specifies the number of sequences that are processed in one batch. Using many sequences in a batch is only for performance reasons. The sequences in a batch are processed independently. This is the same situation as with the previous CNNs, where the images in a batch are also processed independently. When calculating the loss function, the results of those different sequences in a batch are averaged.

Let's look at an example. You want to predict the daily maximum temperature for tomorrow. You have 12 years of historical data, and you want to take the last 10 days into account to predict tomorrow's temperature. You choose a batch size of 128. In that case, the input tensor has the following shape: (128, 10, 1). Let's refine the model. Maybe there's information in the daily maximum temperature of five nearby cities that can help with your prediction. You also take those temperatures into account, which results in an input tensor of shape (128, 10, 6).

Another application area of ordered data is text analysis. Let's say you want to analyze text with characters as input. The `timestep` dimension specifies the position of a character within a sequence. The `input_feature` dimension holds for each sequence and timestep the actual values.

Let's take another example. Suppose you want to analyze text data in lowercase at the character level. The third sequence in the batch starts with "hello." You could encode "hello" by using the position of the letters in the alphabet as (8, 5, 11, 11, 14). Coding characters like this implies an ordering that's artificial. Therefore, in DL, categorical data is treated using one-hot encoding. See http://mng.bz/7Xrv for a more detailed description of one-hot encoding. The first two elements of this sequence in the 3D input tensor would then be:

```
input [2,0,:] = (0,0,0,0,0,0,0,1,0,0,0,0,0,0,0,0,0,0,0,0,0,0,0,0,0,0)
#                a,b,c,d,e,f,g,h,i,j,k,l,m,n,o,p,q,r,s,t,u,v,w,z,x,z
#the 1 at position 8 indicates the 8th character in the alphabet, which is h

input [2,1,:] = (0,0,0,0,1,0,0,0,0,0,0,0,0,0,0,0,0,0,0,0,0,0,0,0,0,0)
#                a,b,c,d,e,f,g,h,i,j,k,l,m,n,o,p,q,r,s,t,u,v,w,z,x,z
#the 1 at position 5 indicates the 5th character in the alphabet, which is e
```

One-hot encoding is useful if you need to model text at the character level when you have a limited number of characters. If you model text at the word level and do one-hot encoding, you need vectors with as many dimensions as you have words. These vectors would get quite large and sparse, and hence, it's better to find a denser representation. This is a step we call *embedding*, which yields a new representation of the word as a vector of numbers. In chapter 6 of Chollet's book at http://mng.bz/qMGr, you can find more details of transforming text to vectors and some demo code for Keras.

2.3.2 *What's special about ordered data?*

For text and other ordered data, the sequences often have some particular properties. The first property is that there is often no notion of a natural starting point in time. Becoming a bit philosophical, if you forget about the Big Bang for now and consider normal time spans, there's no marked starting point. This has as a consequence that all physical laws must be invariant in time. If you play table tennis, the trajectory of the ball is the same as in the 15th century. The second particularity is that time-ordered data often includes long-range dependencies. Consider the following string (taken from Wikipedia's article on Kant, https://en.wikipedia.org/wiki/Immanuel_Kant):

> *Kant was born on April 22, 1724 into a Prussian German family of Lutheran Protestant faith in Königsberg, East Prussia. . . . [thousands of words left out]. A common myth is that Kant never traveled more than 16 kilometers (9.9 mi) from Königsberg his whole life. . . . [thousands of words left out]. Kant's health, long poor, worsened and he died at _____.*

What's the probability of the next word being one of these: a) lightsaber, b) London, or c) Königsberg? This shows that there are quite long-range dependencies in sequential data. Also, lengthy range dependencies can be found in other ordered data. For example, if you consider the daily maximum temperature at an arbitrary place on earth, it's quite likely that 365 data points later, a similar temperature occurs (at least more likely than 182 days later). The last special property of ordered data occurs especially in time series, where there's a notion of past, present, and future. In this case, the future doesn't have an impact on the past. This feature is true for a time series like the temperatures in a weather forecast but not for tasks in sentiment analysis.

An optimal network should incorporate these hard facts in its design so that it doesn't need to learn them. In the case of causal networks, the architecture ensures that only information from the past has an influence on the present. Similarly, in the case of CNN for images, the architecture with shared weights ensures that the model is invariant to small spatial shifts.

2.3.3 Architectures for time-ordered data

We often analyze time-ordered data using so-called recurrent neural networks (RNNs) like long short-term memory networks (LSTMs). These networks are conceptually a bit more complicated than CNNs. Furthermore, RNNs are a bit harder to train. In many applications, RNNs can be replaced by CNNs, or as the finding of a recent research paper states it (Bai et al., https://arxiv.org/abs/1803.01271):

> *We conclude that the common association between sequence modeling and recurrent networks should be reconsidered, and convolutional networks should be regarded as a natural starting point for sequence modeling tasks.*

Because you don't need RNNs for the rest of the book, refer to chapter 6 of Chollet's book at http://mng.bz/mBea, and proceed with CNNs for sequence modeling.

USING CNNS FOR TIME-ORDERED DATA

An alternative way to handle time-ordered data is to use one-dimensional (1D) CNNs. In these 1D networks, time is treated just like a spatial dimension. You can use these 1D convolutional networks for various sequence-specific tasks like sentiment analysis. Here we demonstrate their use for predicting a time series.

For time series data, the future mustn't have any influence on the present or the past. And further, there should also be no marked starting time. You can apply the learned convolutional kernels to sequences of arbitrary size. These, therefore, can be slid over a sequence and don't treat any time point in a special fashion. Allowing only past and current time points to influence the prediction of a current or future outcome is called *causal.* You can easily apply the causal requirement by letting only values from the previous or current time influence the prediction of the current value. This leads to so-called causal convolutions. Figure 2.26 shows a simple example of a convolution of the input values 10, 20, 30 with a 1D convolution kernel of size 2 having the weight values of 1 and 2.

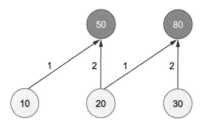

Figure 2.26 **A simple causal convolution for the values 10, 20, 30 with a kernel with weights of 1, 2. The number 50 after convolution only depends on the past and present values (10, 20) but not on the future value of 30.**

You see in figure 2.26 that the second (upper) layer has fewer elements. To make all layers the same size, a zero padding is added to the beginning of the input layer. In that case, figure 2.26 becomes figure 2.27.

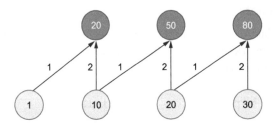

Figure 2.27 A simple causal convolution for the values 10, 20, 30 and the kernel 1, 2 with 0 padding

HANDS-ON TIME If you want to get a better understanding how 1D convolution works, you can go through the notebook http://mng.bz/5aBO. In this notebook, we also introduce time-dilated causal convolution, allowing for long-range time dependencies.

Now you've seen the basic architectural building blocks used in DL: fully connected, convolutional, and recurrent NNs. These are just building blocks, and you can use these in combination with each other. For example, you could feed an image into a convolutional network, then use an RNN to produce ordered output as text. This combination has been successfully used to create captions for images.

But, so far, we've not shown you an important part—how to do the adaptation of the weights in networks. In the next chapter, we take a step back from NNs with millions of weights to training a linear regression with just one or two weights. It's astonishing that all the architectures we discussed so far (from simple linear regression to advanced models like CNNs or time-dilated convolutional networks) can be trained with the same procedure: gradient descent.

Summary

- A fully connected neural network (fcNN) consists of stacked layers of neurons.
- In an fcNN, each neuron connects to each neuron of the previous layer.
- The input to a neuron is given by the weighted sum of the connected neurons in the previous layer.
- That weighted sum passed through an activation function computes the output of a neuron.
- The non-linearity of the activation function is essential because a stack of layers could otherwise be replaced by one layer.
- Use the `relu` activation function for hidden layers. It is known to yield a more efficient training, compared to the sigmoid activation function.
- Use `softmax` as an activation function in the output layer when doing classification. The output of the `softmax` function can be interpreted as probability for a certain class label.
- A convolutional neural network (CNN) consists of a convolutional part, where features are extracted from the input data, and a fully connected part, where the features are combined to the output of the CNN.

- The convolutional part of a CNN consists of stacked layers of feature maps.
- Each neuron in a feature map only connects to a small patch of the previous feature map. This reflects the local structure of image data.
- The high performance of deep NNs relies on the fact that they learn a hierarchy of optimal features for the given task.
- NNs work best when the NN architecture exploits a known structure of the data so that these don't have to learn it from scratch. Therefore,
  - If your data comes from images (or has other 2D structures), use 2D CNNs to exploit the local structure of images by local connections and shared weights.
  - If your data comes from sequences, use 1D convolutions if possible; otherwise, use recurrent NNs.
  - If you have no particular structure, use fcNNs.

Principles of curve fitting

This chapter covers

- How to fit a parametric model
- What a loss function is and how to use it
- Linear regression, the mother of all neural networks
- Gradient descent as a tool to optimize a loss function
- Implementing gradient descent with different frameworks

DL models became famous because they outperformed traditional machine learning (ML) methods in a broad variety of relevant tasks such as computer vision and natural language processing. From the previous chapter, you already know that a critical success factor of DL models is their deep hierarchical architecture. DL models have millions of tunable parameters, and you might wonder how to tune these so that the models behave optimally. The solution is astonishingly simple. It's already used in many methods in traditional ML: you first define a loss function that describes how badly a model performs on the training data and then tune the parameters of the model to minimize the loss. This procedure is called *fitting*.

In ML models that have simple loss functions, it's often possible to provide a formula that lets you compute the optimal parameter values from the data. Yet, this isn't the case for complex models. For complex models, it took several decades to develop sophisticated optimization procedures. DL almost exclusively uses an approach to determine the parameters: this is called *gradient descent*. In this chapter, you'll see that gradient descent is an astonishingly simple technique. It's still kind of a miracle that this technique works so well in DL, while more advanced procedures for optimization fail.

All the components needed for DL—a model with weights and a loss function used to fit the weights to the (training) data—are already present in much simpler models like linear regression. In order to give you a clear picture of the gradient descent method, we demonstrate step by step how it works for fitting a simple linear regression model. This, in fact, is the smallest neural network (NN) possible. We introduce the loss function, which is most often used to fit a linear regression model, and show how to determine the parameter values that minimize this loss function. Think of linear regression as the "hello world" of machine and deep learning. Let's have a look at linear regression through the eyes of DL.

3.1 *"Hello world" in curve fitting*

Let's look at a simple model in the form of linear regression. Imagine you're a novice medical assistant, and you work together with a gynecologist who asks you to notify her if a patient shows an unusual systolic blood pressure (SBP) during routine checks. For this purpose, she provides you with a table that shows a normal range of SBP values for each age category. According to this table, it's normal that the SBP increases with age. This raises your curiosity. You wonder whether the data is consistent with actual data measured during past routine checks. To follow up on this, you want to look at some other data. Fortunately, you're allowed to use the data from your patients for internal analysis.

As a first step, you randomly select a set of 33 patients, who during at least one visit were diagnosed as healthy by the doctor. From each of the selected patients, you note information on age and blood pressure recorded during one of the routine checks, where the patient was diagnosed as healthy. To get an impression of the data, you can produce a scatter plot where you graph the SBP value versus the age (see figure 3.1).

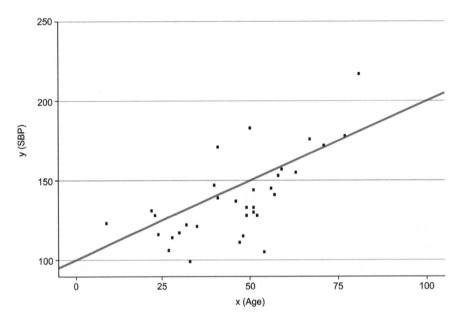

Figure 3.1 Scatter plot showing the systolic blood pressure (SBP) versus age (for women)

From figure 3.1, you can see that most SBP values are in the range 100 to 220. The scatter plot reveals that, similar to the table your boss gave you, there is indeed a trend indicating that for healthy women, blood pressure increases with age. It also makes sense that the table gives a range of normal blood pressures for each age because the relationship between age and SBP is far from deterministic. (Two healthy women with similar ages can have quite different blood pressure values.) Information in the table thus seems consistent with your observations.

You now want to go a step further and look for a model that describes how the blood pressure depends on age. Independent from individual variations in blood pressure, it seems that, on average, the SBP values somehow increase linearly with the age of the women. You can manually draw a straight line through the points to end up with something similar to the line in figure 3.1. We can describe such a straight line by the linear model

$$y = a \cdot x + b$$

where a represents the slope of the line and b is the intercept with the y-axis. Another way (which is more DL-like) is to look at the model of the graph shown in figure 3.2.

This graph is probably the smallest fully connected network (fcNN) you can think of. At the same time, it's a part of the more complicated one that was shown in figure 1.2 in chapter 1. Moreover, it graphically represents the computational steps that

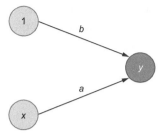

Figure 3.2 Linear regression model ($y = a \cdot x + b$) as a fully connected neural network (fcNN) or a computational graph

you need to take to compute a value for y when you have a value for x and you know the parameter values a and b:

- Take x and multiply it by a ($a \cdot x$)
- Take 1 and multiply it by b ($b \cdot 1$)
- Add both results to get $y = a \cdot x + b$

Regardless of whether you interpret the model as a line equation or as an fcNN, you can only use the model to compute an estimate for the mean y based on a given value of x when the values for a and b are fixed. Therefore, a and b are called the parameters of the model. Because the parameters enter the model linearly, we call the model a *linear model*, and because there's only one input feature x, we call it a *simple linear model*. How can you get appropriate values for the parameters a (slope) and b (intercept) of the linear model that best describes the data?

3.1.1   *Fitting a linear regression model based on a loss function*

You can use your gut feeling to manually draw a straight line through the points in the scatter plot. If you do, you might end up with a line like that shown in figure 3.1, which has a slope of $a = 1$ and an intercept of $b = 100$. You can now use this model to make predictions, say, for example, for a new patient who is 31 years old.

- If you use the network or equation representation of the model, you multiply 31 with 1 and add 100, resulting in a predicted mean SBP value of 131.
- If you use the graphical representation of the fitted line in figure 3.1, you go from $x = 31$ vertically up until you reach the fitted line and then horizontally left until you reach the y-axis.

From here, you can read the fitted value of approximately $\widehat{\text{SBP}} \simeq 130$. Fitted values are often indicated with a hat on top (see figure 3.3. and table 3.1). For convenience, we often drop these hats, and we frequently neglect the hat when reporting estimated or fitted parameter values.

If you ask different persons for an eyeball analysis and let them draw a straight line through the points in figure 3.1, you'll probably get similar but not identical linear models. To decide how good the different suggested models fit the data and to eventually find the best fitting model, you need a clear and quantitative criterion.

In figure 3.3, we show the real data points, y_i (dots), with the differences from the values predicted by the model (the many vertical lines). Statisticians call these differences between observed values and estimated values *residuals*.

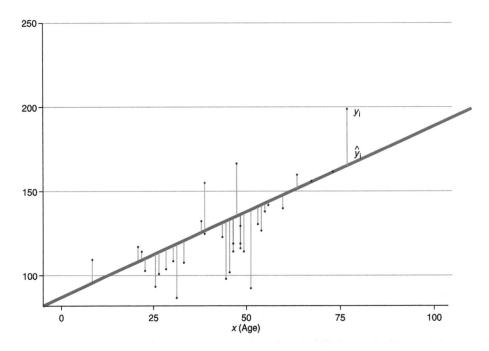

Figure 3.3   Measured data points (dots) and linear model (straight line). The differences between the data points and the linear model (vertical lines) are called residuals. Do you see the "hat" on the right?

Table 3.1   Data and derived quantities for the first 5 entries in figure 3.3, calculated with slope = 1 and intercept = 100

x	y	$\hat{y} = a \cdot x + b$	Residual	Squared residual
22	131	122	9	81
41	139	141	−2	4
52	128	152	−24	576
23	128	123	5	25
41	171	141	30	900

One famous rule, first used by Gauss in the 1790s and first published by Legendre in 1805, is the squared error criterion. You may remember this from introductory statistics courses. Simply choose *a* and *b* so that the sum of the squared errors is minimal. Why squared and not absolute or cubed values? We come to that point later in chapter 4. This is often called the *residual sum of squared errors* or RSS for short. Let's calculate the RSS for the 5 data points in figure 3.3, assuming *a* = 1 and *b* = 100.

Summing up all terms in the column Squared Residual results in an RSS of 1,586. In general the RSS is computed as:

$$\text{RSS} = \sum_{i=1}^{n} (y_i - \hat{y}_i)^2 = \sum_{i=1}^{n} (y_i - (a \cdot x_i + b))^2$$

The RSS quantifies the deviation between the observed target values y_i and the modeled values $\hat{y}_i$. It's a criterion that measures how poorly a model fits the data. Therefore, it's clear that the best fitting model has the smallest RSS. The RSS is 0 if the model perfectly fits all data points; otherwise, it's larger than 0.

You saw from the plot in the blood pressure example (figure 3.1) that RSS can't be 0 because a straight line won't go through all points. But what would be an acceptable RSS? That is almost impossible to tell because the RSS increases with each additional data point used for the fit (which doesn't lie directly on the regression line).

But the fit doesn't get worse when you use more data. If you divide RSS by the number of data points, you get the mean squared deviation of a modeled value $\hat{y}_i$ from the observed value y_i. This quantity does not systematically increase (or decrease) with the number of data points. This is called the *mean squared error* (MSE). Because the number of data points *n* is constant, the MSE is just the RSS divided by *n* and has for the same model the minimum value as the RSS (see equation 3.1). The computed *RSS* as 1,586 transforms to an *MSE* of 1,586 / 5, which equals 317.2. You get this value for the MSE if each modeled blood pressure deviates from the observed blood pressure value by $\sqrt{1586/5} = 17.8$.

Usually you don't have the same error at each data point. Because the errors contribute squared to the loss, some large errors need to be balanced by many small errors. The MSE doesn't depend on the sample size of the data and has a nicer interpretation than the RSS, so it's often preferred. We finally look at our first loss function with pride—the MSE:

$$\text{loss} = \text{MSE} = \frac{1}{n} \sum_{i=1}^{n} (y_i - \hat{y}_i)^2 = \frac{1}{n} \sum_{i=1}^{n} (y_i - (a \cdot x_i + b))^2 \qquad \textbf{Equation 3.1}$$

A close look at the formula reveals that this loss function measures the mean of the squared deviation of the observable target values, y_i, and the modeled values, $\hat{y}_i$. The model parameters *a* and *b* are the variables of the loss function for which you want to find the values that minimize the loss. Besides the parameters, the loss function depends also on the data x and y.

Now let's look at some code (see listing 3.1). For determining the value of the loss for the whole data set (not only 5 points), you need to fix the model parameters to some values (here $a = 1$ and $b = 100$) and use the formula in equation 3.1 to compute the MSE loss. (In DL, we make heavy use of linear algebra to speed up the computations.) You can write the squared residual vector in Python as follows:

$$(y - (a \cdot x + b))^2 = (y - a \cdot x - b)^2$$

This expression corresponds to the last column in table 3.1 as a vector.

Note that we dropped the row number i. The quantities y and x are now vectors; consequently, $y - a \cdot x$ is also a vector. If you look closely at the expression, you might wonder about the compatibility of the dimensions. If $y - a \cdot x$ is a vector, how can you add (or subtract) a scalar b to (or from) it? This is called *broadcasting*, and basically what happens is that b is also transformed into a vector having the same length as y with all elements having the value b. See section 2.3.2 in François Chollet's *Deep Learning with Python* (Manning, 2017) at http://mng.bz/6Qde. The following listing shows how you can compute the MSE in Python.

Listing 3.1   Calculation of the MSE in Python with NumPy

```
a = 1
b = 100
y_hat = a*x + b        ◁——  Column 3 in table 3.1
r = (y - y_hat)              (note the vector notation
MSE = np.sum(np.square(r)) / len(y)   ◁——  and broadcasting)
MSE
```

Column 3 in table 3.1 (note the vector notation and broadcasting)

MSE calculated from column 5 in table 3.1 (created, summed, and divided by the number of data points in the data set).

Column 4 in table 3.1

HANDS-ON TIME   Open the notebook http://mng.bz/oPOZ and step through the code to see how you can simulate some data, fit a linear regression model to it, and determine the MSE for a linear model with the specified parameter values. You will soon reach the first exercises in the notebook, indicated by a pen icon. In this exercise, we ask you to experiment with different parameter values. The goal is to manually find the values that yield the smallest MSE for the parameters a and b.

As described previously, you can use the data from 33 women with known age and measured blood pressure in the notebook. With this information, you can easily compute the loss for a proposed model with $a = 1$ and $b = 100$.

Let's find the best-fitting linear model! In figure 3.1, you saw that in this example, you can't find a straight line that runs through all data points. Therefore, it won't be possible to reduce the loss to zero. Instead, you want to find the parameter values for a and b that minimize the MSE.

Closed form solution for the optimal parameter estimates in a simple linear regression model

Now, you'll see a derivation of a formula that lets you directly compute the optimal parameter values from the training data. Finding the minimum of the loss function requires finding the variable values for which the first derivative gets 0. This requires solving the following two conditions for a and b:

$$\frac{\partial \text{loss}}{\partial a} = 0 \text{ and } \frac{\partial \text{loss}}{\partial b} = 0$$

You can do the calculation as an exercise resulting in a linear equation system with two equations and two unknowns: parameter a (slope) and b (intercept).

$$\hat{a} = \frac{\sum_{i=1}^{n}(x_i - \bar{x})(y_i - \bar{y})}{\sum_{i=1}^{n}(x_i - \bar{x})^2} \text{ and } \hat{b} = \bar{y} - \hat{a} \cdot x$$

As soon as you have at least two data points with different values for x_i, you can determine the solution with a formula that directly yields the parameter values after plugging in the values of the training data.

This is called a *closed-form solution*. In the previous formula, the hat above a and b indicates that these values are estimated from the data. This result is simple. It allows you to directly compute the optimal parameter estimates for $\hat{a}$ and $\hat{b}$, which minimize the MSE. All you need for that is the data (x and y). In our blood pressure example, this yields the value $\hat{a} = 1.1$ for the slope and $\hat{b} = 87.67$ for the intercept.

For this example, it's quite easy to derive the formula that lets you determine the optimal parameter values (see sidebar). This is only possible because the model has a simple loss function, and we worked with quite few data. If you work with complex models like NNs, it isn't possible to directly compute the parameters that optimize the loss from the training data (like we did in the sidebar). Another reason that hinders direct calculations for the parameters are huge data sets. With DL, you usually have too many data points and no closed-form solution. In such cases, you need to use an iterative approach. For this purpose, we use gradient descent, which we explain in the next section.

3.2 Gradient descent method

Gradient descent is the most often used iterative optimization method in ML and for almost all optimizations in DL. You'll learn how this method works, first with one parameter and then with two. Be assured that the same method also works to optimize the millions of parameters in DL models.

3.2.1 Loss with one free model parameter

To give you a clear picture of gradient descent, we want to start with the particular case where you only have to optimize one model parameter. For that, we'll stay with our blood pressure example and assume that you somehow know that the optimal value for the intercept is $b = 87.6$. In order to minimize the loss function, you only need to find the value of the second parameter, a. In this case, the loss, which we discussed previously, looks as follows:

$$\text{loss} = \frac{1}{n} \sum_{i=1}^{n} (y_i - \hat{y}_i)^2 = \frac{1}{n} \sum_{i=1}^{n} (y_i - (a \cdot x_i + 87.6))^2 = \frac{1}{n} \sum_{i=1}^{n} (y_i - a \cdot x_i - 87.6)^2$$

Based on this equation, it's easy to compute the loss for x and y from the training data for each proposed parameter a.

INTUITION OF GRADIENT DESCENT

Figure 3.4 plots the relationship between the loss and the value of the parameter a. In the figure, you can see that the minimum of the loss achieved for the value a is slightly larger than 1.

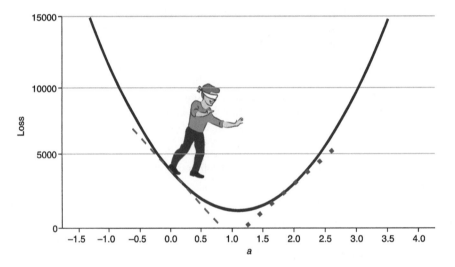

Figure 3.4 A plot of the loss (see equation 3.1) versus the free regression model parameter *a*, with *b* fixed to the optimal value. At the position *a* = 0, the tangent is plotted as a dashed line; at *a* = 2, the tangent is plotted as a dashed line.

How can you systematically find the value of the parameter a for where the loss is minimal? It might be helpful for you to imagine that the loss function is a 1D landscape in which a blind wanderer from the 1D world wants to go to the minimum. If the landscape is bowl-shaped like the loss in figure 3.4, this is quite an easy task. Even if the wanderer is blind and can only explore the local environment, it's quite clear that walking in the direction that points downwards is needed. But what does this mean with respect to (w.r.t.) the value a? That depends on the local slope. If the local slope is negative as in the position of the wanderer in figure 3.4 (see the negative slope of the dashed tangent at the position $a = 0$), a step in the direction of a larger value a

leads towards the minimum. At a position with positive local slope (see the positive slope of the dotted tangent at position $a = 2$), a step in the direction of a smaller value a leads towards the minimum.

The derivative of the function gives the slope of the tangent. Because we're looking at the loss in dependency of a, this derivative is called *gradient* and denoted by $\text{grad}_a(\text{loss})$. Its sign (positive or negative) indicates the direction where the loss function is increasing.

You can see in figure 3.4 that the curve is flatter closer to the minimum and gets steeper for points further away from that. The steeper the slope, the larger the absolute value of the gradient. If your wanderer is a mathematician, you should provide the advice to take a step in a direction that is given by the negative sign of the $\text{grad}_a(\text{loss})$ function. The step size would be proportional to the absolute value of the gradient. The wanderer should take large steps if farther from the minimum, where the slope is steep. And to avoid overstepping, taking smaller steps is needed when getting closer to the minimum, where the slope becomes flatter. Only at the minimum is the slope zero.

How do you choose the proportional factor, which is called the *learning rate*: η (eta)? This might sound picky, but you'll soon see that getting the learning rate (η) right is probably the most critical ingredient for a successful optimization using gradient descent.

The example of the blind wandering mathematician should help you develop a feel for how to systematically tune the parameter a to get to the minimum of the loss function. The wordy description presented here can be transformed into crisp mathematical instructions on how to iteratively change the parameter value, which in gradient descent is called the *update rule*.

THE UPDATE RULE IN GRADIENT DESCENT

Here's the parameter update formula according to the gradient descent optimization procedure:

$$a_{t+1} = a_t - \eta \cdot \text{grad}_a(\text{loss}) \qquad \text{\textbf{Equation 3.2}}$$

This update rule summarizes the iterative procedure of gradient descent: you first start with a random guess a_0 for the parameter value a (for example, $a_0 = 0$). Then you determine the value of the gradient of the loss function w.r.t. the parameter a. A negative sign in $\text{grad}_a(\text{loss})$ indicates the direction in which parameter a needs to be changed in order to go in the direction of decreasing loss. (You'll see in section 3.4 how to compute gradients.) The update step size is proportional to the absolute value of the gradient and to the learning rate, η (eta). Equation 3.2 ensures that you take a step in the direction of decreasing loss. You repeat this stepwise updating of parameter a until convergence. Using the found model for the parameter a leads to the model that fits the data best.

How large a learning rate, η (eta), in the update formula (equation 3.2) should you choose? You might be tempted to use a large learning rate in order to reach the minimum much sooner.

HANDS-ON TIME   Again, open the notebook http://mng.bz/oPOZ and continue to work through the code after exercise 1. This lets you see how you can determine the values for the slope and the intercept via a closed formula and how you can implement the gradient descent method to tune one parameter when the second parameter is fixed. At the end of the notebook, you will find a second exercise, where your task is to study the impact of the learning rate on the convergence. Do it.

What do you observe? You probably see that with large learning rates, the loss function gets larger and larger instead of decreasing. It finally reaches NaN or infinity in a few iterations. What happened?

Take a look at figure 3.5, which shows the dependency of the loss to parameter a, the slope in our blood pressure example. (The intercept was fixed at its optimal value of 87.6.) The only task remaining is to find the optimal value for parameter a. This is done via gradient descent. In figure 3.5, you can see the development of the value a when starting from a first guess of $a_1 = 0.5$, using three different learning rates.

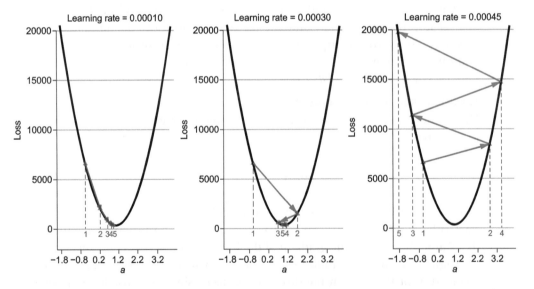

Figure 3.5   Plots of the loss from equation 3.1 versus the free regression model parameter a. It shows the results of 5 steps of gradient descent, starting with $a = 0.5$ with different learning rates. With a learning rate of 0.00010, the minimum is approximately reached in 5 steps without overshooting. With a learning rate of 0.00030, the minimum is also reached after approximately 5 steps but overshooting the position of the minimum twice. With a learning rate of 0.00045, the updates for parameter a always overshoot the position of the minimum. In this case, the updated values for a are more and more apart from the minimum. The corresponding loss grows without bounds.

In figure 3.5, you can see that the learning rate is a critical hyperparameter. If you choose a value too small, a lot of update steps are needed to find the optimal model parameter. However, if the learning rate is too large (see figure 3.5, right panel), it's impossible to converge to the position of the optimal parameter value *a* for which the loss is minimal. If the learning rate is too large, the loss increases with each update. This leads to numerical problems, resulting in NaNs or in infinity. When you observe that the loss gets infinity or NaN, there's a saying that goes, "Keep calm and lower your learning rate." The next time you see that your loss in the training set gets higher and higher instead of lower and lower, try decreasing the learning rate (dividing it by 10 is a good guess to begin with).

3.2.2 Loss with two free model parameters

Now the somewhat artificial condition of parameter *b* that's fixed at its optimal value is lifted, and the loss function is simultaneously optimized for the two parameters *a* and *b*. We've already computed the optimal values $a = 1.1$, $b = 87.67$. In figure 3.6, you see the loss function of the blood pressure example for the different values *a* and *b*.

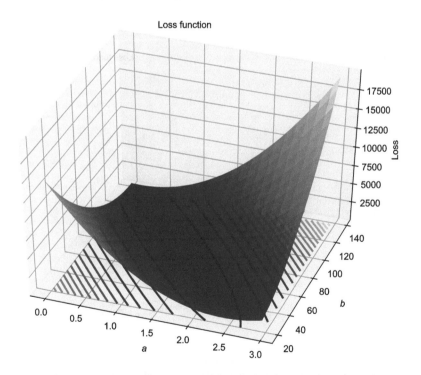

Figure 3.6 The loss function for the blood pressure data for the different values *a* and *b*. You can see that the loss function is shaped more like a ravine than a bowl. The isolines at the bottom indicate positions of equal loss values.

If you recall the parabolic shape of the 1D loss function in figure 3.4, it probably comes as a surprise to you that the 2D loss surface isn't shaped like a bowl, but rather looks like a ravine. It turns out that in most examples of linear regression, the loss surface looks more like a ravine or, to be more precise, an elongated bowl. Although these loss surfaces do have a minimum, it's flat in some directions. Ravine-like loss surfaces are hard to optimize because these need many optimization steps to reach the minimum (see later in this chapter for a more detailed example).

Let's explain the optimization for the two variables *a* and *b* with a simulated example of linear regression that has a well-behaved loss with a bowl shape and not a ravine. You return to the ravine-like shape of the loss function for the blood pressure example later.

HANDS-ON TIME   Open the notebook http://mng.bz/nPp5 and work through it until the section with the title "The gradients." You'll see how to simulate data for a simple linear regression fit where the loss function has a bowl-like shape. Figure 3.7 is produced with the code of this notebook and shows the loss surface of the simulated data set. Indeed, it's shaped like a bowl.

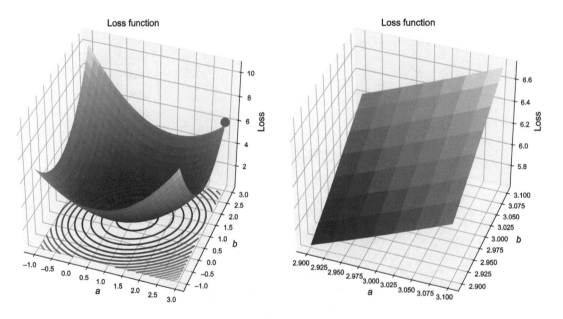

Figure 3.7   The loss function for the simulated data for the different values *a* and *b*. You can see that the loss function is shaped more like a bowl. The contour lines at the bottom indicate positions of equal loss values. The large dot indicates the position of the start value (*a* and *b* = 3). The right side shows a zoom of that region.

The optimization procedure via gradient descent is similar to the case where one variable remains fixed. Let's start with the initial values of $a = 3$ and $b = 3$; the loss function at that position is 6.15. The first step in the optimization is to find which direction shows the steepest descent and then take a small step downhill in that direction.

If you zoom very close to the initial starting point, you'll see that the bowl looks like a plate; this is true for any point of the bowl. If asked to take a small step downhill, starting from $a = 3$ and $b = 3$, you'll probably agree that it should be in the direction towards the center. How can you calculate this direction? Let's use a marble to determine this direction for us.

We place the marble at the upper right corner ($a = 3$, $b = 3$). The marble can only roll in the direction of the resultant force acting on it. As you might recall from high school physics, the resultant force is based on the forces acting in different directions (see figure 3.8). As the force in a certain direction gets stronger, the steeper the slope in that direction. We know that the slope in the direction a is grad_a. Hence, the force on the marble in direction a is proportional to (the operator $\propto$) the negative slope or gradient (as in the 1D example) in that direction:

$$f_a \propto -\mathrm{grad}_a$$

For the physics nerds, the force is given by the mass of the marble times the acceleration of gravity ($g \approx 9.81 \frac{m}{s^2}$) times grad_a. Similarly, the force in the direction b is

$$f_b \propto -\mathrm{grad}_b$$

The total force on the marble is given by this equation:

$$\vec{F} = (f_a, f_b) = -(\mathrm{grad}_a, \mathrm{grad}_b)$$

If you now release the marble, it'll roll a step in the direction of the steepest descent, which is usually not along one single axis a or b (see figure 3.8). The learning rate η

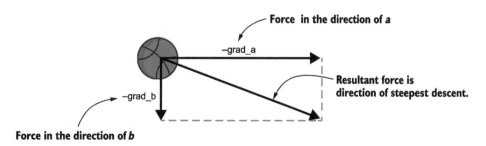

Figure 3.8 The forces dragging on the marble and the resultant direction of the steepest descent

times the gradient gives the step size. For the concrete example, this results in a new coordinate with the update formula:

$$a_{t+1} = a_t - \eta \cdot \text{grad}_a$$

$$b_{t+1} = b_t - \eta \cdot \text{grad}_b \qquad \text{Equation 3.3}$$

This shows that for determining the new position in the 2D parameter space, you need to calculate the 1D derivation twice. First, you keep b fixed at 3 and just vary a. In more mathematical terms, "You calculate the partial derivative of the loss function w.r.t. a." You keep the parameter b fixed and do the derivation of the loss function (MSE) w.r.t. a to get:

$$\text{grad}_a = \frac{\partial}{\partial a}\left(\frac{1}{n}\sum_{i=1}^{n}(a \cdot x_i + b - y_i)^2\right) = \frac{2}{n}\sum_{i=1}^{n}(a \cdot x_i + b - y_i) \cdot x_i \quad \text{Equation 3.4}$$

This is the same formula as in the 1D case (see equation 3.1). You may have noticed that we've swapped the observed y and the fitted value $ax + b$ in the squared error. However, this neither changes the value of the loss nor of the gradient, but it facilitates the notation and differentiation. To determine the partial derivative of the loss w.r.t. b, you can keep the parameter a fixed and do the derivation w.r.t. b:

$$\text{grad}_b = \frac{\partial}{\partial b}\left(\frac{1}{n}\sum_{i=1}^{n}(a \cdot x_i + b - y_i)^2\right) = \frac{2}{n}\sum_{i=1}^{n}(a \cdot x_i + b - y_i) \quad \text{Equation 3.5}$$

Now you can plug these numbers into the update formula (see equation 3.3) to get the new values for a and b. You reach the minimum of the loss function if you choose a learning rate that's small enough. If you have a bowl-like structure, you reach the minimum quite fast. But for ravine-like landscapes with a flat minimum, you finally reach the minimum value with more effort—it just takes longer.

HANDS-ON TIME Open again the notebook http://mng.bz/nPp5 and continue to work through it from the section "The gradients" onward. You'll see how to compute the gradient of the loss w.r.t parameters via the gradient formula and how to update the parameter values via the update formula. To perform the gradient descent method manually, you repeat the update step several times until you arrive close to the minimum of the loss function. The provided code uses the data that was simulated in the beginning of the notebook. At the end of the notebook, you reach an exercise indicated by the pen symbol, where your task is to perform the manual gradient method for the blood pressure data and compare the number of needed steps with the case of simulated data. You'll see that you need many more steps in the blood pressure case. The loss function has a ravine-like shape rather than a bowl-like shape as in the case of the simulated data.

Note that while the direction of the steepest descent is probed by using the marble, a real marble would follow a different path. This is due to the fact that a real marble gathers some momentum and, thus, doesn't follow the steepest descent when moving. There are some advanced methods that include the idea of momentum in gradient descent, but a standard gradient descent has no momentum. This is often misunderstood in optimization.

Similar to the simple 1D example, the learning rate is a critical parameter. Hopefully you've noticed this in the exercise and set it correctly. Another question is whether you always reach the minimum regardless of the starting values. Recall what you're doing: you start at a certain position, calculate the local direction of the steepest descent, and then go one step in that direction. The length of the step depends on the steepness and the learning rate. The steeper the descent, the larger the gradient, which corresponds to a larger step. Closer to a minimum, the curve gets flatter and the gradient smaller. This means that you should take a small step to avoid overshooting. Figure 3.9 shows this quite remarkably for a more complex landscape.

Figure 3.9 A wanderer undertaking gradient descent. At a certain position, he seeks the direction of the steepest descent. Note that the wanderer can't see the whole landscape; he just knows his altitude and the local direction of the steepest descent. He then goes down a bit (depending on the learning rate and the steepness) in the direction of the steepest descent. Do you believe he'll reach the valley? Figure inspired by the Stanford Deep Learning course (cs231n).

Concerning your simple linear regression problem, if you look at figure 3.7, you see that the loss function is shaped like a bowl, which has only one minimum. We call that a *convex* problem. It's obvious and can be shown that regardless of the starting values, the gradient descent (with a sufficiently small learning rate) always finds the (single) minimum in convex problems.

A DL model is much more flexible than a linear regression model. The loss function looks much more complicated than a higher dimensional bowl. It rather resembles the landscape with the wanderer shown in figure 3.9, which has several local minima (like the lake). It's thus quite a miracle that the simple gradient descent algorithm works fine to fit these complex DL models. Some recent research shows that usually all minima in the loss landscape of a DL model are equally good and, therefore, getting stuck in local minima isn't really a problem.

3.3   *Special DL sauce*

Simple linear regression already includes almost all ingredients necessary for training a DL model. There are only three more special tricks you need to know:

- Using mini-batch gradient descent to calculate the loss function in a typical DL setting that has millions of data points
- Using variants of the stochastic gradient descent (SGD) to speed up the learning
- Automating the differentiation process

The first two tricks are easy; the third one is a bit involved. But don't worry we will go slow. Let's start with the easy ones first.

3.3.1   *Mini-batch gradient descent*

The first trick is called *mini-batch gradient descent.* It lets you calculate the loss function in a typical DL setting with millions of data points. As you can see, the loss function depends on all data points:

$$\text{loss} = \frac{1}{n} \sum_{i=1}^{n} (y_i - \hat{y}_i)^2$$

The same applies for the gradients. In DL, you typically do the calculations on a graphics processing unit (GPU). These devices have limited memory, often too small to fit all the data on it. A solution is to use a randomly chosen subset (a mini-batch) of the data points for approximately calculating the loss function and its gradient. The gradient calculated when using a mini-batch is sometimes higher and sometimes lower than the gradient you get when using all data points. This is why mini-batch gradient descent is also referred to as stochastic gradient descent (SGD).

On an average, the gradients calculated with this mini-batch procedure don't systematically deviate from those calculated using all data points. Statisticians call this an *unbiased estimate* of the gradient. When using this unbiased estimate, the values of the parameters are updated as before. You could even just use a mini-batch of size 1 and update the weights after each training instance. In fact, some people restrict the name SGD to cases where only a single data point is used at a time to calculate the gradients and refer to the methods described as mini-batch gradient descent instead.

Deep NNs have up to many millions of parameters, and it's known that the shape of the loss landscape is far from looking like a smooth bowl (it's a non-convex problem). For non-convex problems, the gradient descent procedure might get stuck in a local minima, like the wanderer in figure 3.9 who ends up getting wet in the lake instead of reaching the global minimum at the bottom of the valley. Nevertheless, SGD works great to fit DL models.

So far, it hasn't been completely understood why the simple gradient descent procedure works so well in DL. It has been suggested that one of the reasons is that you don't need to reach the absolute global minimum but that many other minimas are fine as well. It has even been suggested that the gradient descent in DL tends to find solutions that generalize well to unseen novel data, better than the global minimum would do. DL is still in its infancy; it works, but we don't know why. Mini-batch gradient descent is one of the main ingredients to the secret sauce of DL.

3.3.2 *Using SGD variants to speed up the learning*

The second trick is a bit less spectacular and deals with variants of the SGD to speed up the learning. If you did the exercise with the blood pressure data and not the simulated one, you might wonder whether it's really necessary to have 100,000 iterations for an easy problem like linear regression. There are more advanced methods of optimization that also just calculate the local gradient, no further derivative is used, but do some more or less clever tricks. These apply the heuristics of using the values of previous iterations to speed up performance. You can think about this with reference to the marble, where the momentum depends on the direction of the steepest gradients in the previous steps.

Two prominent algorithms are RMSProb and Adam. They are included in all DL frameworks like TensorFlow, Keras, PyTorch, and others. These methods aren't fundamentally different from SGD but are of great use in speeding up the learning process, which is achieved by taking the last couple of updates into account. But for understanding the principles of DL, you don't need to know the details of these variants of SGD. We, therefore, just provide a reference that explains these techniques excellently: https://distill.pub/2017/momentum/.

3.3.3 *Automatic differentiation*

The third trick is automatic differentiation. While it's possible to calculate the gradient for the linear regression analytical by hand, this gets practically impossible for DL models. Luckily, there exist several approaches to do the dull procedure of differentiation automatically. The underlying method is nicely explained in Chollet's book, *Deep Learning with Python*:

> *In practice, a neural network function consists of many tensor operations chained together . . . , each of which has a simple, known derivative.*

Calculus tells us that such a chain of functions can be derived using the following identity, called the chain rule*:*

$$\Big(f\big(g(x)\big)\Big)' = f'\big(g(x)\big) \cdot g'(x).$$

When applying the chain rule to the computation of the gradient values of a neural network we get an algorithm called Backpropagation (also sometimes called reverse-mode differentiation). Backpropagation starts with the final loss value and works backwards from the output layer to the input layer, applying on the way the chain rule iteratively to compute the gradient of the loss with respect to each of the model parameters.

You can use these gradients to compute the updated parameter value by using the update rule. Note that the update formula, introduced earlier in this chapter (see equation 3.2), is valid for each parameter independently, regardless of how many parameters a model has. Basically, all you need is the gradient of the functions within each layer and the chain rule to glue these together. Modern DL frameworks know how to automatically apply the chain rule. These also know the gradient of the basic functions used within a NN. You usually don't have to care about those details when fitting a DL model. Let's still do it to get an idea what's going on under the hood.

3.4   *Backpropagation in DL frameworks*

In most parts of the book, you use the high-level library Keras. This library abstracts from the nasty details and lets you quickly build complex models. But as every architect should know how to lay bricks and the limits in building mechanics, a DL practitioner should understand the underlying principles. So let's get our hands dirty!

DL libraries can be grouped according to how they handle automatic differentiation. The two approaches for tackling the calculation of the gradients needed for gradient descent are as follows:

- Static graph frameworks
- Dynamic graph frameworks

Static graph frameworks like Theano were the first frameworks used in DL. But these are a bit clumsy to work with and were currently replaced or augmented with dynamic frameworks such as PyTorch. We start with the description of the static framework because it gives you a good idea what is going on under the hood. TensorFlow v2.x can handle both approaches. However, in TensorFlow v2.x, static graphs are hidden quite a bit, and you usually do not encounter these. Therefore, we now switch back to TensorFlow v1.x in the accompanying notebook http://mng.bz/vxmp. Note that this notebook does not run in the provided Docker container. We suggest that you run it in Colab. If you want to see the computational graph in TensorFlow v2.x, you can use the notebook: http://mng.bz/4AlR. However, as said, the computational graph is a bit more hidden in TensorFlow v2.0.

3.4.1 Static graph frameworks

Static graph frameworks use a two-step procedure. In the first step, the user defines the computations, like multiply *a* by *x*, add *b*, and call this *y_hat_*, and so on. Under the hood this results in a structure called a *computational graph*. The first steps in listing 3.2 show how the construction is done, but the code isn't executed yet. The code describes the construction phase of a static graph for the linear regression problem using TensorFlow v1.x (see also the notebook http://mng.bz/vxmp).

Listing 3.2 Construction of the computational graph in TensorFlow

**Variables with initial values can be optimized later.
We name them so that they look nicer in the graph.**

```
# x,y are one dimensional numpy arrays
# Defining the graph (construction phase)
tf.reset_default_graph()              ◁—  Constructs a new graph
a_    = tf.Variable(0.0, name='a_var')    from scratch
b_    = tf.Variable(139.0, name='b_var')
x_    = tf.constant(x, name='x_const')   Constants that are fixed
y_    = tf.constant(y, name='y_const')   tensors, which hold the
                                         data values
y_hat_ = a_*x_ + b_
mse_ = tf.reduce_mean(tf.square(y_ - y_hat_))   Symbolic operations
writer = tf.summary.FileWriter("linreg/",       create new nodes in the
              tf.get_default_graph())            computational graph.
writer.close()      Writes the graph
                    for visualization
```

Listing 3.2 defines the building of the static computational graph for the linear regression problem in TensorFlow. After the graph is defined, it can be written to disk. This is done in the last two lines of the listing.

> **NOTE** Google provides a component called TensorBoard, where you can visualize the computational graph. To learn more about TensorBoard, you can refer to Chollet's book at http://mng.bz/QyJ6.

Figure 3.10 displays the output of the computational graph. In addition, we added some comments (shown with arrows). If you want to reproduce it, just follow the steps in the notebook http://mng.bz/vxmp.

Say namaste to the computational graph, meditate, and feel the tensors flowing! TensorFlow lays out computational graphs from bottom to top. Let's start at the lower left corner with the variable *a_* (named a_var in the graph). This corresponds to line 2 of listing 3.2. This variable is multiplied by the constant 1D tensor (vector) *x_* (named x_const in the figure), which holds the 33 values. This is done in the node Mul of the computational graph. This is defined in the tiny a_*x_ part of line 6 of listing 3.2.

In general, in figure 3.10, the edges are the flowing tensors, and the nodes are operations like multiplication. After the multiplication, the result of *a* times *x* is still a

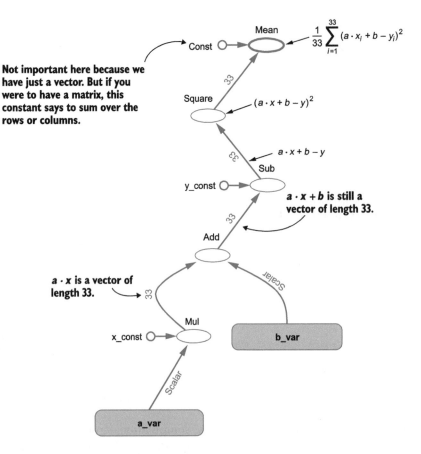

Figure 3.10 The static graph built using listing 3.2 as displayed in TensorBoard with some additional annotations (indicated by arrows).

1D tensor holding 33 values. Going up the graph, b is added, y is subtracted, and finally the expression is squared. When entering the Mean node, we still have a 1D tensor holding 33 values, which are then summed and divided by 33.

A minor detail in figure 3.10 is the constant Const entering from the left side. Usually the tensors in DL are more complex than 1D tensors; for example, 2D tensors (matrices). The Mean node then needs to know whether to average over the rows or the columns.

After you stepped through the computational graph, let's now flow the numbers $a = 0$ and $b = 139$ through the graph (139 is the mean of the blood pressure, and the slope $a = 0$ implies that the model predicts this mean for each woman regardless of her age). For this, we need a materialization/instantiation of the graph—in TensorFlow lingo, a session. The next listing shows this.

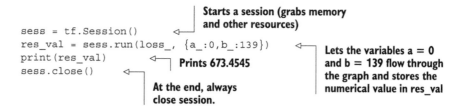

Listing 3.3 Let the tensors flow, a feed-forward pass

```
sess = tf.Session()
res_val = sess.run(loss_, {a_:0,b_:139})
print(res_val)
sess.close()
```

Starts a session (grabs memory and other resources)

Lets the variables a = 0 and b = 139 flow through the graph and stores the numerical value in res_val

Prints 673.4545

At the end, always close session.

Now that the computation graph is defined, it's easy for TensorFlow to calculate the gradients. The loss here is the MSE (see equation 3.1), which is calculated at the very top of the graph. You have seen in the computational graph shown in figure 3.10 that the MSE can be computed by performing a couple of basic operations: addition, subtraction, multiplication, and squaring. For the gradient descent update rule, you need the gradient of the MSE w.r.t. a and b. The chain rule from calculus guarantees that this can be calculated by going back through the graph. Every node you pass on your way back to a (or b) contributes an additional factor. This factor is the derivative of the output of the node w.r.t to its input. It's called the *local gradient*.

You'll now see how this is done, step by step, for a concrete example. This example shows that when you lower the MSE via the gradient update rule, the better the fit. Additionally, you can calculate the gradients in two ways: directly via equations 3.3 and 3.4 and step-by-step via backpropagation in the computational graph.

We demonstrate this fitting procedure with our blood pressure example via SGD. To keep the discussion simple, we use a mini-batch size of 1 (pick a single training example) and do one update step manually. We start with the mean blood pressure 139 and the slope 0 ($b = 139$ and slope $a = 0$); see the solid line in figure 3.11. For the first round of SGD, we randomly pick a patient, say number 15. This patient is $x = 58$ years old and has a blood pressure of $y = 153$ (see the only filled data point in figure 3.11). The initial model predicts for that age a blood pressure of 139. The resulting residuum is visualized by the vertical line between the data point and the model prediction. The current loss for this data point is the square of the residuum. We now update the model parameters a and b to lower the loss for the selected patient. To do so, we use the update rule (see equation 3.2) for which we need to compute the gradients of the loss w.r.t. the two model parameters a and b.

Let's calculate the gradients in two ways. First, you use the formulae for the gradients that you get with $n = 1$, $a = 0$, $b = 139$, $x = 58$, and $y = 153$:

$$\frac{\partial \text{MSE}}{\partial a} = \frac{2}{n} \sum_{i=1}^{n} (a \cdot x_i + b - y_i) \cdot x_i = 2 \cdot (0 \cdot 58 + 139 - 153) \cdot 58 = -1624$$

and

$$\frac{\partial \text{MSE}}{\partial b} = \frac{2}{n} \sum_{i=1}^{n} (a \cdot x_i + b - y_i) = 2 \cdot (0 \cdot 58 + 139 - 153) = -28$$

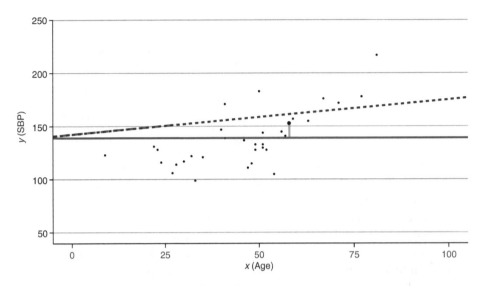

Figure 3.11   The blood pressure data set where we use only one data point in the first round of SGD fitting. This picked data point is visualized as a filled dot. The initial linear model is represented by the solid line and has a slope a = 0 and intercept b = 139. The dashed line represents the linear model after the first update and has a slope a = 0.3 and an intercept slightly larger than b = 139.

Knowing that these values of the gradients of the MSE loss w.r.t. to the parameters a and b are both negative tells you that you need to increase the parameter values to lower the loss in order to get closer to the picked data point. You can check that this makes sense by looking at figure 3.11. The modeled value on the line should go up at the position $x = 58$ to get closer to the observed value $y = 158$. This can be achieved in two ways: by increasing the intercept and by increasing the slope. We updated the values of a and b by using the formula in equation 3.2 with a learning rate $\eta = 0.0002$ to get:

$$b_{t+1} = b_t - \eta \cdot \text{grad}_b = 139 - 0.0002 \cdot (-28) = 139.0056$$

and

$$a_{t+1} = a_t - \eta \cdot \text{grad}_a = 0 - 0.0002 \cdot (-1624) = 0.3248$$

The dashed line in figure 3.11 shows the resulting linear model with updated values a and b. Now let's update the parameter values the TensorFlow way by using the computational graph and then check to see if we get the same results.

You first start to calculate the loss in what's called the forward pass. The intermediate results are written on the left side of figure 3.12. You do the computation step by step and give the intermediate term names to keep track of those. (You'll need them later in the backward pass.) You start on the lower left side by multiplying a by

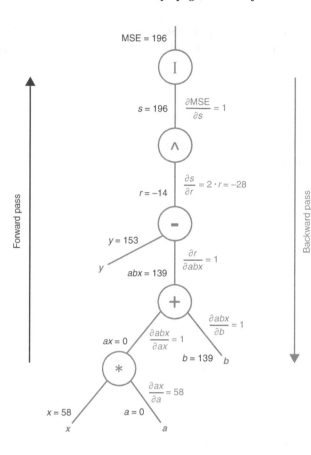

Figure 3.12 The forward and backward pass for the concrete blood pressure example with one data point ($x = 58$, $y = 153$) and the initial parameter values $a = 0$ and $b = 139$. The left side of the graph shows the flowing values in the forward pass; the right side shows the flowing values of the gradients during the backward pass.

x: $ax = a \cdot x = 0 \cdot 58 = 0$. Then you add $b = 139$ to it and get 139. Working your way further up the graph, you subtract $y = 153$, yielding $r = -14$. Then you square that to get $s = 196$.

In this case ($n = 1$), the mean operation does nothing. It's just the identity (written with I in figure 3.12), and the final loss is 196.

Let's do the backward path to calculate the partial derivatives of the loss w.r.t of the parameters. You want to keep track of the intermediate quantities (s, r, abx, and ax) shown in figure 3.12. Hence, you build the partial derivatives of the MSE loss according to those intermediate quantities you pass on your way back to the parameters a and b. To determine the partial derivative of the loss function MSE w.r.t. b, you simply walk down the graph from MSE to b and multiply the local gradients as you encounter those on your way back. The local gradients are the derivatives of the outcomes of a certain operation w.r.t. its incoming value:

$$\frac{\partial \text{MSE}}{\partial b} = \frac{\partial \text{MSE}}{\partial s} \cdot \frac{\partial s}{\partial r} \cdot \frac{\partial r}{\partial abx} \cdot \frac{\partial abx}{\partial b}$$

Let's verify that this is indeed the gradient of MSE w.r.t to b. We treat symbols like ∂s as variables (shocking real mathematicians) and cancel these out on the right side of the formula:

$$\frac{\partial \text{MSE}}{\partial b} = \frac{\partial \text{MSE}}{\cancel{\partial s}} \cdot \frac{\cancel{\partial s}}{\cancel{\partial r}} \cdot \frac{\cancel{\partial r}}{\cancel{\partial abx}} \cdot \frac{\cancel{\partial abx}}{\partial b}$$

You can see that the terms in the product of partial derivatives are the local gradients. To calculate the local gradients, you need the derivatives for the basic operations that are shown in figure 3.13.

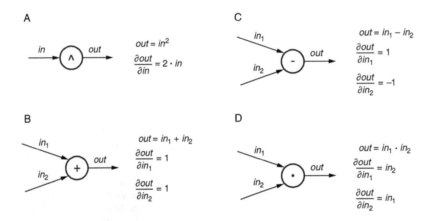

A

$$out = in^2$$
$$\frac{\partial out}{\partial in} = 2 \cdot in$$

B

$$out = in_1 + in_2$$
$$\frac{\partial out}{\partial in_1} = 1$$
$$\frac{\partial out}{\partial in_2} = 1$$

C

$$out = in_1 - in_2$$
$$\frac{\partial out}{\partial in_1} = 1$$
$$\frac{\partial out}{\partial in_2} = -1$$

D

$$out = in_1 \cdot in_2$$
$$\frac{\partial out}{\partial in_1} = in_2$$
$$\frac{\partial out}{\partial in_2} = in_1$$

Figure 3.13   Local gradients for the backward pass in the linear regression example. The circles contain the operations you need, which are square (^), addition (+), subtraction (−), and multiplication (·).

Let's do the calculation with the current values ($x = 58$, $y = 153$, $a = 0$, and $b = 139$) and determine the terms needed to compute the partial derivative of the MSE w.r.t. b:

$$\frac{\partial \text{MSE}}{\partial b} = \frac{\partial \text{MSE}}{\partial s} \cdot \frac{\partial s}{\partial r} \cdot \frac{\partial r}{\partial abx} \cdot \frac{\partial abx}{\partial b}$$

You start on the top of the computational graph with:

$$\text{MSE} = s \Rightarrow \frac{\partial \text{MSE}}{\partial s} = 1$$

The next local gradients are

$$s = r^2 \Rightarrow \frac{\partial s}{\partial r} = 2 \cdot r = 2 \cdot (-14) = -28 \qquad \textbf{(see "A" in figure 3.13)}$$

$$r = abx - y \Rightarrow \frac{\partial r}{\partial abx} = 1 \qquad \text{(see "C" in figure 3.13)}$$

$$abx = a \cdot x + b \Rightarrow \frac{\partial abx}{\partial b} = 1 \qquad \text{(see "B" in figure 3.13)}$$

This yields the gradient of the loss along the *b* axis:

$$\frac{\partial \text{MSE}}{\partial b} = \frac{\partial \text{MSE}}{\partial s} \cdot \frac{\partial s}{\partial r} \cdot \frac{\partial r}{\partial abx} \cdot \frac{\partial abx}{\partial b} = 1 \cdot (-28) \cdot 1 \cdot 1 = -28$$

Multiplying the local gradients together gives you the same value as the closed formula. Similarly, you can calculate the gradient w.r.t. to *a*. You don't need to walk down the graph from scratch, however, but can take a shortcut, starting at the value of –28 and multiplying it with $\frac{\partial ax}{\partial a} = 58$ to yield –1,624. This is the expected value for the gradient of the MSE w.r.t. *a*. This static graph approach is used under the hood when TensorFlow (or any other DL framework using static graphs, like Theano) calculates the gradients.

 HANDS-ON TIME Open the notebook http://mng.bz/XPJ9 and verify the numerical values of the local gradients. Note that we calculated all the intermediate values and gradients just for demonstration of the backpropagation procedure. If you want to use gradient descent to get the fitted parameter values, you use a simpler code like the example in the notebook http://mng.bz/vxmp.

Usually you don't need to apply the gradients in the gradient descent update formula by hand. Instead, you can use an optimizer like `tf.train.GradientDescent-Optimizer()` for that. Listing 3.4 shows the optimizer for the graph. Calling it once will do a single gradient descent step with a given learning rate. This is shown at the very end of the notebook http://mng.bz/vxmp.

Listing 3.4 Fitting the computational graph in TensorFlow

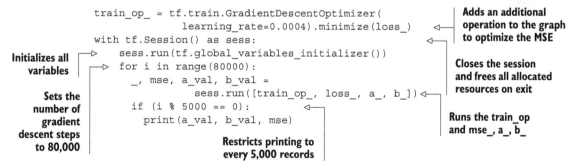

```
train_op_ = tf.train.GradientDescentOptimizer(
        learning_rate=0.0004).minimize(loss_)
with tf.Session() as sess:
    sess.run(tf.global_variables_initializer())
    for i in range(80000):
        _, mse, a_val, b_val =
                sess.run([train_op_, loss_, a_, b_])
        if (i % 5000 == 0):
            print(a_val, b_val, mse)
```

Adds an additional operation to the graph to optimize the MSE

Closes the session and frees all allocated resources on exit

Initializes all variables

Sets the number of gradient descent steps to 80,000

Restricts printing to every 5,000 records

Runs the train_op and mse_, a_, b_

As you can see in the listing, that's quite some code. For that reason, higher-level frameworks were developed to work in conjunction with TensorFlow; Keras is one such framework to work on top of TensorFlow (and other) DL libraries. Keras is also included in the TensorFlow distribution, so you don't have to install anything to use it. Chollet's book, *Deep Learning with Python*, covers Keras in detail.

You can view linear regression as a simple NN, having a dense layer with no applied activation function. (Keras uses the word *linear* to mean no activation.) The second line in listing 3.4, the Dense layer, holds the instruction for a linear combination of x weighted with the parameter a and the bias parameter b to determine the output $ax + b$ of the only node in the output layer. Further, you can build the whole graph and the optimizer with four lines of Keras code as shown in the following listing.

Listing 3.5   Construction of the computational graph in Keras

```
model = Sequential()                                    ◄─────────  Starts building the model
model.add(Dense(1,input_dim=1, activation='linear'))    ◄─┐
opt = optimizers.SGD(lr=0.0004)                           │ Adds a single
model.compile(loss='mean_squared_error',optimizer=opt)    │ dense layer with no
                                                          └ activation function
```

Adding a dense layer with no activation function in this listing is linear regression (see also listing 2.1 and figure 3.2). The following listing shows the training in Keras for fitting the computational graph.

Listing 3.6   Fitting the computational graph in Keras

```
for i in range(0,80000):
    model.fit(x=x,y=y,batch_size=33,
                    epochs=1,
                    verbose = 0)
    a,b=model.get_weights()
    if i % 5000==0:
        mse=np.mean(np.square(model.predict(x).reshape(len(x),)-y))
        print("Epoch:",i,"slope=",a[0][0],"intercept=",b[0],"MSE=",mse
```

 HANDS-ON TIME   Open the notebook http://mng.bz/yyEp to see the complete code of listings 3.5 and 3.6. Go ahead and play with these.

3.4.2   *Dynamic graph frameworks*

The main issue with static libraries is that due to the two-step procedure (first building the graph and then executing it), debugging is quite cumbersome. In dynamic graph frameworks, the graph is defined and evaluated on the fly. You therefore have access to the real numerical values at every point in the code. This has tremendous advantages when it comes to debugging. Moreover, static graphs have the disadvantage that you can't include conditionals and loops in these in order to react dynamically for different input. Chainer and Torch were two of the first frameworks that allowed such dynamical computations. The downside of Torch is that the host language is Lua, a programming language not commonly used. In 2017, Torch switched from Lua to

PyTorch, and many DL practitioners started using that framework. As a reaction, TensorFlow now also includes the possibility of a dynamic graph, called *eager execution.*

Listing 3.7 displays the TensorFlow code for the linear regression problem using eager execution (see also the notebook http://mng.bz/MdJQ). The framework doesn't need to build a static graph anymore. You can stop at any point and each tensor has a value associated with it. TensorFlow in eager mode still needs to calculate the gradients for the individual operations but does this in parallel to executing the code. TensorFlow internally stores the intermediate values needed for calculation of the gradients in an entity called `tape`.

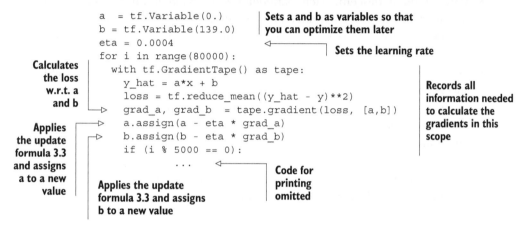

Listing 3.7 Linear regression with `TF.eager`

```
a  = tf.Variable(0.)          Sets a and b as variables so that
b = tf.Variable(139.0)        you can optimize them later
eta = 0.0004
for i in range(80000):                      Sets the learning rate
  with tf.GradientTape() as tape:
    y_hat = a*x + b                              Records all
    loss = tf.reduce_mean((y_hat - y)**2)        information needed
    grad_a, grad_b  = tape.gradient(loss, [a,b]) to calculate the
    a.assign(a - eta * grad_a)                   gradients in this
    b.assign(b - eta * grad_b)                   scope
    if (i % 5000 == 0):
        ...                    Code for
                               printing
                               omitted
```

Calculates the loss w.r.t. a and b

Applies the update formula 3.3 and assigns a to a new value

Applies the update formula 3.3 and assigns b to a new value

As you can see, there's no separation between the construction and execution of the code. The line `with tf.GradientTape() as tape:` tells TensorFlow to keep track of all differentiations using a so-called tape mechanism. Because it takes some time to store the intermediate values, you only want this to take place when you really need it. This is great for debugging and developing complex networks. However, there is a price to pay. Especially if you use many small operations, the eager approach can get quite slow. But there is a solution. If you put all the relevant code in a function and decorate this function with the `@tf.function` decorator, the code in the function gets compiled into a graph and then runs much faster.

With TensorFlow v2.0, you have the best of both worlds: eager execution during development and a graph-based framework in production. The following notebook contains an example of how to use `@tf.function`; further details can be found at https://www.tensorflow.org/guide/function.

In addition to the notebooks discussed, we also provide a notebook using the `autograd` library in Python to automatically calculate the gradient; see the notebook http://mng.bz/aR5j. In the next chapter, we'll really start our journey and encounter the first principle with which loss functions can be derived—the principle of maximum likelihood (MaxLike).

Summary

- Linear regression is the mother of all parametric models and is one of the smallest neural networks (NNs) you can think of.
- You can fit a parametric model by minimizing a loss function that quantifies the deviation between the model and the data.
- The mean square error (MSE) is an appropriate loss function for regression models.
- Gradient descent is a method for finding the parameter values that minimize the loss function. Gradient descent is a simple, general method that you can use for all kinds of parametric models, as long as the loss function is differentiable.
- With gradient descent, each parameter is updated iteratively and independently from the other parameters. This requires determining the gradient of the loss function with regard to each parameter. In addition, you need to define a learning rate.
- Getting the learning rate right (not too low or too high) is most important for successful fitting. With DL, you can perform a stochastic version of gradient descent (SGD) that estimates the gradients based on a random subset of the data (a mini-batch) instead of using all the data.
- DL frameworks like TensorFlow or Keras use backpropagation to determine the required gradients.
- The optimizers used in DL are variants of SGD that accelerate the learning process by additionally taking advantage of past gradients.

Part 2

Maximum likelihood approaches for probabilistic DL models

Part 2 of this book focuses on using neural networks (NNs) as probabilistic models. You might remember from chapter 1 that there is a primary difference between a non-probabilistic and probabilistic model. A *non-probabilistic model* outputs only one best guess for the outcome, whereas a *probabilistic model* predicts a whole probability distribution over all possible outcomes. In the cab driver example (see section 1.1), the predicted outcome distribution for the travel time for a given route was a Gaussian. But until now, you haven't learned how to set up an NN for a probabilistic model. You learn different methods to do so in this part of the book.

In the case of classification, you already know how to get a probability distribution for the outcome. In the fake banknote example (see section 2.1), you set up an NN that predicted for a given banknote a probability for the class *fake* and for the class *real*. In the MNIST classification example (see sections 2.1.3 and 2.2.4), you used different NN architectures to predict for a handwritten digit ten probabilities for ten possible classes. To do so, you defined an NN that had in the last layer as many nodes as there are classes. Further, you used a softmax activation to ensure that the output can be interpreted as a probability: the values that are between zero and one and that add up to one. Thus, classification NNs are probabilistic models by construction.

What about regression problems? In chapter 3, we looked at linear regression. It turns out that all regression problems can be seen as probabilistic models. While classification problems are by definition probabilistic models, regression problems need to be interpreted a little bit to become probabilistic models.

In this part of the book, you learn how to choose for different regression tasks an appropriate distribution and how to estimate its parameters by an NN. Why are we so excited about introducing probabilistic models? Recall the cab driver from section 1.1. He increased his chances of getting the tip using a probabilistic satnav (GPS). There are many other applications in which it is critical to quantify the uncertainty of a prediction. Imagine, for example, a DL model that takes as input an X-ray image of your chest and outputs one of two treatments: surgery or wait and see. Now, feed your image into the model. The non-probabilistic model outputs surgery. The probabilistic model outputs 51% for surgery being the best treatment and 49% for just waiting as the best treatment. Well, we guess with such an uncertain prediction, you would give it a second thought if you want to get the operation. At least, you would like to get a second opinion by a real doctor who might also spot the reason for this untypical high uncertainty. The second great property of probabilistic models is that there is a single, unique way to calculate the loss functions and to rate the performance of the probabilistic model. This unique way is the *likelihood* function.

In this part, you learn about the maximum likelihood approach and see how to use it to determine an appropriate loss function for classification tasks and regression tasks. As you will see, the maximum likelihood approach is a very mighty and intuitive principle. You'll learn how to use the maximum likelihood approach for more advanced probabilistic models, such as prediction models for count data, text-to-speech models, or a model that generates realistic-looking facial images. As it turns out, the maximum likelihood principle is behind almost all loss functions used in DL.

Building loss functions with the likelihood approach

THIS CHAPTER COVERS

- Using the maximum likelihood approach for estimating model parameters
- Determining a loss function for classification problems
- Determining a loss function for regression problems

In the last chapter, you saw how you can determine parameter values through optimizing a loss function using stochastic gradient descent (SGD). This approach also works for DL models that have millions of parameters. But how did we arrive at the loss function? In the linear regression problem (see sections 1.4 and 3.1), we used the mean squared error (MSE) as a loss function. We don't claim that it is a bad idea to minimize the squared distances of the data points from the curve. But why use squared and not, for example, the absolute differences?

It turns out that there is a generally valid approach for deriving the loss function when working with probabilistic models. This approach is called the *maximum likelihood approach* (MaxLike). You'll see that the MaxLike approach yields for the linear regression the MSE as loss function for some assumptions, which we discuss in detail in this chapter.

Concerning classification, you used a loss function called categorical cross entropy (see section 2.1). What is categorical cross entropy and how do you get to it in the first place? You probably can guess by which approach you can derive this loss function. It turns out that the likelihood function is your friend. It yields cross entropy as an appropriate loss function in classification tasks.

4.1 Introduction to the MaxLike principle: The mother of all loss functions

The fact that the MaxLike is the key to the "secret" behind almost all DL and ML applications is sketched in figure 4.1.

Figure 4.1   Unmasking the secrets of almost all loss functions in machine learning (ML in the figure) and in deep learning (DL). After https://www.instagram.com/neuralnetmemes/.

To demonstrate this principle, we start with a simple example far away from DL. Consider a die with one face showing a dollar sign ($) and the remaining five faces displaying dots (see figure 4.2).

Figure 4.2   A die with one side showing a dollar sign and the others displaying a dot

What is the probability that the dollar sign comes up if you throw the die (we assume fair die here)? On average, you get a dollar sign in one out of six cases. The probability of seeing a dollar sign is thus $p = 1/6$. The probability that this won't happen and you see a dot is $5/6 = 1 - p$. Let's throw the die ten times. What is the probability that you see the dollar sign only one time and the dot nine times? Let's assume first, that you see the dollar sign in the first throw and you see dots in the next nine throws. You could write this in a string as:

$.........

The probability for that particular sequence to happen would be $\frac{1}{6} \cdot \frac{5}{6} \cdot \frac{5}{6} \cdot \frac{5}{6} \cdot \frac{5}{6} \cdot \frac{5}{6} \cdot \frac{5}{6} \cdot \frac{5}{6} \cdot \frac{5}{6} \cdot \frac{5}{6} = \frac{1}{6} \cdot \frac{5}{6}^9 = 0.032$ or with $p = \frac{1}{6}$ as $p^1 \cdot (1 - p)^{10-1}$. If we only ask for the probability that a single dollar sign and nine dots occur in the ten throws regardless of the position, we have to take all of the following ten results into account:

```
$.........
.$........
..$.......
...$......
....$.....
.....$....
......$...
.......$..
........$.
.........$
```

To occur, each of these ten distinct sequences have the same probability of $p \cdot (1 - p)^9$. This yields a probability of $10 \cdot p \cdot (1 - p)^9$ for the event that you observe one out of these ten sequences. In our example, we use $p = 1/6$ and we get 0.323 for the probability that one dollar sign occurs during the ten throws. You might get curious and ask yourself what is the probability for two dollar signs in ten throws? The probability for a particular ordering (say $$........) is $p^2 \cdot (1 - p)^8$. It turns out that there are now 45 possible ways[1] to rearrange a string like $.$....... or $..$......: the total probability of two dollar signs and eight dots is thus $45 \cdot (\frac{1}{6})^2 \cdot (\frac{5}{6})^8 = 0.2907$.

---

[1]   Although it's not important for the rest of the book, if you are curious how to get the number 45, it is the number of all permutations 10! corrected by (divided by) the number of indistinguishable permutations. That is 10! / (2! · 8!) = 45 in our case. For more details, see for example, http://mng.bz/gyQe.

The die-throwing experiment where we count the successful throws with upcoming dollar signs is an example of a general class of experiments called *binomial experiments*. In a binomial experiment, you count the number of successes (here seeing a $) in n trials (here throwing a die), where all the trials are independent from each other and the probability for success is the same in each trial. The number of successes in a binomial experiment with n trials is not fixed but can usually take any values between 0 and n (if p is not exactly 0 or 1). For this reason, the number of successes, k, is called a *random variable*. To emphasize that k is a random variable coming from a binomial distribution, one writes:

$$k \sim \text{binom}(n, p)$$

The ~ symbol reads "stems from" or "is distributed like" a binomial with n equal to the number of tries and p equal to the probability of success in a single try. In the context of this book, it is not so important how to derive the probability of a certain k. But there is a SciPy function called `binom.pmf` to calculate this with the arguments k equals the number of successes, n equals the number of tries, and p equals the probability for success in a single try. Using this function, we can plot the probability that 0 to 10 dollar signs occur in 10 throws. See listing 4.1 for the code and figure 4.3 for the result.

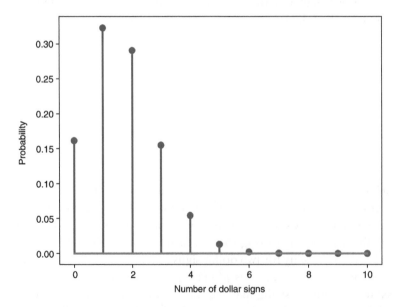

Figure 4.3   Probability distribution for the number of observed dollar signs in 10 die throws. The probability of a dollar sign in an individual throw is $p = 1/6$. The probabilities for one and two dollar signs turning up (0.323 and 0.2907) is the same as that calculated by hand. This figure is created using the code in listing 4.1.

Listing 4.1 The probability for 0 to 10 thrown dollar signs using the `binom` function

```
from scipy.stats import binom
ndollar = np.asarray(np.linspace(0,10,11)\
            , dtype='int')
pdollar_sign = binom.pmf(k=ndollar, n=10, p=1/6)
plt.stem(ndollar, pdollar_sign)
plt.xlabel('Number of dollar signs')
plt.ylabel('Probability')
```

◁─┤ **The numbers of successes (thrown dollar signs), 0 to 10 as 11 integers**

◁─┐ **The probability of throwing 0, 1, 2..., dollar signs, each with the probability p = 1/6**

So far, so good. You might remember this from your probability class. Now we turn the tables. Consider the following situation: you are in a casino and play a game in which you win if the dollar sign appears. You know that there are a certain number of faces (0 to 6) with the dollar sign, but you don't know how many. You observe ten throws of the die and two dollar signs come up in those throws. What do you guess for the number of dollar signs on the die? Surely it cannot be zero because you observed a dollar sign, and on the other hand, it cannot be six either because you would have observed no dots. But what would be a good guess?

Looking at listing 4.1 again, you suddenly have a genius idea. Simply calculate the probabilities to observe two dollar signs in ten throws again, but this time assume that your die has not only one face with a dollar sign, but it's on two faces. Then assume your die has a dollar sign on three faces and again determine the probability to see two dollar signs in ten throws and so on. Your observed data is fixed (two dollar signs in ten throws), but your assumed model of how the data is generated changes from a die with zero dollar faces to a die with 1, 2, 3, 4, 5, or 6 dollar faces. The probability to observe a dollar sign in one throw can be seen as a parameter in your model of the die. This parameter takes the values $p = 0/6, 1/6, 2/6, \ldots, 6/6$ for your different die models. For each of these die models, you can determine the probability to observe two dollar signs in ten throws and plot it in a chart (see figure 4.4).

HANDS-ON TIME Open http://mng.bz/eQv9. Work through the code until you reach the first exercise. For this exercise, it is your task to determine the probability of observing a dollar sign twice in 10 die throws if you consider a die that has dollar signs on 0, 1, 2, 3, 4, 5, or all 6 faces. Plotting the computed probabilities yields the plot in figure 4.4.

What do we see in figure 4.4? Starting from the left, if you have zero dollar signs on the die then the probability that you observe two dollar signs in ten throws is zero. Well, that was expected. Next, compute the probability to observe two times a dollar sign in ten throws, assuming that you have only one dollar sign on the die ($p = 1/6$). This is nearly 0.3. If you assume a die with two dollar signs, then the probability to observe two dollar signs in ten throws is approximately 0.20 and so on. What would you guess is the number of dollar signs on the die? You would guess one because a die with one dollar sign has the highest probability to yield two dollar signs in ten throws. Congratulations! You have just discovered the MaxLike principle.

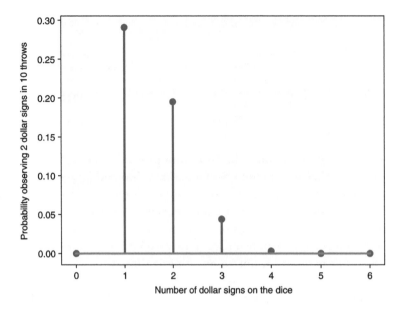

Figure 4.4   Likelihoods for observing *k* = 2 dollar signs in *n* = 10 throws for the different number of dollar signs on the die

THE MAXLIKE MANTRA   Choose the model's parameter(s) so that the observed data has the highest likelihood.

In our case, the parametric model is the binomial distribution that has two parameters: the success probability, p, per trial and the number of conducted trials, n. We observed the data $k = 2$ dollar signs at $n = 10$ throws. The parameter of the model is p, the probability that a single die throw shows a dollar sign. The likelihood for different numbers of dollar signs on the die is shown in figure 4.4. We choose the value with maximal likelihood ($p = 1/6$), corresponding to one dollar sign on the die.

There is one small subtlety. The probabilities in figure 4.4 are unnormalized probabilities in the sense that these do not add up to 1 but to a constant factor instead. In our case, this factor is 0.53. Therefore, the probabilities are not probabilities in the strictest sense, which must add up to 1. This is the reason we speak of likelihoods instead of probabilities. But we can still use these likelihoods for ranking, and we pick the model yielding the highest likelihood as the most probable model. Also, for simple cases such as ours, we could divide each likelihood by the sum of all likelihoods to transform those into proper probabilities. Let's recap the steps in this MaxLike approach for determining the best parameter values:

1 You need a model for the probability distribution of the observed data that has one or several parameters.

   Here the data was the number of times you saw the dollar sign when throwing the die ten times. The parameter p of the binomial distribution was the probability p of the die showing a dollar sign (the number of faces on the die showing dollar signs divided by six).

2 You use the model to determine the likelihood to get the observed data when assuming different values of the parameter in the model.

Here you computed the probability to get two dollar signs in ten throws when your assumed die has either 0, 1, 2, 3, 4, 5, or 6 dollar faces.

3 You take the parameter value for which the likelihood to get the observed data is maximal as the optimal parameter value. This is also called the Max-Like *estimator*.

Here the ML estimator is that the die has one side with a dollar sign.

4.2 Deriving a loss function for a classification problem

In this section, we show you how to apply the MaxLike principle to derive the loss function for classification problems and to demystify the ten-dollar word *categorical cross entropy*. It turns out that this quantity is quite simple to calculate, and you will see how you can use it for sanity checking your models.

4.2.1 Binary classification problem

Let's revisit the fake banknote example from chapter 2 (see listing 2.2, which we repeat here).

> **Listing 2.2 Definition of a classification network with two hidden layers**

```
model = Sequential()
model.add(Dense(8, batch_input_shape=(None, 2),
                     activation='sigmoid'))
model.add(Dense(2, activation='softmax'))
# compile model
model.compile(loss='categorical_crossentropy',
                     optimizer=sgd)
```

This loss, the 'categorical_crossentropy', from listing 2.2 is now explained.

You also used 'categorical_crossentropy' for all classification problems in chapter 2: the fcNN, the CNN applied to the MNIST handwritten digits classification problem, and the CNN for detecting stripes in an art piece. This loss function is generally used for classification problems in DL.

To explain 'categorical_crossentropy', let's start with the banknote example. In that case, the output of the first neuron (labeled p_0 in figure 4.5) is the probability that the model "thinks" a given input x belongs to a class 0 (a real banknote). The output of the other neuron (labeled p_1 in the figure) is the probability that x describes a fake class. Of course, p_0 and p_1 add up to one. This is assured by the softmax activation function (see chapter 2).

We now use the MaxLike principle to derive the loss function. What is the likelihood of the observed data? The training data in classification problems comes in pairs (x_i and y_i). In the banknote example, x_i is a vector with two entries and y_i is the true

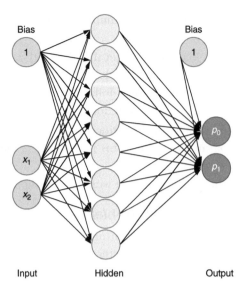

Bias

Bias

p_0

p_1

x_1

x_2

Input   Hidden   Output

Figure 4.5   The classification network for banknotes described by the features x_1 and x_2 with two outputs yielding the probability for a real banknote (p_0) or a fake banknote (p_1). This is the same as figure 2.8 in chapter 2.

class of the example (banknote is fake or real). The CNN (see figure 4.5) takes an input x and outputs a probability for each possible class. These probabilities define the conditional probability distribution (CPD) for a given x (see the figure in the following sidebar). The likelihood of the observed (true) outcome class, y_i, is given by the CPD for the true class y_i. For an NN with known weights and a given input x_i, the likelihood is given by $p_0(x_i)$ if the true class is $y_i = 0$ or by the output $p_1(x_i)$ if the true class is $y_i = 1$.

> **IMPORTANT**   Keep this in mind: the likelihood of a classification model for a given training example (x_i, y_i) is simply the probability the network assigns to the correct class y_i.

As an example, a well-trained network returns a high value for p_1 if the training example is from class 1 (fake banknote). What is the probability for the training set as a whole? Here we make the assumption that all the examples in the training are independent from each other. Then the probability of the whole training data set is simply the product of the individual probabilities. For example, imagine you throw a regular die twice and you ask for the probability to have a 1 in the first throw and a 2 in the second. This is simply $1/6 \cdot 1/6$ because the throws are independent. This carries on and, in general, the likelihood of the whole training set is the product of all individual examples. We go from one training example after another and look at what is the probability for the true class. Then we take the product of all those probabilities.

We could also order the probabilities as follows: first, in our example, we take the real banknotes (for which $y = 0$) and multiply the predictions p_0 together. Then, we take the fake ones and multiply p_1 together. Let's say you have five banknotes in your training set. The first three examples come from real banknotes, the last two examples from fake ones. You get from the NN for all banknotes the probabilities to belong to class zero (p_0) or to class one (p_1). Then the likelihood of all five banknotes is

$$P(\text{Training}) = p_0(x_1) \cdot p_0(x_2) \cdot p_0(x_3) \cdot p_1(x_4) \cdot p_1(x_5) = \prod_{j=1}^{3} p_0(x_j) \cdot \prod_{j=4}^{5} p_1(x_j)$$

The $\prod$ in the equation tells you to take the product, and Σ tells you to take the sum. In general, this can be written as:

$$P(\text{Training}) = \prod_{j \text{ with } y=0} p_0(x_j) \prod_{j \text{ with } y=1} p_1(x_j) \qquad \textbf{Equation 4.1}$$

We can also explain equation 4.1 in a slightly different way, based on formulating the probability distribution for an outcome Y (see the sidebar). Because this point of view can help you to digest the ML approach from a more general perspective, we give this explanation in the following sidebar.

MaxLike approach for the classification loss using a parametric probability model

The NN with fixed weights in figure 4.5 outputs the probabilities for all possible class labels y when feeding in a certain input x. This can be written as the probability distribution for the outcome Y, which depends on the input value x and the weights of the NN:

$$P(Y = k | X = x, W = w) = \begin{cases} p_0(x, w) & \text{for } k = 0 \\ p_1(x, w) & \text{for } k = 1 \end{cases} \text{ with } \sum p_i = 1$$

$Y = k$ states that the random variable Y takes a specific value k. In the equation, you can further read the vertical bar as "with given" or "conditioned on." To the right of the bar comes all given information, which is used to determine the probability of the variable to the left of the bar. Here you need to know the value of the input x and the weight W of the NN to compute the outputs of the NN, which are p_0 and p_1. Because the probability distribution depends on x, it is called a *conditional probability distribution* (CPD). Often you see a simpler version of this equation that skips the part to the right of the bar (either only $W = w$ or both $X = x$ and $W = w$) and that assumes this is self-evident.

$$P(Y = k) = \begin{cases} p_0 & \text{for } k = 0 \\ p_1 & \text{for } k = 1 \end{cases} \text{ with } \sum p_i = 1$$

This probability distribution where the outcome Y can only take the value 0 or 1 is known as *Bernoulli distribution*, which has only one parameter p. From this, you can directly compute $p_0 = 1 - p_1$. The following figure shows this probability distribution for the binary outcome Y.

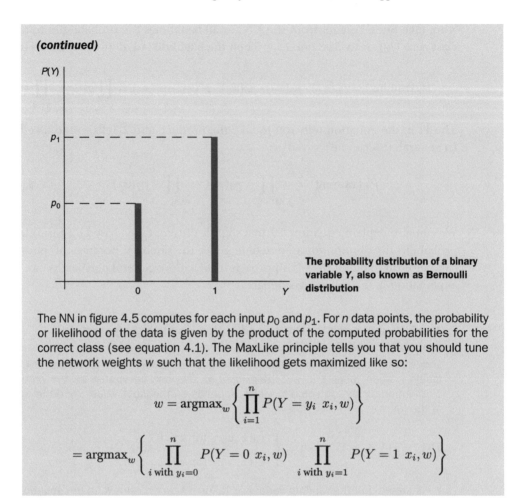

(continued)

The probability distribution of a binary variable Y, also known as Bernoulli distribution

The NN in figure 4.5 computes for each input p_0 and p_1. For n data points, the probability or likelihood of the data is given by the product of the computed probabilities for the correct class (see equation 4.1). The MaxLike principle tells you that you should tune the network weights w such that the likelihood gets maximized like so:

$$w = \text{argmax}_w \left\{ \prod_{i=1}^{n} P(Y = y_i \mid x_i, w) \right\}$$

$$= \text{argmax}_w \left\{ \prod_{i \text{ with } y_i=0}^{n} P(Y = 0 \mid x_i, w) \prod_{i \text{ with } y_i=1}^{n} P(Y = 1 \mid x_i, w) \right\}$$

In principle, we are now done. We could maximize equation 4.1 by tuning the weights of the network. You do not need to do this by hand, but you can use any framework such as TensorFlow or Keras. Both of these can do (stochastic) gradient descent.

There is still a practical issue remaining. The p_0 and p_1 in equation 4.1 are numbers between 0 and 1, and some of these might be small. Multiplying many numbers in the range 0 to 1 yields numerical problems (see listing 4.2).

Listing 4.2   Numerical instabilities when multiplying many numbers between 0 and 1

```
import numpy as np
vals100 = np.random.uniform(0,1,100)
vals1000 = np.random.uniform(0,1,1000)
x100 = np.product(vals100)
x1000 = np.product(vals1000)
x100, x1000
```

Multiplies 100 numbers randomly between 0 and 1.0

Multiplies 1,000 numbers randomly between 0 and 1.0

A typical result (7.147335361549675e-43, 0.0) for 1,000 numbers gives you 0.

If we take more than a few hundred examples, the product is so close to zero that it is treated as a zero due to the limited precision of the floating-point numbers in a computer. DL uses typical floating-point numbers of type float32, and for those, the smallest number (next to zero) is approximately 10^{-45}.

There is a trick to fix this issue. Instead of $P(\text{Training})$ in equation 4.1, you can take the logarithm of the likelihood. Taking the logarithm changes the values of a function but does not change the position at which the maximum is reached. As a side note, the property that the maximum stays the same is due to the fact that the logarithm of x is a function that strictly grows as x gets larger. Functions with this property are called *strictly monotonic* functions. In figure 4.6, you see an arbitrary function $f(x)$ and its logarithm $\log(f(x))$. The maximum of both $f(x)$ and $\log(f(x))$ is reached at $x \approx 500$.

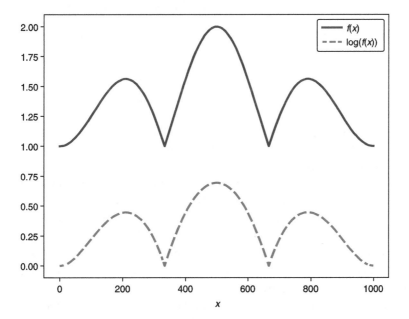

Figure 4.6 An arbitrary function **f(x)** with non-negative values (solid line) and the logarithm of that function (dashed line). While the maximum value (approximately 2) changes if you take the logarithm, the position at which the maximum is reached (approximately 500) stays the same regardless of whether or not you take the logarithm.

What have you gained by taking the logarithm? The log of the product of any numbers is the sum of the logs, which means $\log(A \cdot B) = \log(A) + \log(B)$. This formula can be extended to an arbitrary number of terms: $\log(A \cdot B \cdot C \cdot \ldots) = \log(A) + \log(B) + \log(C) + \cdots$, so the products in equation 4.1 become the sums of the logarithms. Let's look at the consequences for numerical stability.

You now add the log of numbers between 0 and 1. For 1, you get $\log(1) = 0$; for 0.0001, you get $\log(0.0001) \approx -4$. The only numerical problem arises if you really get a probability of 0 for the correct class, then the log of zero is minus infinity. To prevent this, sometimes a small number like 10E-20 is added to the probabilities. But let's not bother here about this extremely unlikely situation. What happens if you change listing 4.2 from products to sums of logs? You get a numerically stable result (see listing 4.3).

Listing 4.3   Fixing numerical instabilities by taking the log

```
log_x100 = np.sum(np.log(vals100))      ⟵┤ The product based on the same
log_x1000 = np.sum(np.log(vals1000))        sampled numbers as in listing 4.2
log_x100, log_x1000   ⟵┐                     becomes the sum of the logs.
                       └ A typical result (–89.97501927715012, –987.8053926732027)
                         for 1,000 numbers gives you a valid value.
```

Using the log trick transforms the MaxLike equation (4.1) to the maximum log likelihood equation shown here:

$$\log(P(\text{Training})) = \sum_{j \text{ with } y_j=0} \log(p_0(x_j)) + \sum_{j \text{ with } y_j=1} \log(p_1(x_j)) \quad \textbf{Equation 4.2}$$

This log trick does not depend on the bases you work with, but it is useful to know that Keras uses the natural logarithm to calculate the loss function. We are now nearly at the end, just two more minor details.

In equation 4.2, you add as many numbers as training data. Equation 4.2 therefore depends on the number of training data n. To have a quantity that does not depend systematically on the number of training data, you can divide the equation by n. In this case, you consider the mean log-likelihood per observation. The last point is instead of maximizing, DL frameworks are usually built to minimize a loss function. So instead of maximizing $\log(P(\text{Training}))$, you minimize $\log(P(\text{Training}))$. And voilà! You have derived the negative log likelihood (NLL) function for a binary classification model, which is also called *cross entropy*. You will see in the next section where the name cross entropy comes from. After achieving our goal to derive the loss function of a binary classifier, let's write it down once more:

$$\text{crossentropy} = -\frac{1}{n}\left(\sum_{j \text{ with } y_j=0} \log(p_0(x_j)) + \sum_{j \text{ with } y_j=1} \log(p_1(x_j)) \right) \quad \textbf{Equation 4.3}$$

You can now verify that this is indeed the quantity that gets minimized in DL.

 HANDS-ON TIME   Open http://mng.bz/pBY5 and run the code where you create a subset of the MNIST digits with only two classes (0 and 1). Your task in this first exercise is to use the function `model.evaluate` to determine the cross entropy loss of the untrained model and to explain the value that you obtain.

With the untrained model, you achieve a cross entropy of around 0.7. Of course, this is a random result because the weights of the network have their initial random values and no training has happened yet. Expect some random deviation from 0.7. Can you explain that value of 0.7 with what you just learned? The network knows nothing at the beginning. What mean hitting rate would you expect? About 50% right? Let's calculate $ln(0.5)$. That's 0.69, which looks about right. (Keras uses the natural logarithm to calculate the loss function.)

Loss function for classification of two classes with a single output

For the special case where you have two classes, like in the banknote example, there is the possibility of having a network with one output neuron. In that case, the output is the probability for class p_1. The probability for the other class, p_0, is then given by $p_0 = 1 - p_1$. Because of that, we do not need a one-hot encoding for y_i. It is either $y_i = 0$ for class 0 or $y_i = 1$ for class 1. Using that we can rewrite equation 4.3 as:

$$\text{crossentropy} = -\frac{1}{n}\left(\sum_{j=1}^{n}\left(y_i \cdot \log(p_1(x_i)) + (1 - y_i) \cdot \log(1 - p_1(x_i))\right)\right)$$

In contrast to this equation, we don't have to check to which class an example belongs. If example *i* belongs to class 1 ($y_i = 1$), the first part is taken containing p_1. Otherwise, if example *i* belongs to class 0 ($y_i = 0$), the second part where $p_0 = 1 - p_1$ is active.

4.2.2 Classification problems with more than two classes

What happens if you have more than two classes? Nothing special, you might think, and you are right. You've already done this in several exercises in chapter 2 where you tackled the task of discriminating between the ten digits in the MNIST data set. Recall, when setting up the DL models for the MNIST task, you used the same loss as in a binary classification model: `loss='categorical_crossentropy'`. Let's check out how you can use the MaxLike approach to derive the loss function and show that using cross entropy is appropriate.

Recall the probabilistic modeling you did for the binary classification task. You used an NN with two output nodes (see figure 4.5) yielding, for each input, the corresponding probabilities p_0 and p_1 for the classes 0 and 1, respectively. You can interpret these two probabilities as the parameters of the CPD for a binary classification task (see the figure in the first sidebar of this chapter). The model of this CPD is the Bernoulli distribution (see the first sidebar in this chapter). In principle, the Bernoulli distribution only needs one parameter: the probability of class one, p_1. This parameter is given by the second output node. You can derive the probability for class 0 from p_1 by $p_0 = 1 - p_1$; the usage of the `softmax` activation function ensures that the first output of the NN returns p_0. When following the MaxLike approach, the loss for a binary classification task is given by the mean NLL of the Bernoulli distribution (see equations 4.2 and 4.3).

Let's use the same procedure for a classification task with more than two classes. In the MNIST example, you have ten classes and you use an NN with ten output nodes, one for each class. Recall, for example, the architecture that we used in chapter 2 for the MNIST handwritten digit classification task shown in figure 2.12, which we repeat in figure 4.7.

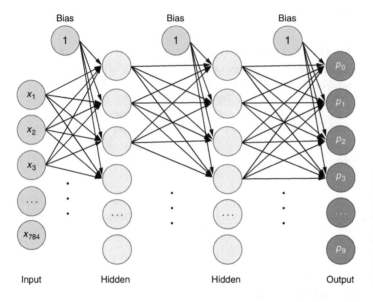

Figure 4.7   A fully connected NN (fcNN) with two hidden layers. For the MNIST example, the input layer has 784 values for the 28 × 28 pixels. The output layer has ten nodes, one for each class.

In this MNIST task, you want to discriminate between ten classes $(0, 1, \ldots, 9)$. Therefore, you set up an NN with ten output nodes, each providing the probability that the input corresponds to the respective class. These ten probabilities define the ten parameters of the CPD in the MNIST classification model. The model of the classification CPD is called *multinomial distribution,* which is an extension of the Bernoulli distribution to more than two classes. In the case of the MNIST classification task with ten classes, the multinomial CPD can be expressed as follows:

$$P(Y = k|x, w) = \begin{cases} p_0(x, w) & \text{for } k = 0 \\ p_1(x, w) & \text{for } k = 1 \\ \quad\vdots & \quad\vdots \\ p_9(x, w) & \text{for } k = 9 \end{cases} \text{ with } \sum_{i=0}^{9} p_i(x, w) = 1$$

Depending on the weights w, the NN yields for each input image x ten output values that define the parameters of the corresponding multinomial CPD that assigns a probability to each possible outcome.

Before training the NN, you initiate the weights with small and random values. The untrained NN assigns a probability close to 1/10 to each class similar to a uniform distribution (see figure 4.8), regardless of the image that is passed through the NN.

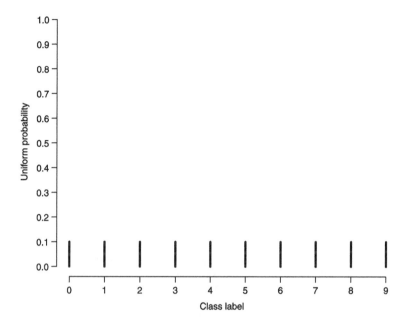

Figure 4.8 **A uniform probability distribution that assigns a probability of 0.1 to each of the ten class labels. An untrained classification NN for ten class labels results in a CPD similar to this uniform distribution, regardless of the label of the classified image.**

If you then train the NN with a couple of labeled images, the CPD already carries some information. A CPD that results after passing through an image with the label 2 can, for example, look like what's shown in figure 4.9.

Let's look at figure 4.9. What is the likelihood of this observed image with label 2? The likelihood is the probability that the CPD assigns to the label, here approximately 0.3. Note that only the probability that the CPD assigns to the correct label contributes to the likelihood. If you have classified several images with your NN and you know the true label of each image, you can determine the joint NLL. To do so for each image, evaluate the probability that the CPD assigns to the correct class label with this equation:

$$\text{NLL} = -\left(\sum_{j \text{ with } y_j=0} \log(p_0(x_j)) + \sum_{j \text{ with } y_j=1} \log(p_1(x_j)) \right.$$
$$\left. + \cdots + \sum_{j \text{ with } y_j=K-1} \log(p_{k-1}(x_j)) \right)$$

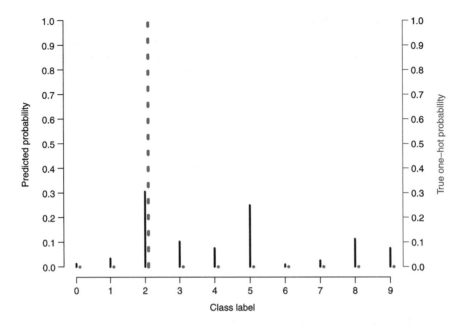

Figure 4.9   The multinomial CPD that corresponds to an image of label 2, which was passed through a NN (distribution with solid lines). Here the distribution of the ground truth (the dotted line) assigns a probability of 1 to the true label 2.

The mean NLL per observation is the NLL divided by the number of samples. This again results in the formula of the cross entropy:

$$\text{crossentropy} = -\frac{1}{n}\Bigg(\sum_{j \text{ with } y_j=0} \log(p_0(x_j)) + \sum_{j \text{ with } y_j=1} \log(p_1(x_j))$$

Equation 4.4

$$+ \cdots + \sum_{j \text{ with } y_j=K-1} \log(p_{k-1}(x_j)) \Bigg)$$

You can write this more compactly if you use the one-hot encoded vector $^{\text{true}}p_i$ for the true class of example i. The vector $^{\text{true}}p_i$ is 1 for the true class of the training example i and 0 for the remaining components (see figure 4.9).

$$\text{crossentropy} = -\frac{1}{n}\sum_{i=1}^{n} {}^{\text{true}}p_i \cdot \log(p_i)$$

What value for the loss do you expect from an untrained NN that was set up for the MNIST task? Pause for a second and try to find the answer by yourself before you read on.

In the full MNIST data set, you have ten classes. An untrained network would assign ~1/10 to each class. This leads to $p_i \approx 1/10$ for all classes, and we get $-\log(1/10) \approx 2.3$ for the loss. To debug your training, it's good practice to always check this number for classification problems.

HANDS-ON TIME Open http://mng.bz/OMJK and work through the code until you reach the exercise indicated by a pen icon, then do the exercise. Your task in the exercise is to use the digit predictions on MNIST images made by an untrained CNN and compute the value of the loss by hand. You'll see that you get a value close to the value 2.3 that we previously calculated.

4.2.3 Relationship between NLL, cross entropy, and Kullback-Leibler divergence

You might have wondered why DL people call the NLL in classification problems cross entropy. Maybe you have also wondered if it is possible in classification problems to quantify the "badness" of a fit by a difference between the true and a predicted value, similar to the MSE in regression. In this section, you learn about the answers to both questions.

What entropy means in statistics and information theory

We use the term *entropy* in different disciplines including information theory, statistical physics, and statistics. Here you'll learn about the first instance, where it's used to describe the information content of a probability distribution. You'll see it's useful to understand the origin of the term *cross entropy* for the loss in classification.

Let's start with the term *entropy*. The basic idea behind entropy is how much does the distribution tell you about the quantity at hand and how much uncertainty or surprise is left? In the following equation, you can measure the entropy H by the spread or "roughness" of a distribution. It's defined as

$$H(P) = -E_p\big(\log(p)\big) = -\sum_k p_k \log \cdot (p_k)$$

Take a look at the two distributions in figure 4.9. The CPD (black) is quite flat. You don't learn too much about the possible class label. You can take this to the extreme and consider uniform distribution (see figure 4.8). Indeed, it can be shown that the uniform distribution has the maximum entropy. For 10 classes with $p_i = \dfrac{1}{10}$ each, the entropy is equal to $H = -10 \cdot \dfrac{1}{10} \cdot \log(\dfrac{1}{10}) \approx 2.3$. The ground-truth distribution (figure 4.9, dotted line) tells you as much about the labels as possible. The distribution has only one peak, and you can be 100% sure that the true class label is 2. The corresponding entropy is $H = 0$, because for the correct class, you have $p_i = 1$ and with that $p_i \cdot \log(p_i) = 1 \cdot 0 = 0$.

CROSS ENTROPY AND KULLBACK-LEIBLER DIVERGENCE

Cross entropy comes into play if you have two distributions q and p and you calculate the expected value of $\log(q)$ given the distribution p. For the discrete case, this is as follows:

$$H(P, Q) = -E_p(\log(q)) = -\sum_k p_k \log(q_k)$$

With cross entropy, you can compare the two distributions.

KULLBACK-LEIBLER DIVERGENCE AS THE MSE PENDANT IN CLASSIFICATION

Let's again inspect figure 4.9, which shows the predicted CPD (black line) and the ground-truth distribution (dotted line), which is the one-hot encoded ground-truth label. If the model is perfect, the predicted CPD matches the ground-truth distribution. Let's try to quantify the "badness" of the model, which should be some measure of the distance between the current predicted CPD and the ground truth. A naive way is to determine at each class label the difference of its CPD and ground-truth probabilities, maybe square them, and then take the mean. This would mimic MSE in regression, which is the expected value of the squared differences between true and predicted values.

But be aware that the MSE doesn't give you the MaxLike estimate for classification. For classification, subtracting the true versus the predicted value doesn't correspond to the MaxLike principle. Here, you need to compare two distributions: the true distribution and the predicted distribution. For this purpose, the Kullback-Leibler (KL) divergence is often used. The KL divergence is the expected value of the differences of the log probabilities. By using some basic log calculus rules and the definition of the expected value, you can show that the KL divergence is the same as the cross entropy:

$$
\begin{aligned}
\mathrm{KL}(^{\mathrm{true}}p \,\|^{\mathrm{pred}} p) &= E_{^{\mathrm{true}}p}\left(\log(^{\mathrm{true}}p) - \log(^{\mathrm{pred}}p)\right) \\
&= E_{^{\mathrm{true}}p}\left(\log\left(\frac{^{\mathrm{true}}p}{^{\mathrm{pred}}p}\right)\right) \\
&= \sum_k {}^{\mathrm{true}}p_k \cdot \log\left(\frac{^{\mathrm{true}}p_k}{^{\mathrm{pred}}p_k}\right) \\
&= \sum_k {}^{\mathrm{true}}p_k \cdot \log\left(^{\mathrm{true}}p_k\right) - \sum_k {}^{\mathrm{true}}p_k \cdot \log\left(^{\mathrm{pred}}p_k\right) \\
&= 0 - \sum_k {}^{\mathrm{true}}p_k \cdot \log\left(^{\mathrm{pred}}p_k\right) \\
&= \mathrm{crossentropy}
\end{aligned}
$$

As you can see in the preceding derivation, the KL divergence between the ground truth and the predicted distribution strips down to the sum of the entropy of the ground truth and the cross entropy. Because the first term (entropy of the ground truth) is zero (dotted distribution in figure 4.9), you indeed minimize the KL divergence if you minimize the cross entropy. You'll encounter the KL divergence again in this book. But at the moment, let's appreciate that the KL divergence is to classification what the MSE is to regression. As with cross entropy and the KL divergence: the two probability distributions don't have the same role, and you get a different result if you swap the two distributions. To indicate that $KL(^{\mathrm{true}}p \,\|^{\mathrm{pred}}p) \neq KL(^{\mathrm{pred}}p \,\|^{\mathrm{true}}p)$, we write it with two bars. By the way, that wouldn't be a good idea. Why? (Try to answer the question before reading on.) Well, $^{\mathrm{true}}p_i$ is mostly zero, and taking the log of zero is not such a good idea because it returns minus infinity.

4.3 *Deriving a loss function for regression problems*

In this section, you use the MaxLike principle to derive the loss function for regression problems. You start off by revisiting the blood pressure example from chapter 3, where the input was the age of an American healthy woman and the output was a prediction of her systolic blood pressure (SBP). In chapter 3, you used a simple NN without hidden layers to model a linear relationship between input and output. As the loss function, you used the MSE. This choice of the loss function was explained by some hand-waving arguments. No hard facts were given to prove that this loss function is a good choice. In this section, you will see that the MSE as a loss function directly results from the MaxLike principle. Further, using the MaxLike principle, we can go beyond the MSE loss and model data with nonconstant noise, known under the scary name of *heteroscedasticity* in the statistics community. Don't be afraid; understanding the Max-Like principle makes modeling (not spelling) heteroscedasticity a piece of cake.

4.3.1 *Using a NN without hidden layers and one output neuron for modeling a linear relationship between input and output*

Let's go back to the blood pressure example from chapter 3. In that application, you used a simple linear regression model, $\hat{y} = a \cdot x + b$, to estimate the SBP y when given the age x of the woman. Training or fitting this model requires you to tune the parameters a and b so that the resulting model "best fits" to the observed data. In figure 4.10, you can see the observed data together with a linear regression line that goes quite well through the data but might not be the best model. In chapter 3, you used the MSE as a loss function that quantifies how poorly the model fits the data. Recall equation 3.1:

$$\text{loss} = \text{MSE} = \frac{1}{n} \sum_{i=1}^{n} (y_i - \hat{y}_i)^2 = \frac{1}{n} \sum_{i=1}^{n} (y_i - (a \cdot x_i + b))^2$$

This loss function relies on the idea that deviations between model and data should be quantified by summing up the squared residuals. Given this loss function, you determined the optimal parameter values by SGD.

In chapter 3, we introduced the MSE loss with the hand-waving argument that a fit is optimal if the sum of the squared residuals is minimal. In the following, you see how you can use the MaxLike principle to derive the appropriate loss for a linear regression task in a theoretically sound way.

SPOILER ALERT You will see that the MaxLike approach leads to the MSE loss.

Let's derive the loss function for the regression task by the MaxLike approach. For a simple regression model, we need only a simple NN (see figure 4.11) without a hidden layer. When using a linear activation function, this NN encodes the linear relationship between the input x and the output: $\text{out} = a \cdot x + b$.

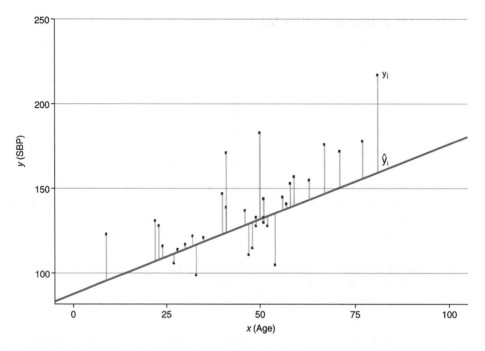

Figure 4.10 Scatter plot and regression model for the blood pressure example. The dots are the measured data points, and the straight line is the linear model. The vertical differences between data points and model are the residuals.

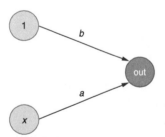

Figure 4.11 Simple linear regression as an fcNN without a hidden layer. This model computes the output directly from the input as out = $a \cdot x + b$.

The training data in regression problems comes in n pairs (x_i, y_i). In the blood pressure example, x_i holds the age of the i-th woman and y_i is the true systolic blood pressure of the i-th woman as well. If you choose certain numbers for the weights of the NN, say $a = 1$ and $b = 100$, then for a given input you can compute, say $x = 50$ and the fitted value $\hat{y} = 1 \cdot 50 + 100 = 150$. You can understand this as the best guess of the model. In our data set, we have a woman age 50, but her blood pressure is 183, not 150. This does not imply that our model is wrong or could be further improved because you do not expect that all women with the same age have the same blood pressure.

As in classification, also in regression. The output of the NN is not the value y you expect to observe when the input has a specific value x. In classifications, the output of the NN is not a class label but the probabilities for all possible class labels, which are the parameters for the fitted probability distribution (see the figure in the first sidebar). In regression, the output of the NN is not the specific value y itself, but again the parameter(s) of the fitted continuous probability distribution. Here we use a Normal distribution; later in chapter 5, we also use different ones like the Poissonian distribution. To recap the properties of a Normal distribution, see the next sidebar.

Recap on Normal distributions

Let's recap how to deal with a continuous variable Y that follows a Normal distribution. First, have a closer look at the density of a Normal distribution: $N(\mu, \sigma)$. The parameter μ determines the center of the distribution, and σ determines the spread of the distribution (see the following figure). You often see something like this

$$Y \sim N(\mu, \sigma)$$

which states the random variable Y (blood pressure at a certain age, for example) follows a Normal distribution. Such a random variable Y has the following probability density function:

$$f(y; \mu, \sigma) = \frac{1}{\sqrt{2\pi\sigma^2}} e^{-\frac{(y-\mu)^2}{2\sigma^2}}$$

This is visualized in the next figure:

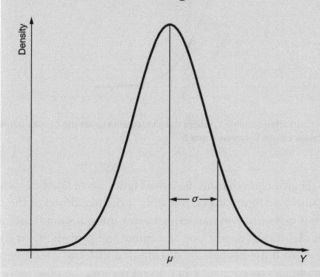

The density of a Normal distribution where μ is the center and σ is the spread of the distribution

Looking at the figure gives one the foresight that Y takes high probability values close to μ and small probability values further away from μ. This intuition is correct. But still, it is a bit harder to read the probability distribution of a continuous variable Y (see the previous figure) than the probability distribution of a discrete variable (see figure 4.2).

(continued)
In the case of a discrete variable, the probability distribution consists of separated bars, corresponding to the discrete outcome values. For discrete probability distributions, the height of the bars directly corresponds to the probabilities, and these probabilities add up to one. A continuous variable can take infinitely many possible values, and the probability for exactly one value like $\pi = 3.14159265359\ldots$ is zero. A probability can, therefore, only be defined for a region of values. The probability to observe a value y in the range between a and b, $y \in [a, b]$, is given by the area under the density curve between a and b (see the shaded region in the following figure). The range of all possible values has a probability of 1; therefore, the area under a probability density curve is always 1.

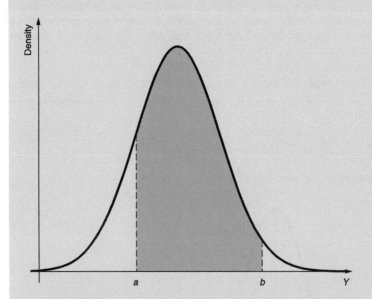

The density of a Normal distributed variable *Y*, where the shaded area under the density curve gives the probability that *Y* takes values between *a* and *b*

You can use the MaxLike principle to tune the two weights $w = (a, b)$ of the NN used to perform linear regression (see figure 4.11). But what is the likelihood of the observed data? For regression, it is just a little bit harder to answer this question than for classification. Remember, in classification, you can determine the probability or likelihood for each observed value from the probability distribution with the parameters p_i. The NN controls these parameters (see figure 4.11). In regression, the observed value y_i is continuous. Here you need to work with a Normal distribution. (Other distributions besides Normal are also sometimes adequate and we deal with those later in chapter 5, but for now, we stick to the Normal distribution.)

Normal distribution has two parameters: μ and σ. To start with, we leave the parameter σ fixed (let's say, we set it to $\sigma = 20$) and let the NN control only the parameter μ_x. Here, the subscript x reminds us that this parameter depends on x. It is determined by the network and, thus, μ_x depends on the parameters (weights) of the network. The simple network in figure 4.11 produces a linear dependency of $\mu_x = ax + b$ on x. Figure 4.12 shows this with a bold line. Older women have, on average, a higher blood pressure. The weights (a, b) themselves are determined (fitted) to maximize the likelihood of the data. What is the likelihood of the data? We start with a single data point (x_i, y_i). Inspect, for example, the data point of the 22-year-old woman who has an SBP of 131. For that age, the network predicts an average value of $\mu_x = 111$; the spread σ is fixed.

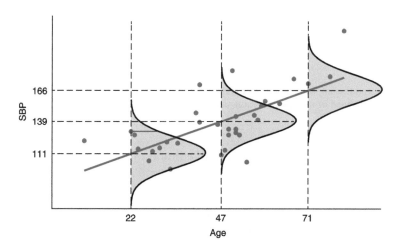

Figure 4.12 **Scatter plot and regression model for the blood pressure example. The dots are the measured data points and the straight line is the linear model. The bell-shaped curves are the conditional probability distributions of the outcome *Y* conditioned on the observed value *x*.**

In other words, a woman of age 22 has (according to the model) most likely a blood pressure of 111. But other values are also possible. The probability density $f(y, \mu = 111, \sigma = 20)$ for different values of the blood pressure y is distributed around the value 111 by a Normal (shown in shaded grey area in figure 4.12 and again in figure 4.13).

The woman in our observation has a blood pressure of 131. As in the discrete case, where we reinterpreted the probability $p(y|x, a, b) = p(y|x, w)$ as a likelihood for the data to occur given the parameters w, we now interpret the probability density $f(y|x, \mu, \sigma) = f(y|x, w)$ as the likelihood for the observed data to occur. Because it is derived from a probability density, the likelihood in the continuous case is a continuous

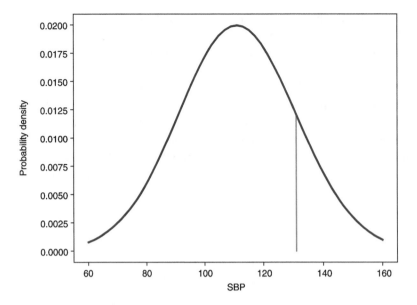

Figure 4.13   **The conditional Normal density function f. The height of the vertical bar indicates the likelihood of the specific value under this model.**

function as well. In our concrete case, the likelihood of this observation is given by the density as follows:

$$f(y = 131; \mu = 111, \sigma = 20) = \frac{1}{\sqrt{2\pi\sigma^2}} e^{-\frac{(y-\mu)^2}{2\sigma^2}} = \frac{1}{\sqrt{2\pi \cdot 400}} e^{-\frac{(131-111)^2}{2\cdot 400}} \approx 0.01209$$

See also the vertical bar in figure 4.13. For each value of the input x, the output y follows another Normal distribution. For example, for a woman aged 47 with an SBP of 110, the parameter is $\mu_x = 139$. The corresponding likelihood of that given blood pressure is determined by $f(y = 110; \mu = 139, \sigma = 20)$. Because the normal probability distribution depends via $\mu_{x_i} = a \cdot x_i + b$ on the value x_i, it is often called a conditional probability distribution (CPD). As before in the classification case, the likelihood of all points (we assume independence) is given by the product of the individual likelihoods as:

$$L(a, b) = f(y_1, \mu_{x_2}, \sigma) \cdot f(y_2, \mu_{x_2}, \sigma) \cdots = \prod_{i=1}^{n} f(y_i; \mu_i, \sigma) = \prod_{i=1}^{n} f(y_i; (a \cdot x_i + b), \sigma)$$

This likelihood depends only on the parameters a and b. The values $\hat{a}$ and $\hat{b}$ maximizing it are our best guess and are known under the name *MaxLike estimates*. (That's also the reason they get their hat.) Practically, we again take the log and minimize the NLL:

$$l(a,b) = -\log(L(a,b)) = -\log\left(\prod_{i=1}^{n} f(y_i; \mu_i, \sigma)\right) = -\prod_{i=1}^{n} \log(f(y_i; (a \cdot x_i + b), \sigma))$$

Equation 4.5

You saw in chapter 3 that you can find the network weights that minimize the loss function by SGD. Let's do this now. We have to define a novel loss function in Keras. You can implement a custom loss function in Keras by defining a function that takes as input the true values and the prediction of the network. As shown in figure 4.11, linear regression is defined as a simple network, which predicts $a \cdot x_i + b$ with one weight a that gives the slope and the bias b that gives the intercept. The loss from the loss function in equation 4.4 is then coded as shown in listing 4.4. (You can find this code in the notebook.)

HANDS-ON TIME Open http://mng.bz/YrJo and work through the code to see how to use the MaxLike approach to determine the parameter values in a linear regression model. For this, the NLL is defined as a loss function that is minimized via SGD.

Listing 4.4 Estimating the MaxLike solution

```
def my_loss(y_true,y_pred):
    loss = -tf.reduce_sum(tf.math.log(f(y_true,y_pred)))
    return loss

model = Sequential()
model.add(Dense(1, activation='linear',
                batch_input_shape=(None, 1)))
model.compile(loss=my_loss,optimizer="adam")
```

Defines a custom loss function → (points to `def my_loss`)

Calculates the sum of all losses (see equation 4.4) → (points to `loss = -tf.reduce_sum...`)

Sets up an NN equivalent to linear regression; includes one linear activation and a bias term → (points to `model.add(Dense...`)

In chapter 3, you already minimized the MSE loss function via SGD, and you received $a = 1.1$ and $b = 87.8$ as optimal parameter values. And, indeed, the MaxLike estimate shown here is identical with the MSE approach of chapter 3. For the detailed derivation, see the following sidebar.

MaxLike-based derivation of the MSE loss in linear regression

Let's follow step-by-step the MaxLike approach to derive the loss for a classical linear regression task. The MaxLike approach tells you that you need to find those values for the weights w in the NN. Here $w = (a, b)$ (see the figure in the sidebar entitled "MaxLike approach for the classification loss using a parametric probability model"), which maximize the likelihood for the observed data. The data are provided as n pairs (x_i, y_i). The following product shows the likelihood of the data:

$$w = \mathrm{argmax}_w \left\{ \prod_{i=1}^{n} f(y_i; x_i, w) \right\} \Rightarrow$$

(continued)

Maximizing this product leads to the same results as minimizing the sum of the corresponding NLL (see section 4.1).

$$w = \text{argmin}_w \left\{ \sum_{i=1}^{n} -\log f(y_i; x_i, w) \right\} \Rightarrow$$

Now you plug in the expression for the Normal density function (see the second equation in the sidebar, "Recap on Normal distributions").

$$w = \text{argmin}_w \left\{ \sum_{i=1}^{n} -\log \left(\frac{1}{\sqrt{2\pi\sigma^2}} \cdot e^{-\frac{(y_i - \mu_{x_i})^2}{2\sigma^2}} \right) \right\} \Rightarrow$$

Then let's use the rule that $\log(c \cdot d) = \log(c) + \log(d)$ and $\log(e^g) = g$, and the fact that $(c - d)^2 = (d - c)^2$:

$$w = \text{argmin}_w \left\{ \sum_{i=1}^{n} -\log \left(\frac{1}{\sqrt{2\pi\sigma^2}} \right) + \frac{(\mu_{x_i} - y_i)^2}{2\sigma^2} \right\} \Rightarrow$$

Adding a constant does not change the position of the minimum and, because the first term $-\log \left(\frac{1}{\sqrt{2\pi\sigma^2}} \right)$ is constant with respect to *a* and *b*, we can drop it:

$$w = \text{argmin}_w \left\{ \sum_{i=1}^{n} \frac{(\mu_{x_i} - y_i)^2}{2\sigma^2} \right\} \Rightarrow$$

$$w = \text{argmin}_w \left\{ \frac{1}{2\sigma^2} \sum_{i=1}^{n} (\mu_{x_i} - y_i)^2 \right\} \Rightarrow$$

Multiplying with a constant factor also does not change the position of the minimum. We can freely multiply with the constant factor $2 \cdot \sigma^2 / n$ so that we finally obtain the formula for the MSE loss:

$$(a, b) = \text{argmin}_w \left\{ \frac{1}{n} \sum_{i=1}^{n} (\mu_{x_i} - y_i)^2 \right\}$$

With this, we have derived the loss, which we need to minimize to find the optimal values of the weights. Note that you only need to assume that σ^2 is constant; you do not need to derive the value of σ^2 to derive the loss function of a classical linear regression model:

$$\text{loss} = \text{MSE} = \frac{1}{n} \sum_{i=1}^{n} (\hat{y}_i - y_i)^2$$

Ta-da! We ended the task to find the parameter values for *a* and *b*, which minimize the sum of the squared residuals. This can be done by minimizing the MSE.

> The MaxLike approach did indeed lead us to a loss function that is nothing else other than the MSE! In the case of simple linear regression, the fitted value is $\hat{y}_i = \mu_{x_i} = a \cdot x_i + b$ yielding:
>
> $$\text{loss} = \text{MSE} = \frac{1}{n} \sum_{i=1}^{n} (a \cdot x_i + b - y_i)^2$$

Let's take a step back and reflect on what we have done so far. First, we used an NN to determine the parameters of a probability distribution. Second, we chose a Normal distribution to model our data. A Normal probability distribution has two parameters: μ and σ. We keep σ fixed and only model μ_{x_i} using the simplest model possible, the linear regression: $\mu_{x_i} = a \cdot x_i + b$. The corresponding y value (SBP) to an x value (age) is distributed like a Normal:

$$Y_{x_i} \sim N(\mu_{x_i} = a \cdot x_i + b, \sigma^2)$$

This reads Y is a random variable coming from a Normal distribution with a mean μ_{x_i} and a standard deviation σ. We can extend this approach in several ways:

1 We can choose a different probability distribution beside a Normal. As it turns out, there are certain situations where a Normal distribution is not adequate. Take count data for example. A Normal distribution always includes negative values. But some data-like count data does not have negative values. We deal with those cases in chapter 5.

2 We can use a full-blown NN instead of linear regression to model μ_{x_i}, which we do in the next section.

3 We do not need to stick to the assumption that the variability of the data is constant over the whole input range, but can also model σ by the NN and allow, for example, the uncertainty to increase. We do this in section 4.3.3.

4.3.2 Using a NN with hidden layers to model non-linear relationships between input and output

An NN without hidden layers (see figure 4.11) models a linear relationship between input and output: out = $a \cdot x + b$. Now you can extend this model and use an NN with one or more hidden layers to model μ_x. Let's still assume that the variance σ^2 is constant. With the NN in figure 4.15, you model for each input x a whole CPD for the output given by:

$$Y_{x_i} \sim N(\mu_{x_i}, \sigma^2)$$

If you add at least one hidden layer to your NN, you see that the mean μ_{x_i} of these CPDs do not need to be along a straight line (see figure 4.15). In listing 4.5, you see how you can simulate some data from a function with a sinusoidal shape and fit an NN with three hidden layers and an MSE loss to the data, resulting in a well-fitting, non-linear curve (see figure 4.14).

Listing 4.5   Using MSE loss to model non-linear relationships in an fcNN

```
x,y = create_random_data(n=300)                        Creates some random
model = Sequential()                                    data (see figure 4.14)
model.add(Dense(1, activation='relu',
batch_input_shape=(None, 1)))                          Defines the fcNN with
model.add(Dense(20, activation='relu'))               3 hidden layers and
model.add(Dense(50,activation='relu'))                ReLU activations
model.add(Dense(20, activation='relu'))
model.add(Dense(1, activation='linear'))
opt = optimizers.Adam(lr=0.0001)
model.compile(loss='mean_squared_error',optimizer=opt)
history=model.fit(x, y,
                  batch_size=n,                        Fits the NN using
                  epochs=10000,                        the MSE loss
                  verbose=0,
                  )
```

With this extension, you can model arbitrary, complicated non-linear relationships between input and output such as, for example, a sinus (see figure 4.14).

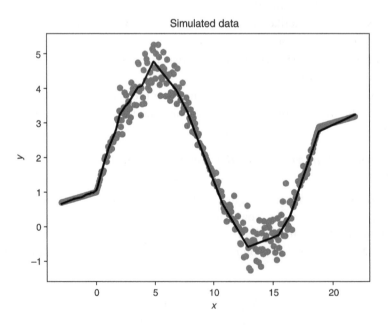

Figure 4.14   A sinus-shaped curve (solid line) fitted to the data points (see dots) by using an fcNN with three hidden layers and an MSE loss

How does this work? The model in figure 4.11 was only able to draw a straight-line model. Why is the slightly extended NN (see figure 4.15) able to model such a complex curve? In chapter 2, we discussed that hidden layers allow us to construct in a non-linear manner new features from the input feature. For example, an NN with one hidden layer holding eight neurons (see figure 4.15) allows the NN to construct eight new features from the input x.

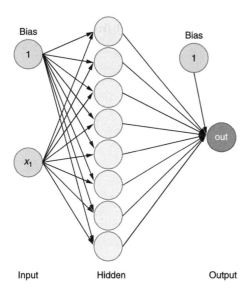

Figure 4.15   Extended linear regression. The eight neurons in the hidden layer give the features from which the output "out" is computed.

Then the NN models a linear relationship between these new features and the outcome. The derivation of the loss function stays the same and leads to the MSE loss formula:

$$\text{loss} = \text{MSE} = \frac{1}{n} \sum_{i=1}^{n} (\hat{y}_i - y_i)^2 \qquad \textbf{Equation 4.6}$$

In the case of an NN with a hidden layer (see, for example, figure 4.12), the modeled output $\hat{y}_i = f_{NN_{4.11}}(x_i, w)$ is a quite complicated function of the input x_i and all weights in the NN. This is the only difference to a simple linear model that is encoded by an NN without a hidden layer (see figure 4.11), where the fitted value is a simple linear function of the weights and the input $\hat{y}_i = f_{NN_{4.6}}(x_i, a, b) = a \cdot x_i + b$.

4.3.3   Using an NN with additional output for regression tasks with nonconstant variance

One assumption in classical linear regression is *homoscedasticity*, meaning that the variance of the outcome does not depend on the input value x. Therefore, you need only one output node to compute the first parameter μ_x of the conditional Normal distribution (see figures 4.11 and 4.15). If you also allow the second parameter, σ_x, to depend on *x*, then you need an NN with a second output node. If the variance of the output's CPD is not constant but dependent on *x*, we talk about heteroscedasticity.

Technically, you can easily realize this by adding a second output node (see figure 4.16). Because the NN in figure 4.15 also has a hidden layer, it allows for a nonlinear relationship between the input and the output. The two nodes in the output layer provide the parameter values μ_x and σ_x of the CPD $N(\mu_x, \sigma_x{}^2)$. When working with a linear activation function in the output layer, you can get negative and positive output values. Thus, the second output is not directly taken as standard deviation σ_x, but as $\log(\sigma_x)$. The standard deviation is then computed from out$_2$ via $\sigma_x = e^{\text{out}_2}$, ensuring that σ_x is a non-negative number.

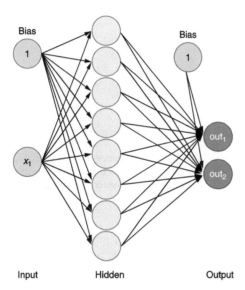

Figure 4.16   You can use an NN with two output nodes to control the parameters μ_x and σ_x of the conditional outcome distribution $N(\mu_x, \sigma_x)$ for regression tasks with nonconstant variance.

Because the classical linear regression assumes that the variance σ^2 is constant (called the homoscedasticity assumption), you might suspect that it makes things much more complicated if you want to allow for varying σ^2 (called *heteroscedasticity*). But luckily, this is not the case. The homoscedasticity assumption is only used in the derivation of the loss function to get rid of the terms containing σ^2 leading to the MSE loss. But if you do not assume constant variance, you can't do this step. The loss is still given by the NLL defined in equation 4.4

$$w = \operatorname{argmin}_w \left\{ \sum_{i=1}^{n} -\log\left(\frac{1}{\sqrt{2\pi\sigma(x_i, w)^2}} \right) + \frac{(\mu(x_i, w) - y_i)^2}{2\sigma(x_i, w)^2} \right\}$$ **Equation 4.7**

with the loss

$$\text{loss} = \text{NLL} = \sum_{i=1}^{n} -\log\left(\frac{1}{\sqrt{2\pi\sigma_{x_i}{}^2}}\right) + \frac{(\mu_{x_i} - y_i)^2}{2\sigma_{x_i}{}^2}$$

Equation 4.8

If you want to analytically solve this loss as it is done in traditional statistics, the fact that σ is nonconstant causes problems. But if you renounce from a closed-form solution, optimizing this loss is not a problem at all. You can again use the SGD machinery to tune the weights for a minimal loss. In TensorFlow or Keras, you can realize this by defining a custom loss and then using this custom loss for the fitting procedure (see listing 4.6), which uses the loss function from equation 4.8.

Why you do not need to know the ground truth for the variance

Presenting the MaxLike principle to students, we are frequently asked the question, "How can you determine the variance if you don't have a ground truth for it?" Let's have a look again at the architecture in figure 4.16. The network has two outputs: one directly corresponds to the expected value μ_{x_i} of the outcome distribution and the other corresponds to a transformation of the standard deviation σ_{x_i} of the outcome distribution. While it somehow feels natural to choose the μ_{x_i} that is closer to the values y_i, you might wonder how you can fit, for example, the standard deviation of the outcome distribution without having this information given as ground truth. You only have for each input x_i the observed outcome y_i. But the MaxLike approach is beautiful and is doing the trick for you!

Recall the blood pressure data set (see figure 4.12), where it was assumed that the data spread is the same over the whole range of ages. Let's forget the regression task for a moment and turn to an easier task: you only want to model the blood pressure for 45-year-old women by a Normal distribution. Let's imagine that all four women have a blood pressure of roughly 131 (say, 130.5, 130.7, 131, 131.8). As a distribution for blood pressure at age 45, you would probably want to use a Gaussian bell curve that has the parameter values μ_{x_i} at the observed (mean) value 131 and σ_{x_i} close to zero. This should yield a maximum likelihood for observations at 131 (see the left panel in the following figure). It feels kind of natural that μ_{x_i} is determined by the ground truth y_i. But how would you handle a situation where your data shows high variability?

Imagine for example that the four 45-year-old women in your data set have blood pressures of 82, 114, 117, and 131. In such situations, you would probably not like to use the Gaussian bell curve shown in the left panel of the figure because only the observation with the blood pressure 131 has a high likelihood; the other three observations have tiny likelihoods leading to a small overall (joint) likelihood. To maximize the joint likelihood, it is much better to use a Gaussian curve where all four observations have reasonably high likelihoods (see the right panel of the following figure).

(continued)

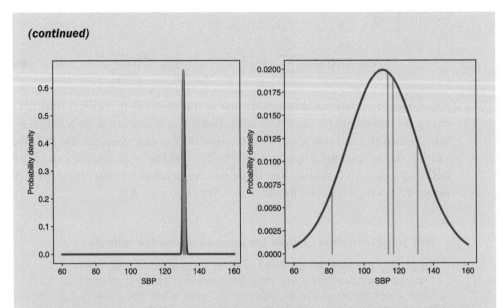

The Normal distribution that maximizes the joint likelihood of four observed SBP values in the case of almost no data variability (left), where all four observations have values close to 131, or a large data variability (right), where the four observed SBP values of 82, 114, 117, and 131 are quite different. The height of the line indicates the likelihood of the observed SBP values.

OPTIONAL EXERCISE   Open http://mng.bz/YrJo and step through the code until you reach exercise 2, then work on exercise 2. Plot a Normal distribution along with the likelihood of the observed values as shown in the figure in the previous sidebar. Manually adapt the parameter values of a Normal distribution to achieve a maximal joint likelihood or minimal NLL. Develop code which determines the optimal parameter via gradient descent.

If you did the exercise, you saw that the likelihood is maximized when the curve has a similar spread to the data, and indeed, it is at its maximum when you use the standard deviation of the four observations as parameter σ_x. This means that the distribution $N(\mu_{x_i}, \sigma_{x_i})$ you are modeling with your NN reflects the distribution of the data as well as possible. In case of a regression, the situation is more complicated because you have neighboring points at different x values. The parameter σ_{x_i} cannot have a completely different value at the neighboring x values, but it should be a smooth curve. If the network has enough flexibility, it holds that in regions where the spread of the observed outcomes is large (like at around $x = 5$ and $x = 15$ in figure 4.17), you should use a quite broad conditional Normal distribution that is a larger parameter σ_{x_i}. In contrast, in regions where there is a small spread (for example, around $x = 0$ in figure 4.17), σ_{x_i} should be small. In this way, the likelihood approach allows you to estimate the parameters of the conditional Normal distribution without having these values as ground truth.

Let's hold on and recall the original question. Why did you think you had a ground truth for the mean and not for the variance in the first place? All you have is data and a model from which you assume the data has been created. In our case, the model is the Gaussian distribution $N(\mu_{x_i}, \sigma_{x_i})$ and the network determines its parameters μ_{x_i}, σ_{x_i}. You optimize the weights of the NN so that the likelihood of the data is maximal. There is no such thing as a ground truth for the mean either. An NN would just estimate μ and σ for the conditional distribution, and both are indeed just estimates. There is no ground truth neither for μ nor for σ. There is no spoon.

Listing 4.6   Non-linear heteroscedastic regression model from equation 4.5

```
import math                          Defines a custom loss
def my_loss(y_true,y_pred):                              Extracts the first
  mu=tf.slice(y_pred,[0,0],[-1,1])                       column for μ
  sigma=tf.math.exp(tf.slice(y_pred,[0,1],[-1,1]))       Extracts the second
                                                         column for σ
  a=1/(tf.sqrt(2.*math.pi)*sigma)
  b1=tf.square(mu-y_true)
  b2=2*tf.square(sigma)
  b=b1/b2
  loss = tf.reduce_sum(-tf.math.log(a)+b,axis=0)    Defines an NN with 3 hidden
  return loss                                       layers as in listing 4.4 but
                                                    now with 2 outcome nodes
model =  Sequential()
model.add(Dense(20, activation='relu',batch_input_shape=(None, 1)))
model.add(Dense(50, activation='relu'))
model.add(Dense(20, activation='relu'))
model.add(Dense(2, activation='linear'))
model.compile(loss=my_loss,\             Uses the custom
optimizer="adam",metrics=[my_loss])      loss for the fitting
```

You can now graph the fit by not only plotting the curve of the fitted values but also the curves for the fitted values plus/minus 1 or 2 times the fitted standard deviation. This illustrates the varying spread of the fitted CPD (see figure 4.17).

You can design this network arbitrarily deep and wide to model complex relationships between x and y. If you only want to allow for linear relationships between inputs and outputs, you should use an NN without hidden layers.

 OPTIONAL EXERCISE   Open http://mng.bz/GVJM and work through the code until you reach the first exercise indicated by a pen icon. You'll see how to simulate the data shown in figure 4.17 and how to fit different regression models. Your task in this exercise is to experiment with different activation functions.

You have now seen how to derive a loss function with the MaxLike approach. You only need a parametric model for your data. If you want to develop a prediction model, then you need to pick a model for the CPD $p(y|x)$. The CPD yields the likelihood of the observed outcomes. To follow this modeling approach in a DL manner, you design an NN that outputs the parameters of the probability distribution (or value from

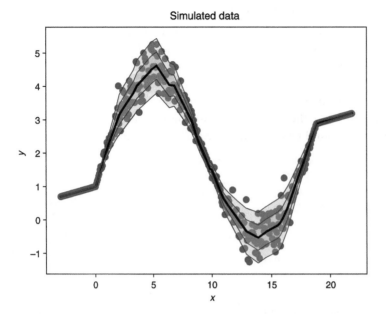

Figure 4.17   The fitted values follow a sinus-shaped curve. The solid middle line gives the position of fitted μ_x with varying standard deviation. The two thin outer lines correspond to a 95% prediction interval ($\mu - 2\sigma$, $\mu + 2\sigma$). We use an NN with three hidden layers, two output nodes, and a customized loss to fit the data points (see the dots).

which these parameters can be derived). The rest is done by TensorFlow or Keras. You use SGD to find the value of weights in the NN, which lead to modeled parameter values that minimize the NLL. In many cases, the NLL is provided as a predefined loss function, such as the cross entropy or the MSE loss. But you can also work with arbitrary likelihoods by defining a customized loss function that corresponds to the NLL. You saw in listing 4.6 a customized loss function defining the NLL for regression problems with nonconstant variance.

Summary

- In the maximum likelihood (MaxLike) approach, you tune the parameter of a model such that the resulting model can produce the observed data with a higher probability than all other models with different parameter values.
- The MaxLike approach is a versatile tool to fit the parameters of models. It is widely used in statistics and provides a sound theoretical framework to derive loss functions.
- To use the MaxLike approach, you need to define a parametric probability distribution for the observed data.
- The likelihood of a discrete variable is given by a discrete probability distribution.

- The likelihood of a continuous outcome is given by a continuous density function.
- The MaxLike approach involves:
  - Defining a parametric model for the (discrete or continuous) probability distribution of the observed data
  - Maximizing the likelihood (or minimizing the NLL) for the observed data
- To develop a prediction model, you need to pick a model for the conditional probability distribution (CPD) of the outcome y given the input x.
- Using the MaxLike approach for a classification task is based on a Bernoulli or multinomial probability distribution like CPD and leads to the standard loss for the classification known as cross entropy in Keras and TensorFlow.
- The Kullback-Leibler (KL) divergence is a measure between the predicted and the ground-truth CPD. Minimizing it has the same effect as minimizing cross entropy. In that sense, the KL divergence is the pendent of the MSE for a classification model.
- Using the MaxLike approach for a linear regression task that is based on a Normal probability distribution like CPD leads to the mean squared error (MSE) loss.
- For linear regression with a constant variance, we can interpret the output of the network with input x as the parameter μ_x of a conditional Normal distribution $N(\mu_x, \sigma)$.
- Regression with nonconstant variance can be fitted with a loss that corresponds to the negative log-likelihood (NLL) of a normal probability model, where both parameters (mean and standard deviation) depend on the input x and can be computed by an NN with two outputs yielding the CPD $N(\mu_x, \sigma_x)$.
- Non-linear relationships can be fitted with the MSE loss by introducing hidden layers.
- Generally, likelihoods of arbitrary CPDs can be maximized in the framework of NNs by interpreting the output of the NN as the parameter of the probability distributions.

5

Probabilistic deep learning models with TensorFlow Probability

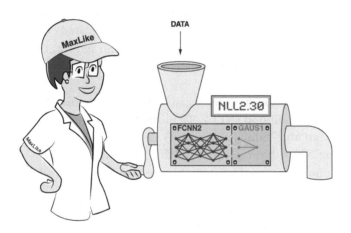

This chapter covers

- Introduction to probabilistic deep learning models
- The negative log-likelihood on new data as a proper performance measure
- Fitting probabilistic deep learning models for continuous and count data
- Creating custom probability distributions

In chapters 3 and 4, you encountered a kind of uncertainty that's inherent to the data. For example, in chapter 3, you saw in the blood pressure example that two women with the same age can have quite different blood pressures. Even the blood pressure of the same woman can be different when measured at two different times within the same week. To capture this data-inherent variability, we used a conditional probability distribution (CPD): $p(y|x)$. With this distribution, you captured the outcome variability of y by a model. To refer to this inherent variability in the DL community, the term *aleatoric uncertainty* is used. The term *aleatoric* stems from the Latin word *alea*, which means dice, as in *Alea iacta est* ("the die is cast").

In this chapter, we focus further on developing and evaluating probabilistic models to quantify the aleatoric uncertainty. Why should you care about uncertainties? It's not only about theoretical baublery; it has real practical importance for making critical or costly decisions based on the predictions. Think, for example, about a situation where a New York taxi driver transports an art dealer to a great art auction that starts in 25 minutes. The art dealer promises a generous tip ($500) if she arrives there in time. That matters to the taxi driver! He, fortunately, has the newest gadgets, and his travel-time prediction tool is based on a probabilistic model yielding probabilistic proposals for the travel-time prediction.

The tool proposes two routes leading to the auction. Route 1 has a predicted average travel time of $\mu_1 = 19$ min but a high uncertainty (standard deviation of $\sigma_1 = 12$ min), and route 2 has an average travel time of $\mu_2 = 22$ min but a small uncertainty (standard deviation of $\sigma_2 = 2$ min). The taxi driver decides to take the second route, which is a really smart decision. The probability of getting the tip is about 93%[1] when taking route 2 even if the mean travel time of route 2 is substantially longer than that of route 1. The chance of getting the tip when choosing the first route with 19 minutes mean travel time is about 69%.[2] But such information can only be derived from a probabilistic model that predicts not a single value, but a reliable probability distribution over all possible travel times.

From chapter 4, you know how to fit a probabilistic model. You use a neural network (NN) to determine the parameters of the predicted CPD for the outcome. In principle, developing a probabilistic DL model is easy:

1. You pick an appropriate distribution model for the outcome.
2. You set up an NN that has as many output nodes as the model has parameters.
3. You derive from the picked distribution the negative-log-likelihood (NLL) function and use that function as the loss function to train the model.

---

[1] This probability can be computed as follows:
```
import tensorflow_probability as tfp
dist = tfp.distributions.Normal(loc=22, scale=2)
dist.cdf(25) #0.933
```
[2] The probability can be computed as follows:
```
import tensorflow_probability as tfp
dist = tfp.distributions.Normal(loc=19, scale=12)
dist.cdf(25) #0.691
```

NOTE To get our terminology straight, when we talk about *output*, we mean a node in the last layer of the NN; when we talk about an *outcome*, we mean the target variable *y*.

Chapter 4 focused on the maximum likelihood (MaxLike) approach for fitting a model. This approach leads to the NLL as the loss function. You can determine the NLL for a chosen probability distribution manually. We did this in chapter 4 in section 4.2 for classification problems and in section 4.3 for standard regression problems. But as you saw in chapter 4, we quickly needed some calculus and programming to derive the NLL as the loss function.

In this chapter, you'll get to know TensorFlow Probability (TFP), an extension of TensorFlow that makes it easy to fit a probabilistic DL model without requiring you to manually define the corresponding loss function. You'll see how to use TFP for different applications, and you'll gain an intuitive understanding of what's going on behind the scenes. Fitting probabilistic models allows you to easily incorporate your field knowledge: you simply pick an appropriate outcome distribution (in figure 5.1, it's sketched as a distribution plate in the DL machine) and so model the randomness of real-world data.

In this chapter, you'll also develop highly performant probabilistic DL models for different tasks. Probabilistic models can be optimized in two ways. First, we choose an appropriate architecture, the network shelf in figure 5.1, for example. (We covered this aspect in chapter 2.) Second, and this is the focus of this chapter, we enhance the model by choosing the right distribution for the outcome. But how does one determine the performance of a probabilistic model in the first place? You'll see that the criterion for selecting the best performing probabilistic model is easy! The model with the lowest NLL on new data is the best performing probabilistic prediction model.

5.1 Evaluating and comparing different probabilistic prediction models

The goal of a probabilistic prediction model is to yield accurate probabilistic predictions on new data. This means that the predicted CPD at a given *x* should match the observed distribution as well as possible. The correct measure is simple. You already saw it in chapter 4; it's the NLL that's minimized on the training data. But now, it's evaluated on new data (test data) not used in the training. The lower the NLL on this test data, the better the model performance is expected for new data in general. It can even be proved mathematically that the test NLL is optimal when assessing the prediction performance of a model.[3]

In the process of model development, you usually tune your models. In that process, you repeatedly fit several models to your train data and evaluate the performance on the validation data. In the end, you select the model with the highest prediction performance on the validation data. But when you always use the same validation data

---

[3] Just to give you an idea for the proof, in this proof, it's assumed that the data is generated from a true distribution. In practice, the true distribution is never known. It then can be shown that the NLL is a so-called proper score that reaches only its minimal value if the predicted distribution is equal to the true distribution.

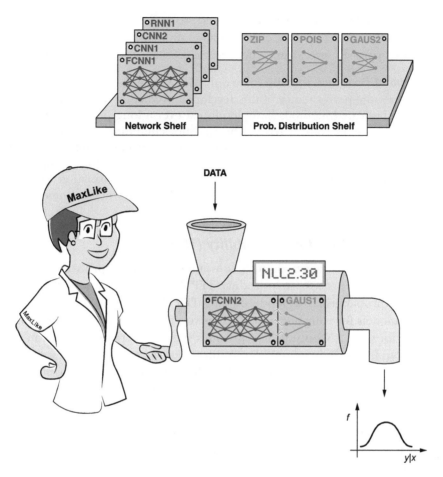

Figure 5.1 **Principle idea of probabilistic modeling in deep learning (DL). The network determines the parameters of a probability distribution. We fit the model using the mighty MaxLike principle. In the figure, the outcome is modeled by a Normal distribution, where the NN is used to control one parameter (see the chosen last plate with one output node), usually the mean value.**

to check the performance of the model, it's possible that you overfit on the validation data. It's, therefore, good practice in DL, as well as in machine learning (ML), to work with three data sets:

- A training data set to fit the model
- A validation data set to check the prediction performance of the model
- A test data set that's not touched at any point in the model selection procedure and that's only used to evaluate the prediction performance of the final model

Sometimes, it's not possible to get all three data sets. In statistics, it's quite common to work only with train and test data, where the test data takes the role of the validation and test data. Another approach commonly used in ML and statistics is cross-validation. In that technique, you split the training repeatedly into two parts and use one for training and the other for validation. Because this cross-validation procedure requires us to repeat a time-costly training process several times, deep learners usually don't apply this technique.

> **WARNING**   In statistics, sometimes we only use a single data set. To still be able to evaluate the performance of the developed prediction model on the same data, sophisticated methods have developed over a long period of time and are still in use in some parts of the statistics community. These methods account for the fact that the model saw the data during fitting and applied corrections to account for that. These methods include, for example, the Akaike Information Criterion (AIC) or the Bayesian Information Criterion (BIC). Don't get confused. If you have a validation set, you don't need these methods.

5.2   *Introducing TensorFlow Probability (TFP)*

In this section, you'll learn about a convenient way to fit probabilistic models to your data. For this process, we introduce TFP that's built on top of TensorFlow and tailored for probabilistic DL models. Using TFP allows you to think in terms of distribution models for your outcome. It frees you from handcrafting appropriate loss functions for your NN output. TFP provides special layers where you can plug in a distribution. It lets you compute the likelihood of the observed data without setting up any formulas or functions. In the last chapter, you set up probabilistic models without TFP, which is possible but sometimes cumbersome. Remember the procedure in chapter 4?

1 You pick an appropriate distribution for the outcome.
2 You set up an NN with as many outputs as you have parameters in your selected outcome distribution.
3 You define a loss function that yields the NLL.

In the case of linear regression, you pick a Gaussian distribution as a model for the CPD (see figure 5.2 that shows the blood pressure example). In this case, your CPD is $N(\mu_x, \sigma_x)$, which has only two parameters: the mean (μ_x) and the standard deviation (σ_x). For a Gaussian distribution, you can define a 95% prediction interval that gives you a range that covers 95% of the occurring outcomes. The borders of the 95% prediction interval $[q^{2.5\%}, q^{97.5\%}]$ are usually the 0.025 and 0.975 quantiles. These quantities are also called the 2.5% and 97.5% percentile. The 0.975 quantile ($q^{97.5\%}$) is that value in the outcome distribution for which 97.5% of all occurring outcomes are smaller or equal to this value. In a Normal distribution, $N(\mu_x, \sigma_x)$, the 97.5% quantile is given by $q^{97.5\%} = \mu_x + 1.96 \cdot \sigma_x \approx \mu_x + 2 \cdot \sigma_x$.

If you assume a constant standard deviation, then the derivation of the loss gets quite easy. That's because when minimizing the NLL, you can ignore in the likelihood all parts that depend on the standard deviation. After some derivation, it turns out that minimizing the mean NLL is the same as minimizing the mean squared error

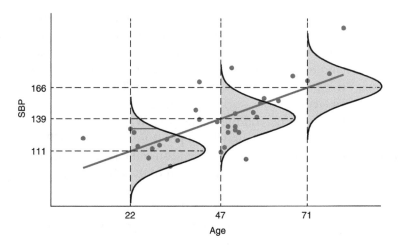

Figure 5.2   Scatter plot and regression model for the blood pressure example. The bell-shaped curves are the conditional probability distributions (CPDs) of the outcome SBP, which is conditioned on the observed value *x* (age). The length of the solid horizontal bar indicates the likelihood of an observed SBP of 131 for a 22-year-old woman.

(MSE) (see the sidebar titled "MaxLike-based derivation of the MSE loss in linear regression" in chapter 4):

$$\text{loss} = \frac{1}{n} \sum_{i=1}^{n} \left(a \cdot x_i + b - y_i \right)^2$$

where *x* is the age in our example. After the slope and intercept is optimized, you can derive the constant standard deviation from the residuals. You need to know this standard deviation to get a probabilistic model with known CPD $p(Y|X = x) = N(y; \mu_x, \sigma)$, allowing you to determine the likelihood of an observed outcome.

But if you want to allow the standard deviation to depend on *x*, the derivation of the loss gets more complicated. The terms in the likelihood that depend on the variance can no longer be ignored when minimizing the NLL. The resulting loss isn't the MSE anymore but a more complicated expression (for a derivation, see the sidebar titled "MaxLike-based derivation of the MSE loss in linear regression" in chapter 4):[4]

$$\text{loss} = \frac{1}{n} \sum_{i=1}^{n} -\log \left(\frac{1}{\sqrt{2\pi\sigma_{x_i}^2}} \right) + \frac{(x_i - y_i)^2}{2\sigma_{x_i}^2}$$

---

[4] In contrast to this sidebar mentioned here from chapter 4 (section 4.3), we divided by *n*. This is OK because it does not change the position of the minimum.

This isn't a standard loss function in Keras; therefore, you needed to define a custom loss function that then compiles into the model. In chapter 4, you saw how to derive the NLL and how to work with customized loss functions. Doing this manually gives you a good understanding and full control over the whole fitting procedure. But it also is sometimes error-prone and not really convenient. Therefore, you'll now learn about TFP, which can facilitate your work considerably.

TFP allows you to concentrate on the model part. When thinking in probabilistic models, you try to find a prediction model that predicts for new data CPDs that assign high likelihoods to the observed outcomes. To measure the performance of a probabilistic model, you, therefore, use the joint likelihood of the observed data. Accordingly, you use the negative log-likelihood as a measure for the "badness" of probabilistic models, which is the reason why you use the NLL as the loss function.

See figure 5.2 for an example where the CPD is a Normal $N(\mu_x, \sigma)$ distribution with a constant variance σ. The parameter is modeled by $\mu_x = a \cdot x + b$, the linear regression in its standard form.

You'll see later in this chapter that for other tasks like modeling discrete count data with low average counts, the Normal distribution isn't the best choice. You might want to pick another distribution family for the CPD; for example, a Poisson distribution. Within the TFP framework, this isn't a big deal. You can simply change the distribution. You'll see how to do this in several examples in this chapter.

HANDS-ON TIME   Open http://mng.bz/zjNw. Step through the notebook while reading.

Because probability distributions are the main tool for capturing uncertainties in probabilistic models, let's check out how to work with a TFP distribution. TFP provides a quickly growing collection of distributions. The Normal distribution is the distribution family that you're probably most familiar with, so let's start with defining a Normal distribution from TFP (see listing 5.1). We'll sample from it and then determine the likelihood of the sampled values.

Listing 5.1 Working with a TFP Normal distribution

```
import tensorflow_probability as tfp
tfd = tfp.distributions
d = tfd.Normal(loc=[3], scale=1.5)
x = d.sample(2)
px = d.prob(x)
print(x)
print(px)
```

Creates a 1D Normal distribution with a mean of 3 and a standard deviation of 1.5

Samples two realizations from the Normal distribution

Computes the likelihood for each of the two sampled values in the defined Normal distribution

---

You can use TFP distributions for different purposes. See table 5.1 and the notebook for some important methods that you can apply to TFP distributions.

Table 5.1   Important methods for TFP distributions[a]

Methods for TensorFlow distributions	Description	Numerical result when calling the method on `dist = tfd.Normal(loc=1.0, scale=0.1)`
`sample(n)`	Samples *n* numbers from the distribution	`dist.sample(3).numpy()` `array([1.0985107, 1.0344477, 0.9714464], dtype = float32)` Note that these are random numbers.
`prob(value)`	Returns the likelihood (probability density in the case of models for continuous outcomes) or probability (in the case of models for discrete outcomes) for the values (tensors)	`dist.prob((0,1,2)).numpy()` `array([7.694609e-22, 3.989423e+00, 7.694609e-22], dtype = float32)`
`log_prob(value)`	Returns the log-likelihood or log probability for the values (tensors)	`dist.log_prob((0,1,2)).numpy()` `array([-48.616352, 1.3836466, -48.616352], dtype = float32)`
`cdf(value)`	Returns the cumulative distribution function (CDF) that this is a sum or the integral of, up to the given values (tensors)	`dist.cdf((0,1,2)).numpy()` `array([7.619854e-24, 5.000000e-01, 1.000000e+00], dtype = float32)`
`mean()`	Returns the mean of the distribution	`dist.mean().numpy()` `1.0`
`stddev()`	Returns the standard deviation of the distribution	`dist.stddev().numpy()` `0.1`

[a] For more methods, see http://mng.bz/048p.

5.3   *Modeling continuous data with TFP*

In this section, you'll use TFP for a linear prediction model. You'll adapt the linear model to optimally fit data that shows a quite complicated variability.

When doing a first model selection experiment, it's best if you start with some simulated data that gives you full control over the structure of the data. You can get train, validation, and test data by randomly splitting the simulated data into three parts, then lock the test data. Visualizing the synthetic training and validation data shows that it looks a little bit like a fish (see figure 5.3). The test data shouldn't be touched; you shouldn't even have a look at it! Figure 5.3 doesn't show the test. If you get this data and manually try to draw a smooth curve through the data, you'd probably end up with a straight line. But there are more things to notice: the data variability isn't a constant but changes over the *x* range. In this and the following chapter, you'll learn how you can set up probabilistic models that account for these properties.

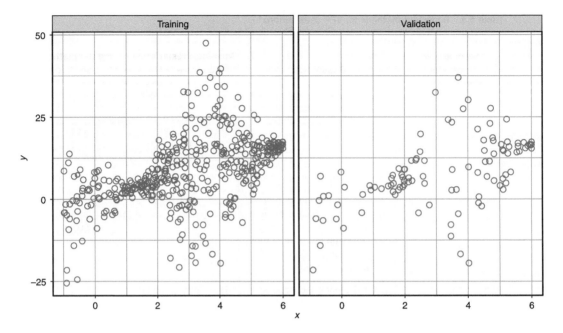

Figure 5.3   Visualization of the train (left) and test (right) data of the synthetic data set

5.3.1   *Fitting and evaluating a linear regression model with constant variance*

Let's assume you want to develop a probabilistic prediction model for the data shown in figure 5.3. After inspecting the data, the first idea is to go for a linear model. Let's use the TFP framework to set up a probabilistic linear regression model (see listing 5.2). For this purpose, you pick a Normal distribution $N(\mu_x, \sigma^2)$ as the CPD.

Let's assume the standard linear regression setting where only the parameter μ_x depends on the input x and the standard deviation is a constant. How do you handle a constant standard deviation in TFP? You saw in chapter 4 (see the sidebar titled "Max-Like-based derivation of the MSE loss in linear regression") that the value of the constant variance doesn't impact the estimation of the linear model. Therefore, you can freely pick any value for the constant variance; for example, 1 when using `tfd.Normal()` (see listing 5.2). Accordingly, your NN needs only to estimate one output for the parameter μ_x.

TFP lets you mix Keras layers with TFP distributions. You can connect the output of the NN with a distribution via the `tfp.layers.DistributionLambda` layer. This layer takes as input two things: a distribution and the values for its parameters. Technically speaking, a distribution like `tf.distributions.Normal` is a realization of `tf.distributions.Distribution`. You can, therefore, call the methods shown in table 5.1. The distribution parameters (such as loc (μ) and scale (σ) for normal) are given by the previous layer.

In listing 5.2, you see how to use a `tfp.layers.DistributionLambda` layer to construct the CPD $P(y|x, w)$. Here we choose a Normal distribution $N(\mu_x, \sigma^2)$ with a location parameter μ_x, depending on x and a fixed-scale parameter $\sigma_x = 1$. The corresponding NLL is directly given by the likelihood that the CPD has assigned to the observed outcome y: $-\log(P(y|x, w))$. Because the result `distr` of `tfp.layers.Distribution-Lambda` is of type `tfd.Distribution`, this translates to `-distr.log_prob(y)` (see the second line in table 5.1). Thus, TFP frees you from deriving and programming the appropriate loss function for your model.

Listing 5.2   Using TFP for linear regression with a constant variance

```
from tensorflow.keras.layers import Input
from tensorflow.keras.layers import Dense
from tensorflow.keras.layers import Concatenate
from tensorflow.keras.models import Model
from tensorflow.keras.optimizers import Adam

def NLL(y, distr):
    return -distr.log_prob(y)

def my_dist(params):
    return tfd.Normal(loc=params, scale=1)
# set the sd to the fixed value 1

inputs = Input(shape=(1,))
params = Dense(1)(inputs)

dist = tfp.layers.DistributionLambda(my_dist)(params)
model_sd_1 = Model(inputs=inputs, outputs=dist)
model_sd_1.compile(Adam(), loss=NLL)
```

Computes the NLL of an observed y under the fitted distribution distr

Uses the output of the last layer (params) as the parameter(s) of a distribution

Sets up the NN with one output node

Calls a distributional layer to take the function my_dist with the argument params

Connects the output of the NN with a distribution

Compiles the model with NLL as a loss function

With the TFP code in listing 5.2, you've fitted a linear regression model. But is it a probabilistic model? A probabilistic model needs to provide a whole CPD for the output for each input x. In the case of a Gaussian CPD, this not only requires an estimated mean μ_x but also a standard deviation σ. In the standard linear regression case, a constant variance is chosen independently of the x position. In this case, we can estimate σ^2 by the variance of the residuals. This means you first need to fit the linear model before you can determine the variance that is used for all CPDs.

Now you're ready to use the trained model to do some probabilistic predictions on your validation data. For each test point, you'll predict a Gaussian CPD. To visualize how the model performs on the validation data, you can draw the validation data along with the predicted mean of the CPD, μ_x (see the solid line in figure 5.4), and the mean plus/minus two times the standard deviation of the CPD, $\mu_{x_i} \pm 2 \cdot \sigma$ corresponding to the 0.025 and 0.975 quantiles (see the dashed lines in figure 5.4).

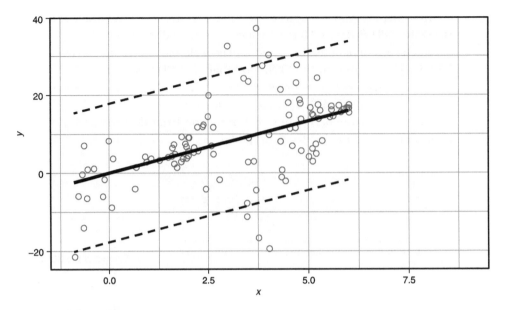

Figure 5.4 The synthetic validation data along with the predicted probabilistic model for linear regression, which is the same as an NN without a hidden layer. The mean μ_x of the CPD is modeled by the NN, and the standard deviation is assumed to be a constant. The black solid line indicates the positions of μ_{x_i}, and the dashed lines show the positions of the 0.025 and 0.975 quantiles.

HANDS-ON TIME Open http://mng.bz/zjNw. Step through the code to solve exercise 1 and follow the code while reading.

- Use TFP to fit a linear model with a constant standard deviation.
- Which constant standard deviation yields the lowest validation NLL?

When checking your fit visually (see figure 5.4), you might be satisfied with the positions of the mean (black solid line). But the varying spread of the outcome isn't captured at all. Does it matter? Yes, for sure. To better see this, let's check out how well the CPD matches the data distribution.

A matching CPD can assign high likelihoods to the observed outcome. For visualization purposes, let's do this for four randomly chosen test points: (−0.81, −6.14), (1.03, 3.42), (4.59, 6.68), and (5.75, 17.06) (see the filled circles in figure 5.5). The x positions of the selected points are indicated by the four dotted vertical lines in figure 5.5. A trained NN predicts the CPD from the x values. You get four Gaussian distributions with four different means but always the same standard deviation. Each CPD gives the probability distribution for all possible outcomes y for a given input of the test point x_{test}: $p(y|\mu_{x_{\text{test}}}, \sigma)$. The likelihood that the CPD assigns to the actually observed y_{test} is indicated by the horizontal line connecting the filled dots with the curved lines: $p(y_{\text{test}}|\mu_{x_{\text{test}}}, \sigma)$.

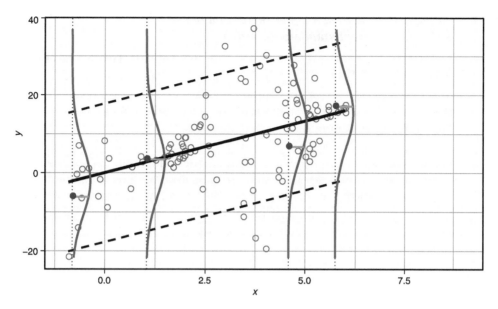

Figure 5.5 Validation data along with the predicted Gaussian CPDs. The model used is the linear model with constant data variability (see listing 5.2). The black solid line indicates the position of the mean, and the dashed lines are the positions of the 0.025 and 0.975 quantiles. For the four picked data points (filled dots), the predicted CPD is shown. The corresponding likelihoods are indicated by the solid horizontal line segments connecting the dots with the curves.

On first viewing figure 5.5, the model seems to assign reasonable likelihoods to the true outcomes. To quantify this, you can determine for each test point the assigned likelihood of the true observation and summarize this by the mean NLL over all points in the validation set, which is in this case:[5]

$$NLL(\text{constant sigma model}) = 3.53$$

How could you get a model that predicts better Gaussian CPDs? Remember, the better the model, the lower the NLL for the validation set. For a given standard deviation, a point gets the optimal likelihood if it's in the center of the Gaussian CPD. OK, the four picked points (see figure 5.5) aren't really in the center of their CPDs. If that were the case, these would lie on the bold line, but they are quite close. A second tuning parameter for the Gaussian is the standard deviation.

---

[5] See the notebook titled "Result: Constant sigma."

5.3.2 *Fitting and evaluating a linear regression model with a nonconstant standard deviation*

Let's try to get a better prediction model for the synthetic data that takes into account the varying spread of the data (see figure 5.3). How can you adapt your model to allow for a Gaussian CPD with a nonconstant standard deviation? No big deal! Just allow the model to learn the data variability too! You still assume a Normal distribution as CPD, but this time you want to learn both parameters.

The output of the NN can, in principle, take any value from minus infinity to plus infinity. One way to ensure that the standard deviation is always positive is to feed the output of the NN through an exponential function. We have done this before. A popular alternative is to use the softplus function. In figure 5.6, you see the softplus function beside the exponential (exp) function. In contrast to the exponential function, the softplus function increases linearly for large x values.

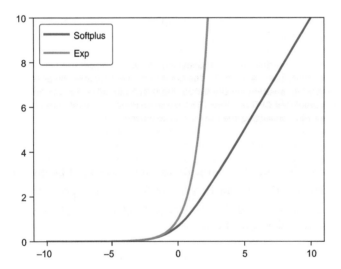

Figure 5.6 The softplus function compared with the exponential (exp) function. Both functions map arbitrary values to positive values.

This only requires a small change in our TFP code. You now have two output nodes (see line 5 in listing 5.3), and you tell the distributional layer the location and scale parameters derived by the NN.

Listing 5.3   A shallow NN for linear regression with nonconstant variance

```
def NLL(y, distr):
    return -distr.log_prob(y)        ⊲—|  Computes the
def my_dist(params):                         NLL of the model
    return tfd.Normal(
```

The first output node defines the mean (loc).

```
loc=params[:,0:1],
scale=1e-3 +
tf.math.softplus(0.05 * params[:,1:2]))

inputs = Input(shape=(1,))
params = Dense(2)(inputs)
dist =    tfp.layers.DistributionLambda(my_dist)(params)
model_monotoic_sd = Model(inputs=inputs, outputs=dist)
model_monotoic_sd.compile(Adam(learning_rate=0.01), loss=NLL)
```

Sets up the NN with two output nodes

The second output defines the standard deviation (scale) via the softplus function. To ensure a non-negative scale, a small constant is added.

Let's display the fitted model along with the data (see figure 5.7). But this isn't what you hoped for! True, the variance isn't modeled to be a constant across the whole x range. But the dashed lines, indicating $\mu_{x_i} \pm 2 \cdot \sigma$, only roughly follow the underlying data variability.

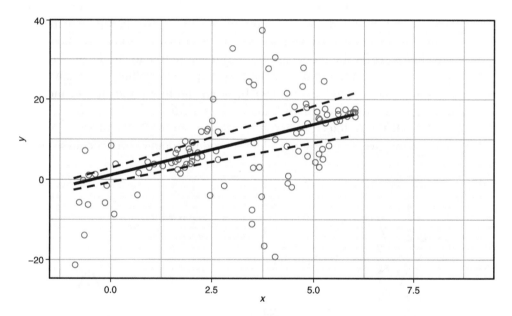

Figure 5.7 The synthetic validation data along with the predicted probabilistic model where the mean and the standard deviation of the CPD is modeled by an NN without a hidden layer. The black solid line indicates the position of the mean, and the dashed lines designate the positions of the 0.025 and 0.975 quantiles.

Can you guess what happened? Let's look at the code in listing 5.3 and think about the used NN architecture, which has no hidden layer. The two nodes in the output layer depend linearly on the input: $out_1 = a \cdot x + b$ and $out_2 = c \cdot x + d$. You can see in listing 5.3 that the first output gives the value of the loc argument, and the second output is put through a softplus function to determine the scale argument. Thus, the standard deviation only depends monotonically on the input, meaning it's impossible for the fitted standard deviation to follow the non-monotonic variance structure of the data. You can quantify the prediction performance by the mean validation NLL (see the notebook titled "Result: Monotonic sigma"):

$$NLL(\text{monotonic sigma}) = 3.55$$

This is comparable with the value 3.53 we got using a constant variance. You would expect a better, or at least an equal, performance for the "monotonic sigma" model because this model is more flexible and is also able to learn a constant variance (the "constant sigma" model). The small performance decrease, therefore, indicates a little overfitting, meaning the training set shows a slightly increasing variance by chance.

How can you improve the model? You need to allow the standard deviation to depend on x in a more flexible manner. You saw in the last chapters the simple recipe of DL to achieve flexibility: stack more layers. If you just introduce a hidden layer between the input and the two output nodes, you'd also allow the mean to depend in a non-linear manner on x. You don't really want to do this because then you wouldn't get a linear regression model anymore. But you're free to choose an architecture that directly connects the input with the first output controlling the mean (out$_1$) and to put one or several hidden layer(s) between the input and the second output controlling the standard deviation (out$_2$) (see figure 5.8).

To code the architecture in figure 5.8, you can use TFP and Keras. The functional API of Keras gives you greater flexibility in coding complex architectures where different

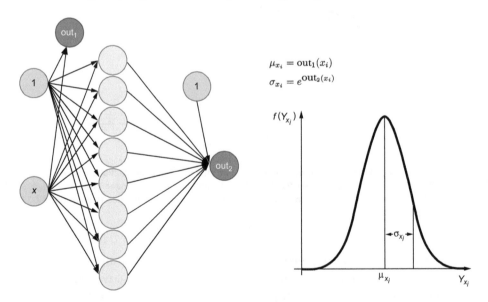

Figure 5.8   An NN architecture (left) for the two parameters μ_x, σ_x of a Gaussian CPD. The first output (out1) determines the mean μ_x of the CPD that linearly depends on x. The second output (out2) controls the standard deviation σ_x of the CPD that depends on x in a flexible manner. In the notebook for listing 5.4, there are three hidden layers.

output nodes can be computed in a very different manner from the input. But this requires that you save the result of each layer in a tensor variable and define (for each layer) which tensor it gets as input (see listing 5.4). The architecture shown in figure 5.8 translates to the code shown in listing 5.4, where you choose three hidden layers: one with 30 and two with 20 nodes between the input and the second output.

> **Listing 5.4 Using an NN with a hidden layer for linear regression with nonconstant variance**

```
def NLL(y, distr):
  return -distr.log_prob(y)
def my_dist(params):
  return tfd.Normal(loc=params[:,0:1],
scale=1e-3 +
tf.math.softplus(0.05 * params[:,1:2]))          ← The first output
                                                     models the mean;
                                                     no hidden layers
inputs = Input(shape=(1,))                           are used.
out1 = Dense(1)(inputs)                         ←
hidden1 = Dense(30,activation="relu")(inputs)
hidden1 = Dense(20,activation="relu")(hidden1)     The second output models
hidden2 = Dense(20,activation="relu")(hidden1)     the spread of the distribution;
out2 = Dense(1)(hidden2)                        ←  three hidden layers are used.
params = Concatenate()([out1,out2])             ←
dist = tfp.layers.DistributionLambda(my_dist)(params)    Combining the outputs
                                                         for the mean and the
model_flex_sd = Model(inputs=inputs, outputs=dist)       spread
model_flex_sd.compile(Adam(learning_rate=0.01), loss=NLL)
```

HANDS-ON TIME Open http://mng.bz/zjNw. Step through the code to solve exercises 2 and 3, and follow the code while reading.

- Fit linear regression models with nonconstant standard deviation.
- How do you pick the best model?
- How does the predicted CPD look outside the range of the training data?

The resulting probabilistic fit is displayed in figure 5.9. Now everything looks very nice! On the average, you have a linear relationship between input and outcome, but the variability of the outcome is different for different inputs. This is reflected by the distance of the two dashed lines in figure 5.9, between which ~95% of all data should fall, which this model seems to fulfill. Also, the predicted CPDs $p(y|\mu_{x_{test}}, \sigma)$ and the resulting likelihoods $p(y_{test}|\mu_{x_{test}}, \sigma)$ for the four test points (–0.81, –6.14), (1.03, 3.42), (4.59, 6.68), (5.75, 17.06) really look good now! Just enjoy for a moment how much an appropriate standard deviation of the Gaussian CPD can improve the likelihood with which the probabilistic model expects the true outcome (compare figures 5.5, 5.7, and 5.9).

To quantify the prediction performance, you can again determine the mean validation NLL (see the topic "Result: Flexible sigma" in the notebook):

$$\text{Validation mean NLL(flexible sigma)} = 3.11$$

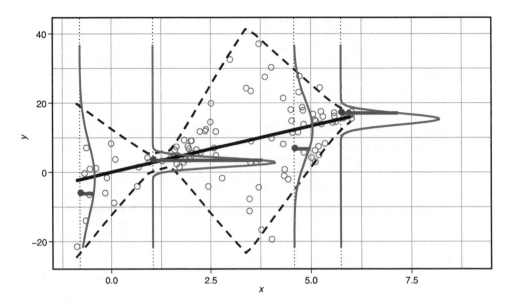

Figure 5.9   Validation data along with the predicted Gaussian CPDs from the linear model that allows for flexible data variability. The black solid line indicates the position of the mean, and the dashed lines represent the positions of the 0.025 and 0.975 quantiles. For four picked data points (the filled dots), the CPD is shown. The corresponding likelihoods are indicated by the solid horizontal line segments. An animated version comparing this approach with figure 5.5 can be found at http://mng.bz/K2JP.

According to the mean NLL on the validation data, you'd pick the last model with a flexible standard deviation of the Gaussian CPD as the winner. Let's do a clean finish and make sure that you avoid the overfitting pitfall when reporting the mean test NLL. Use your winning model to determine again the mean test NLL, which is

$$\text{Test mean NLL(flexible sigma)} = 3.15$$

Let's look back and recap what you learned. If you want to develop a probabilistic prediction model, your goal is to predict the correct CPD on new data. To evaluate if the predicted CPD indeed describes the distribution of the outcome in new data, you computed the mean NLL on the validation data. But what about the well-established MSE or the mean absolute error (MAE)? These two performance measures quantify how much the predicted mean deviates (on average) from the actual observed value. But these completely ignore the variance of the CPD, meaning they don't evaluate the correctness of the full CPD. For this reason, it's not appropriate to report the MSE or MAE alone if you want to assess the quality of a probabilistic model. We recommend that you always report the performance of a probabilistic regression model by the validation NLL and give only additional measures like validation MSE and MAE (or accuracy in case classification).

5.4 *Modeling count data with TensorFlow Probability*

When setting up a probabilistic model, the most challenging task is to pick the right distribution model for the outcome. The data type of the outcome plays an important role in this game. In the blood pressure example, the outcome was continuous. Given a certain age of a woman, you modeled the possible blood pressure values by a continuous Normal distribution, $N(\mu, \sigma)$, which has two parameters: the mean, μ, and standard deviation, σ. In the MNIST example, the outcome was categorical, and your task was to predict from a raw image the probability that the image shows the digits 0, 1, 2, 3, 4, 5, 6, 7, 8, or 9 (see chapter 2). The predicted probabilities for the 10 possible digits make up the categorical outcome distribution, which is called multinomial distribution and has 10 parameters $p_0, p_1, \ldots, p_9$ that add up to 1.

In this section, you'll learn how to model outcomes that are counts. There are many use cases where you want to model count data; for example, counting the number of people y_i that are on a given image x_i, or the number of comments that a blog post receives in the upcoming 24 hours, or the number of deer killed in a road accident during a certain hour based on some features x_i (like the time of day, date, and so on). You'll later have the opportunity to do a case study predicting the number of roadkills. We recommend that you step through the following notebook while working through this section.

 HANDS-ON TIME Open http://mng.bz/90xx. Step through the notebook and try to understand the code. What's the mean NLL on the test data absolute error and the RMSE for linear regression and for Poisson regression?

Let's start with a classical example in count data analysis, taken from https://stats.idre .ucla.edu/r/dae/zip/. Your task here is to predict the number of fish (y) caught by a fishing party in a state park. We have a small data set of 250 groups that we call camper data. The groups of individuals visited a state park and provided the following information:

- How many people are in the group?
- How many children in the group?
- Did the group come with a camper to the park?

To set up a probabilistic model for count data, you'll learn about two new distributions that can only output whole numbers and, thus, are suitable for count data: the Poisson distribution and the zero-inflated Poisson (ZIP) distribution. The Poisson distribution has one parameter; the ZIP distribution has two parameters. Shortly, you'll learn more about their meaning. To use one of these distribution models for predicting a count outcome with a probabilistic DL model, you follow the standard TFP procedure: use an NN with an appropriate architecture and capacity to transform the input into a predicted CPD, and in the TFP, pick the distribution that corresponds to your chosen outcome prediction (see figure 5.10).

Figure 5.10 Count data modeling with probabilistic DL. The network determines the parameters of a probability distribution. Fit the model using the MaxLike principle. In the example shown, the outcome is count data. Here it's modeled by a Poisson distribution, where NN is used to control its rate parameter λ (see the chosen last plate with one output node), which gives the mean and the variance.

Before working through this chapter, your first impulse might be to fit the camper data with a standard NN and a linear activation function at the output node and then train the NN using the MSE loss. Using a linear regression model is, in fact, what many people do in this situation, but it's not the best solution! You can try this naive approach using the code provided in the notebook: http://mng.bz/jgMz.

To check the performance of the model, you can compare the predicted outcome distributions with the actual outcomes. Let's pick the predicted outcome distribution for the test observations 31 and 33 (see figure 5.11). Observation 31 is a group that caught five fish and had the following features: used live bait, had a camper, and were four persons with one child. Observation 33 is a group that caught zero fish and had the following features: used live bait, no camper, four persons, two children. Looking at the predicted CPDs for observations 31 and 33 shows that the likelihood of the observed outcome (five fish and zero fish) is quite good for both observations (the dotted line in figure 5.11). But according to these CPDs, negative numbers of fish caught would also have quite high likelihoods. Common sense tells you that catching –2 fish is rather unlikely. Another problem of the linear regression model for count data is that the predicted outcome distributions are continuous, but the possible number of fish caught are integer numbers—you can't catch half a fish.

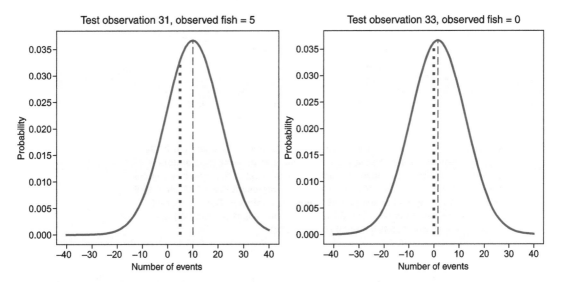

Figure 5.11 The predicted Normal distribution for the test observations 31 (left) and 33 (right) for the camper data. The dashed lines indicate the positions of the predicted means. The thick dotted lines indicate the likelihoods of the observed outcome of observations: 31 (five fish caught) and 33 (zero fish caught).

To compare the observed outcomes with the predicted CPDs simultaneously for all test points in one plot, you need to draw a CPD at each test point. Such a plot would look rather crowded. Instead of the whole CPD, figure 5.12 shows only the mean (solid line), the 2.5% (lower dashed line), and 97.5% percentile (upper dashed line) to characterize it. Because of multiple features, it's no longer possible to put the feature on the horizontal axis (as in the simple linear regression). Instead, the predicted mean of the CPD is plotted on the horizontal axis. Observations 31 and 33 shown in figure 5.11 are highlighted. Again, the problem of predicted negative number of fish caught is visible. The lower dashed line is below zero and even the solid line, representing the predicted mean of the number of fish caught is in some regions below zero. Further, in case of a good fit, the solid line should run through the mean of the

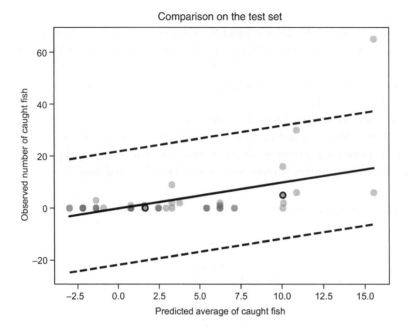

Figure 5.12   Linear regression showing a comparison of the predicted CPDs with the observed data. The observed fish caught in the test camper data is plotted versus the predicted mean number of fish caught. The solid line depicts the mean of the predicted CPD. The dashed lines represent the 0.025 and 0.975 quantiles, yielding the borders of a 95% prediction interval. The highlighted points correspond to observation 33 with zero fish caught (on the left) and observation 31 with five fish caught (on the right).

observed data points, which is obviously not the case. The plot shows only the observed data and not its mean, but still, you can see that the predicted mean (up to 8) is larger than the data average. Besides this, the 95% prediction interval indicated by the dashed lines seems to be unreasonably large for the small numbers of fish predicted.

Linear regression assuming a Gaussian CPD has obviously some flaws. But which distribution is more appropriate? That's the question! Even after realizing that you're dealing with count data, there are different options for count data. In the simplest case, count data can be described by a Poisson distribution.

5.4.1   *The Poisson distribution for count data*

Back in the pre-DL era, around the year 1900, Ladislaus von Bortkiewicz wanted to model the number of soldiers kicked to death by horses each year in each of the 14 cavalry corps of the Prussian army. As training data, they had data from 20 years. In his first statistics book, *Das Gesetz der kleinen Zahlen* (*The Law of Small Numbers*), he modeled the number of soldiers kicked to death by horses by the Poisson distribution, a distribution named after Siméon Denis Poisson. To keep our discussion less bloody, the number of raindrops in a bucket per minute can also be modeled by a Poisson distribution. Or, in our case, the number of fish caught per state park camper group. In all these examples, you count the number of events per unit; these units are often units of time, but they can also be other units like the number of homicides per 100,000 inhabitants.

Often in real life, you have to deal with randomness, and you don't always observe the same number of events each time (unit). But let's assume that, on average, there are two events per unit (two dead soldiers per year, two raindrops in the bucket per minute, or two fish caught per stay). Figure 5.13 shows the resulting probability distribution of possible observed outcomes. The average number of events is the only needed information to fix the distribution (see equation 5.1). This distribution assigns a probability to each possible outcome: a probability to observe zero events per unit or to observe one event per unit, two events per unit, and so on. Because it's a probability distribution, all probabilities add up to one.

Figure 5.13 shows that two events per (time) unit occur with a quite high probability of above 0.25, but other possible outcomes also have some probability. The average number of events per unit plays an important role because it defines the only parameter of the Poisson distribution, which is often called *rate* and is usually indicated in formulas with the symbol λ. In our case, $\lambda = 2$, but because λ is the average number of events per unit, λ isn't always an integer. Just in case you're curious, there's a formula

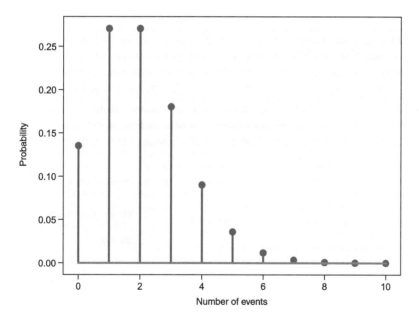

Figure 5.13   Poisson distribution for the case that there are, on average, two events per unit (two dead soldiers, two raindrops in the bucket, or two fish caught). It's quite likely to observe either one or two events. This probability distribution is from the notebook nb_ch05_02.ipynb.

for the Poisson distribution that defines the probability for each possible value k of the counted events. The probability with which it's observed is

$$P(y = k) = \frac{\lambda^k \cdot e^{-\lambda}}{k!}$$

Equation 5.1

where $k!$ indicates the factorial of k ($k! = 1 \cdot 2 \cdot 3 \cdot \ldots \cdot k$). Note that now, in contrast to the Gaussian $P(y = k)$, we have a real probability and not just a density (as the Gaussian). To stress this, it is sometimes also called *probability mass function*. A remarkable property of Poisson distributions is that λ not only defines the center of the distribution (the expected value), but also the variance. The average number of events λ is, therefore, all you need to fix the distribution.

In this listing, you can see how the Poisson distribution can be modeled with TFP.

Listing 5.5   The Poisson distribution in TFP

The standard deviation, yielding sqrt(2.0) = 1.41 . . .
Poisson distribution with parameter rate = 2
Integer values from 0 to 10 for the x-axis in figure 5.13

```
dist = tfd.poisson.Poisson(rate = 2)
vals = np.linspace(0,10,11)
p = dist.prob(vals)
print(dist.mean().numpy())
print(dist.stddev().numpy())
```

Computes the probability for the values

The mean value, yielding 2.0

Now you have a proper distribution for count data. We estimate the parameter rate of the distribution using an NN. We use a very simple network, without a hidden layer, and its task is to predict a Poisson CPD that only requires you to determine the rate parameter. The parameter rate in the Poisson distribution is zero or a positive real value. Because the output of an NN with linear activation could be negative, we take the exponential function as the activation function before using it as the rate. (You could also choose to use a softplus activation, if you would like to do so.) This network is shown in the following listing.

Listing 5.6   Simple Poisson regression for the number of fish caught

Defines a single layer with one output

```
inputs = Input(shape=(X_train.shape[1],))
rate = Dense(1,
             activation=tf.exp)(inputs)
p_y = tfp.layers.DistributionLambda(tfd.Poisson)(rate)

model_p = Model(inputs=inputs, outputs=p_y)


def NLL(y_true, y_hat):
    return -y_hat.log_prob(y_true)
```

We use the exponential of the output to model the rate.

Glues the NN and the output layer together. Note that output p_y is a tf.distribution.

The second argument is the output of the model and thus a TFP distribution. It's as simple as calling log_prob to calculate the log probability of the observation that's needed to calculate the NLL.

```
model_p.compile(Adam(learning_rate=0.01), loss=NLL)
model_p.summary()
```

If you stepped through the code in the notebook, you noticed that the solution with the Poisson distribution is better than using linear regression. The root mean squared error (RMSE) is approximately 7.2 for the Poisson regression, lower than 8.6, which is the RMSE for the linear regression. But more importantly, the NLL is 2.7 for the Poisson regression compared to 3.6 for the linear regression and, thus, is much lower.

Let's have a closer look at the results from the Poisson prediction and use the fitted Poisson model to predict the CPDs for the test observations 31 and 33 (see figure 5.14). The predicted outcome distributions for observations 31 and 33 are Poisson distributions with $\text{rate}_{31} = 5.56$ and $\text{rate}_{33} = 0.55$, respectively. The likelihood of the observed outcomes (five fish and zero fish) is quite good for both observations (the dotted line in figure 5.11).

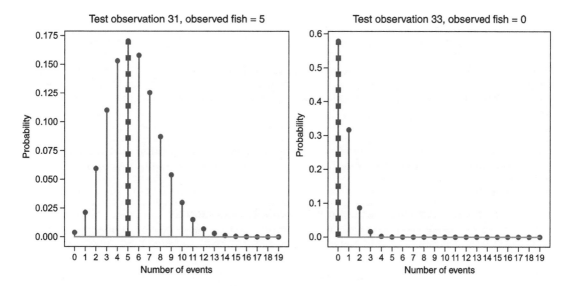

Figure 5.14 The predicted Poisson distribution for the test observations 31 (left) and 33 (right). The thick dotted lines indicate the likelihood of the observed outcome for the observations.

To compare the observed outcomes with the predicted CPDs simultaneously for all the test points in one plot, you can again plot the observed number of fish versus the predicted mean number of fish (see figure 5.15) and indicate the mean of the predicted CPD as a solid line and the 2.5% and 97.5% percentiles of the predicted CPD as dashed lines. You might wonder why the quantile curves aren't smooth but take whole numbers at the position of the predicted CPD (see the right panel in figure 5.15). The answer lies in the nature of the Poisson distribution and the definition of the percentiles: a Poisson model can only assign probabilities to integer values. The 97.5%

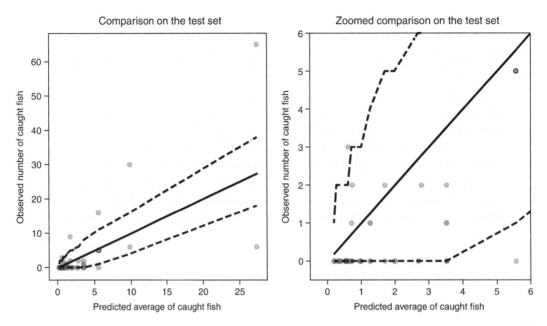

Figure 5.15   **Poisson regression prediction results for the camper example. The observed fish caught in the test sample is plotted versus the predicted mean number of fish caught. To indicate the predicted CPD, the solid lines depict the CPD's mean. The dashed lines represent the 0.025 and 0.975 quantiles, yielding the borders of a 95% prediction interval.**

percentile, for example, is defined as the value in the distribution that can only be an integer for which 97.5% of the values are smaller than or equal to this value.

How to read diagnostic plots for probabilistic models

Here's some hints for reading the diagnostic graphs used to evaluate the performance of probabilistic models. Note that in figures 5.12, 5.15, and 5.17, the observed outcome is plotted versus the mean of the predicted CPD (not versus an input feature as in the simple linear regression with one variable). Because in the camper data we have four features, it's not possible to use a single input feature for the horizontal axis, and the graphical representation gets harder. Also note that different combinations of input features can yield not only the same predicted mean for the CPD, but can potentially have different quantiles. In these cases, you have several CPDs at the same mean positions but with different quantiles, resulting in more than one quantile at the same *x* position. The more data you have, the higher the probability to observe such cases. In chapter 6, you'll see such cases. Also, the jumps in the quantiles (dashed lines in the figures) aren't artifact. Because the *x*-axis doesn't represent a smooth change of an input variable anymore, such jumps are possible. For the same reason, the quantiles don't need to change smoothly (see figure 5.17). The fact that quantiles do not need to show a monotonic behavior was already visible in the simple linear regression example (see figure 5.9). The curve of the CPD's mean (solid line in figure 5.15) is always the main diagonal because it plots the mean versus the mean.

Note that in contrast to the linear regression model, the Poisson model predicts outcome distributions that only assign probabilities to values that can actually be observed: the non-negative and whole numbers of fish caught. In case of an ideal probabilistic prediction model, the mean of the observed values should correspond to the solid line, and 95% of all points should be between the two dashed lines. According to these criteria, the Poisson models seem to be reasonably good, at least for the majority of data. But still, there might be room for improvement.

It seems that there are a lot of groups that didn't catch any fish at all. How can it be that there are so many unlucky fishermen? We can only speculate, but it might also be that camping parties just brought their fishing gear as an excuse to drink vast amounts of beer and not to go fishing at all. Therefore, there might be two reasons to leave the state park with zero fish: bad luck or no fishing at all. A model explicitly taking those lazy fishermen into account is the zero-inflated model. We discuss that model next.

5.4.2 Extending the Poisson distribution to a zero-inflated Poisson (ZIP) distribution

The zero-inflated Poisson (ZIP) distribution takes into account the fact that there are many zeros, more than are compatible with the number of expected zeros in a Poisson distribution. In our examples, these are the lazy camping parties not fishing at all. In the ZIP distribution, you can model the excess of zeros by the introduction of a zero-generating process as follows: you toss a coin. The coin has a probability p to show heads. If this is the case, you have a lazy camping party who yields zero fish. If not, you have a regular fishing group, and you can use a Poisson distribution to predict the number of fishes caught. To fit your count data with a ZIP outcome model in a TFP manner, you set up an NN with a ZIP distributional.

Unfortunately, TFP doesn't yet provide a ZIP distribution. But it's quite easy to define a custom function for a new distribution based on existing TFP distributions (see listing 5.7). The ZIP needs two parameters:

1 The probability p with which additional zeros are produced
2 The rate of a Poisson distribution

The ZIP function takes as input the two output nodes from an NN: one for the rate and one for p. As shown in listing 5.7, we use the exponential transformation on the first component out[:,0:1] of the output out to get a positive value for the rate, and the sigmoid transformation on the output out_2 of the NN to get a value between 0 and 1 for p.

Listing 5.7 Custom distribution for a ZIP distribution

The first component codes the rate. We used exponential to guarantee values > 0 and the squeeze function to flatten the tensor.

The second component codes zero inflation; using the sigmoid squeezes the value between 0 and 1.

```
def zero_inf(out):
    rate = tf.squeeze(tf.math.exp(out[:,0:1]))
    s = tf.math.sigmoid(out[:,1:2])
```

```
                    probs = tf.concat([1-s, s], axis=1)          ◁      The two probabilities
                    return tfd.Mixture(                                  for 0's or Poissonian
                        cat=tfd.Categorical(probs=probs),               distribution
                        components=[
                        tfd.Deterministic(loc=tf.zeros_like(rate)),  ◁   Zero as a
                        tfd.Poisson(rate=rate),       ◁                  deterministic
                    ])                                                   value
```

tfd.Categorical allows creating a mixture of two components.

Value drawn from a Poissonian distribution

The network is then simply a network without a hidden layer and two output nodes. The following listing shows the code to setup the network.

Listing 5.8   An NN in front of a ZIP distribution

```
## Definition of the custom parameterized distribution
inputs = tf.keras.layers.Input(shape=(X_train.shape[1],))
out = Dense(2)(inputs)
p_y_zi = tfp.layers.DistributionLambda(zero_inf)(out)
model_zi = Model(inputs=inputs, outputs=p_y_zi)
```

A dense layer without activation. The transformation is done in the zero_inf function.

You can now use the fitted ZIP model to predict the probability distribution for observations in the test data set. Let's use the fitted ZIP model to predict the CPDs for the test observations 31 and 33 (see figure 5.16).

The most striking feature of the predicted ZIP CPDs is the large peak at 0 (see figure 5.16). This is due to the zero-inflated process modeling a higher number of zeros compared to a Poisson process. The likelihood of the observed outcomes (five fish and zero fish) is quite good for both observations (see the dotted lines in figure 5.16).

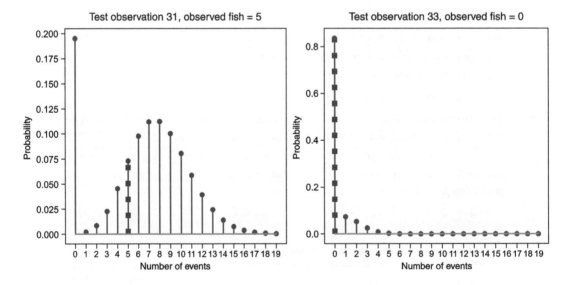

Figure 5.16   The predicted ZIP distribution for the test observations 31 (left) and 33 (right). The thick dotted lines indicate the likelihood of the observed outcome of the observations.

To compare the observed outcomes with the predicted CPDs simultaneously for all test points in one plot, you can again plot the observed number of fish versus the predicted mean number of fish (see figure 5.17). To indicate the shape of the predicted CPD, we plot the mean of the predicted CPD (see the solid lines in figure 5.17) and the 2.5% and 97.5% percentiles of the predicted CPD (see the dashed lines in figure 5.17). In the ZIP model, the 2.5% percentile stays at zero over the whole range. This means that for all groups, the predicted ZIP CPDs assign a probability higher than 2.5% to the outcome zero, which nicely corresponds to the high number of observed zeros.

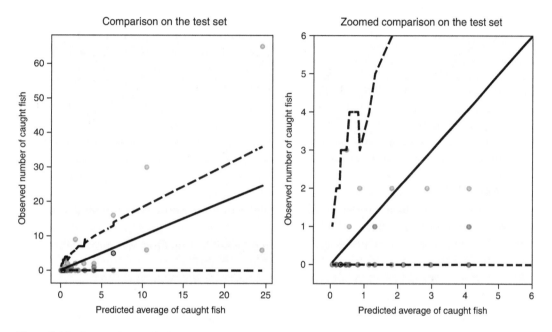

Figure 5.17 **Regression prediction results from the ZIP model for the camper example. The observed fish caught in the test sample is plotted versus the predicted mean number of fish caught. To indicate the predicted CPD, the solid lines depict the CPD's mean. The dashed lines represent the 0.025 and 0.975 quantiles, yielding the borders of a 95% prediction interval.**

In figure 5.17, it seems that the mean of the observed values is close to the solid lines and that 95% of all points are in between the two dashed lines. When quantifying the performance of the ZIP model by its test NLL, it turns out that the zero-inflated model outperforms both the linear regression and the Poisson model (see table 5.2).

For fitting the data of the fishing party, there is no clear consensus to which model is the overall best. Table 5.2 reveals that Poisson is best in terms of RMSE and MAE. The ZIP model is best in terms of NLL. But as discussed in section 5.2, to measure the probabilistic prediction performance, you should use the mean test NLL. The ZIP model is, therefore, the best probabilistic model of all three models' tests. Note that

Table 5.2 Comparison of the prediction performance of different models on validation data. If you run the notebook, you might get slightly different values. There's some randomness involved, and there's not a lot of data. But the overall behavior should be more or less the same.

	Linear Regression	Poisson	Zero-Inflated
RMSE	8.6	7.2	7.3
MAE	4.7	3.1	3.2
NLL	3.6	2.7	2.2

strictly speaking, the NLL should be only compared among discrete models (Poisson or ZIP as CPD) but not between a continuous and a discrete model (Gaussian or Poisson as CPD). Is there a better model? There might be a model with a lower NLL, but you can't tell. In this application, there's no theoretical lower bound of the NLL.

In the end, just for completeness, we'd like to note that there's a third way to deal with count data, and that's using the so-called negative binomial distribution. Like the ZIP distribution, it's a distribution with two parameters that allows not only the mean of the counts, but also the standard deviation of the counts to depend on the input.

Summary

- A probabilistic model predicts for each input a whole conditional probability distribution (CPD).
- The predicted CPD assigns for each possible outcome y, a probability with which it's expected.
- The negative log-likelihood (NLL) measures how well the CPD matches the actual distribution of the outcomes.
- You use the NLL as a loss function when training a probabilistic model.
- You use the NLL on new data to measure and to compare the prediction performance of different probabilistic models.
- Using a proper choice for the CPD enhances the performance of your models.
- For continuous data, a common first choice is a Normal distribution.
- For count data, common choices for distribution are Poisson, negative binomial, or zero-inflated Poisson (ZIP).

Probabilistic deep learning models in the wild

This chapter covers

- Probabilistic deep learning in state-of-the-art models
- Flexible distributions in modern architectures
- Mixtures of probability distributions for flexible CPDs
- Normalizing flows to generate complex data like facial images

Many real-world data like sound samples or images come from complex and high-dimensional distributions. In this chapter, you'll learn how to define complex probability distributions that can be used to model real-world data. In the last two chapters, you learned to set up models that work with easy-to-handle distributions. You worked with linear regression models with a Gaussian conditional probability distribution (CPD) or a Poisson model with its distribution as a CPD. (Maybe you find yourself in the figure at the top of this chapter, where the ranger stands in a protected area with some domestic animals, but the animals out in the world are more wilder than the ones you've worked with up to now.) You also learned enough about different kinds of domestic probabilistic models to join us and journey into the wild to state-of-the-art models that handle complex CPDs.

One way to model complex distributions are mixtures of simple distributions such as Normal, Poisson, or logistic distributions, which you know from the previous chapters. Mixture models are used in state-of-the-art networks like Google's parallel WaveNet or OpenAI's PixelCNN++ to model the output.

- WaveNet generates realistic sounding speech from text.
- PixelCNN++ generates realistic looking images.

In a case study in this chapter, we give you the chance to set up your own mixture models and use these to outperform a recent publicly described prediction model. You also learn another way to model these complex distributions: the so-called *normalizing flows*. Normalizing flows (NFs) allow you to learn a transformation from a simple distribution to a complicated distribution. In simple cases, this can be done with a statistical method called the *change of variable* method. You'll learn how to apply this method in section 6.3.2, and you'll see that TensorFlow Probability (TFP) supports this method with so-called bijectors.

By combining the change of variable method with DL, you can learn quite complicated and high-dimensional distributions as encountered in real-world applications. For example, sensor readings from complex machines are high-dimensional data. If you have a machine that is working correctly, you can learn the corresponding "machine OK" distribution. After you learn this distribution, you can continuously check if the sensor data the machine produces is still from the "machine OK" distribution. If the probability that the sensor data comes from the "machine OK" distribution is low, you might want to check the machine. This application is called *novelty detection*. But you can also do more fun applications, such as modeling the distributions of images of faces and then sampling from this distribution to create realistic-looking faces of people who don't exist. You can imagine that such a facial image distribution is quite complicated. You'll do other fun stuff with this distribution too, like giving Leonardo DiCaprio a goatee or morphing between different people. Sound complicated? Well, it's a bit complicated, but the good thing is that it works with the same principle that you've used so far (and will continue to use for the rest of the book)—the principle of maximum likelihood (MaxLike).

6.1 Flexible probability distributions in state-of-the-art DL models

In this section, you'll see how to use flexible probability distributions for state-of-the-art models in DL. Up to now, you've encountered different probability distributions such as the Normal or uniform distribution for a continuous variable (the blood pressure in the American women data), a multinomial distribution for a categorical variable (the ten digits in the MNIST data), or the Poisson and zero-inflated Poisson (ZIP) for count data (the number of fish caught in the camper data).

The number of parameters defining the distribution is often an indicator of the flexibility of the distribution. The Poisson distribution, for example, has only one parameter (often called rate).The ZIP distribution has two parameters (rate and the mixing proportion), and in chapter 5, you saw that you could achieve a better model for the camper data when using the ZIP distribution instead of the Poisson distribution as the CPD. According to this criterion, the multinomial distribution is especially flexible because it has as many parameters as possible values (or, actually, one parameter less because probabilities need to sum up to one). In the MNIST example, you used an image as input to predict a multinomial CPD for the categorical outcome. The predicted multinomial CPD has ten (or more correctly, nine) parameters, giving us the probabilities of ten possible classes (see figure 6.1).

Indeed, using the multinomial distribution in a digit classification by convolutional neural networks (CNNs) became the first and most heavily used real-world applications for DL models. In 1998, Yann LeCun, who was then working at AT&T

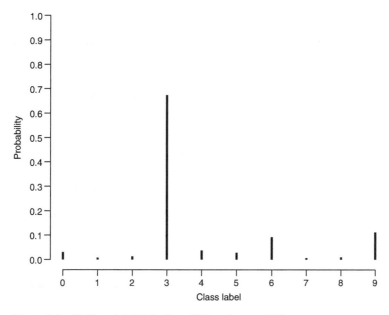

Figure 6.1 Multinomial distribution with ten classes: $MN(p_0, p_1, p_2, p_3, p_4, p_5, p_6, p_7, p_8, p_9)$

Bell Laboratory, implemented a CNN for ZIP code recognition. This is known as LeNet-5.

6.1.1 *Multinomial distribution as a flexible distribution*

In 2016, an example of a real-world task requiring flexible distribution was Google's WaveNet. This model generates astonishingly real-sounding artificial speech from text. Go to https://cloud.google.com/text-to-speech/ for a demonstration on the text of your choice. The architecture is based on 1D causal convolutions, like the ones you saw in section 2.3.3, and their specialization called *dilated convolutions*, which are shown in the notebook http://mng.bz/8pVZ. If you're interested in the architecture, you might also want to read the blog post http://mng.bz/EdJo.

WaveNet works directly on raw audio, usually using a sampling rate of 16 kHz (16 kiloHertz), which is 16,000 samples per second. But you can also use higher sampling rates. The audio signal for each time point t is then discretized (typically one uses 16-bit for this). For example, the audio signal at time t, x_t takes discrete values from 0 to $2^{16} - 1 = 65,535$. But the interesting piece for this chapter is the probability part (stuff from the probability shelf on the right side of figure 5.1 in chapter 5). In Wave-Net, we assume that x_t depends only on the audio signals of samples earlier in time. This gives us:

$$P(x_t) = P(x_t|x_{t-1}, x_{t-2}, \ldots x_0)$$ **Equation 6.1**

You can sample values x_t from previous values as shown in figure 6.2 and then determine the probability distribution of future values. Such models are called *autoregressive* models. Note that you look at a probabilistic model where you can predict a whole distribution of possible outcomes: $P(x_t)$. This lets you determine the likelihood or probability of the observed value x_t under the predicted distribution. Welcome home! You can use the good old MaxLike principle to fit this kind of model.

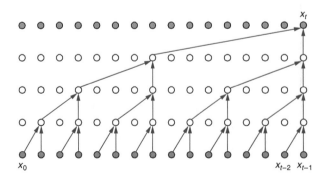

Figure 6.2 The WaveNet principle. The discrete values of the sound x_t at time t (on the top) are predicted from earlier values in time (on the bottom). Go to http://mng.bz/NKJN for an animated version of this figure showing how WaveNet can create samples from the future by successively applying equation 6.1.

But which type of distribution do you pick for $P(x_t)$? The outcome x can take all discrete values from 0 to $2^{16} - 1 = 65,535$. You don't really know how the distribution of these values will look. It probably won't look like a Normal distribution; that would suggest that there's a typical value and that the probability of the outcome values is decreasing quickly with distance to this typical value. You need a more flexible type of distribution.

In principle, you can model the 65,536 different values with a multinomial distribution, where you estimate a probability for each possible value. This ignores the ordering of the values $(0 < 1 < 2 < \ldots < 65,535)$, but it is indeed flexible because you can estimate for each of the 65,536 possible values a probability. The only restriction is that these predicted probabilities need to add up to 1, which can be easily achieved by a softmax layer. Oord et al., the authors of the WaveNet paper, chose to go down this road, but first, they reduced the depth of the signal from 16-bit (encoding 65,536 different values) to 8-bit (encoding 256 different values) after performing a non-linear transformation on the original sound values. All together, the Deep Mind people trained a dilated causal 1D convolutional NN with a softmax output, predicting the multinomial CPD with 256 classes and called it WaveNet.

Now you can draw new samples from the learned distribution. To do so, you provide a start sequence of audio values, x_0, x_1, ..., x_{t-1}, to the trained WaveNet, which will then predict a multinomial CPD: $P(x_t) = P(x_t|x_{t-1}, x_{t-2}, \ldots x_0)$. From that you then sample the next audio value x_t. You can proceed by providing x_1, x_2, ..., x_t and then sample from the resulting CPD the next value x_{t+1}, and so on.

Let's take a look at another prominent autoregressive model: OpenAI's PixelCNN. This is a network that can predict a pixel based on "previous" pixels. While for WaveNet, the ordering of the audio values is simply time, for images, there's no natural way to order the pixels. You could, for example, order them like the characters in text and read them from left to right and from top to button, like you do when reading this text. Then, these models can sample a pixel x_t for a certain color based on all previous pixels $x_{t'}$ with $t' < t$. You again have the same structure as in equation 6.1, where x_t is now a pixel value.

How do you train the models? One can take the same approach as in WaveNet and encode the pixel values with 8-bit, which limits the output to 256 possible values, and use a softmax on an output of 256 one-hot encoded categorical variables. This was indeed done in PixelCNN.

A year later, in early 2017, the engineers from OpenAI improved PixelCNN, which is reported in the paper called "PixelCNN++: Improving the PixelCNN with Discretized Logistic Mixture Likelihood and other Modifications" (see https://arxiv.org/abs/1701.05517). What! You don't know what "Discretized Logistic Mixture Likelihood" means? No worries. You'll learn about that soon. For the moment, let's just appreciate that with this new kind of CPD, OpenAI improved the prediction performance quantified by a test NLL of 2.92 compared to an NLL of 3.14 that was achieved by the original PixelCNN. After that paper on PixelCNN++, the Google engineers also enhanced WaveNet to something called parallel WaveNet (see https://arxiv.org/abs/1711.10433). Among other enhancements, they switched from a multinomial CPD to a discretized logistic mixture distribution as CPD. (You'll see what this means later.) When the parallel WaveNet model was set up, this was quite some work, but now with TensorFlow Probability, it's quite easy as you'll see in the next section.

6.1.2 *Making sense of discretized logistic mixture*

In both applications, WaveNet and PixelCNN, one has to predict discrete values from 0 to an upper value (typically, 255 or 65,535). This is like count data but with a maximum value. Why not take a count distribution like a Poissonian and clamp the maximal values? This would be fine, in principle, but it turns out the distributions need to be more complex. Therefore, in the papers, a mixture of distributions was used. The distributions used for the mixture in the PixelCNN++ paper were discretized logistic functions.

Let's unfold the discretized logistic mixture. You know that the density of a Normal distribution is bell-shaped, and the density of a logistic distribution looks, indeed, quite similar. Figure 6.3 shows the densities of the logistic functions with different values for the `scale` parameter on the left and the corresponding cumulative distribution function (CDF) on the right. The logistic CDF is, in fact, the same as the sigmoid activation function used in chapter 2. Have a look at the following optional notebook to learn more about the logistic functions.

OPTIONAL EXERCISE Open http://mng.bz/D2Jn. The notebook shows the code for figures 6.3, 6.4, and 6.5, and for listing 6.2.

- Read it in parallel with this text.
- Change the parameters of the distributions and see how the curves change.

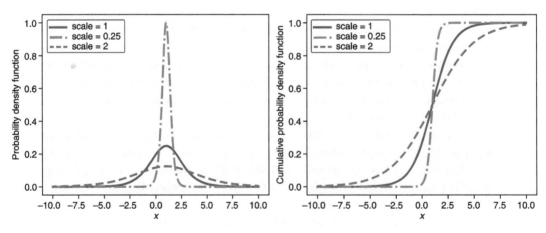

Figure 6.3 Three logistic functions created using `tfd.Logistic(loc=1, scale=scale)` with values of 0.25, 1.0, and 2.0 for the `scale` parameter. On the left is the probability density function (PDF) and on the right, the cumulative probability density function (CDF).

In the WaveNet and PixelCNN models, the outcome is discrete. An appropriate CDF should, therefore, model discrete (and not continuous) values. But the logistic distribution is for continuous values without lower and upper limits. Therefore, we discretize the logistic distribution and clamp the values to the possible range. In TFP, this can be done using the `QuantizedDistribution` function. `QuantizedDistribution` takes a probability distribution (called inner distribution in figure 6.4) and creates a quantized version of it. The optional exercise in the accompanying notebook elaborates on the details of using `QuantizedDistribution`.

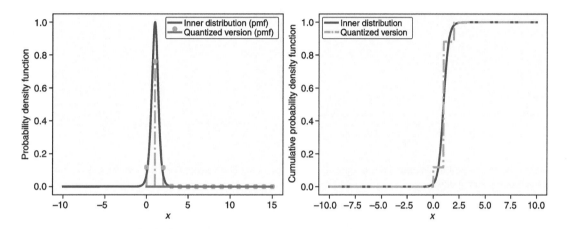

Figure 6.4   A quantized version of a logistic function with the parameters `loc=1` **and** `scale=0.25`

To handle more flexible distributions, we mix several quantized logistic distributions (see figure 6.5). For the mixing, one can use a categorical distribution that determines the weights (mixture proportions) of the different distributions that are mixed. The following listing shows an example.

Listing 6.1   Mixing two quantized distributions

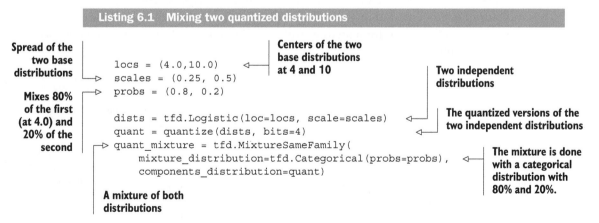

Figure 6.5 shows the resulting distribution. This distribution is appropriate for data like pixel values (in the case of PixelCNN) and sound amplitudes (in the case of WaveNet). You can easily construct more and more flexible outcome distributions if you don't mix only two but, for example, four or ten distributions together.

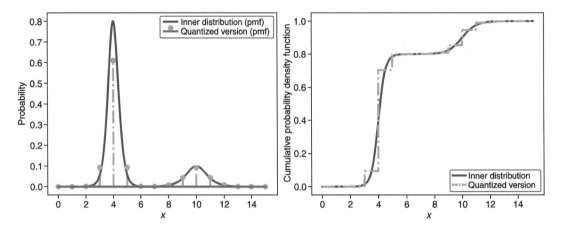

Figure 6.5   **The resulting discrete distribution when mixing two logistic distributions (see listing 6.2 for the code that produces these plots)**

If you want to use this distribution instead of, say, a Poissonian for your own network, you can copy and paste the function `quant_mixture_logistic` from the end of listing 6.2. It's taken from the TensorFlow documentation of `QuantizedDistribution`.

For each mixture component, the NN needs to estimate three parameters: the location and spread of the component, and how much the component is weighted. If you work with *num* logistic distribution components in the mixture, then the output of the NN needs to have 3 · *num* output nodes: three for each component, controlling location, spread, and weight. Note that the function `quant_mixture_logistic` expects an output without activation (as it is by default in Keras). The following listing shows how to use this function for a mixture with two components. In this case, the network has six outputs.

Listing 6.2   Using `quant_mixture_logistic()` as distribution

```
def quant_mixture_logistic(out, bits=8, num=3):
    loc, un_scale, logits = tf.split(out,
                                     num_or_size_splits=num,
                                     axis=-1)
    scale = tf.nn.softplus(un_scale)
    discretized_logistic_dist = tfd.QuantizedDistribution(
        distribution=tfd.TransformedDistribution(
            distribution=tfd.Logistic(loc=loc, scale=scale),
```

Splits the output into chunks of size 3

Transforms into positive values as needed for the scale

Shifts the distribution by 0.5

```
            bijector=tfb.AffineScalar(shift=-0.5)),
        low=0.,
        high=2**bits - 1.)
    mixture_dist = tfd.MixtureSameFamily(
        mixture_distribution=tfd.Categorical(logits=logits),
        components_distribution=discretized_logistic_dist)
    return mixture_dist
```

Using logits, no need for normalizing the probabilities

```
inputs = tf.keras.layers.Input(shape=(100,))
h1 = Dense(10, activation='tanh')(inputs)
out = Dense(6)(h1)
p_y = tfp.layers.DistributionLambda(quant_mixture_logistic)(out)
```

The last layer of the network. Controls the parameters of the mixture model: three for each component (here 2 · 3). Stay with the default linear activation and don't restrict the value range. The transformation ensuring positive values is done by the softplus function above.

6.2 Case study: Bavarian roadkills

Let's apply what we learned about mixtures in the last section to a case study demonstrating the advantages of using an appropriate flexible probability distribution as a conditional outcome distribution. Because it takes quite some computational resources to train NNs like PixelCNN, here we use a medium-sized data set. The data set describes deer-related car accidents in the years 2002 through 2011 on roads in Bavaria, Germany. It counts the number of deer killed during 30-minute periods anywhere in Bavaria. We previously used this data set in other studies for the analysis of count data. It's originally from https://zenodo.org/record/17179. Table 6.1 contains some rows of the data set after some preprocessing.[1]

Table 6.1 Some rows of deer-related car accidents in Bavaria

Wild	Year	Time	Daytime	Weekday
0	2002.0	0.000000	night.am	Sunday
0	2002.0	0.020833	night.am	Sunday
...	...	...	...	...
1	2002.0	0.208333	night.am	Sunday
0	2002.0	0.229167	pre.sunrise.am	Sunday
0	2002.0	0.270833	pre.sunrise.am	Sunday

---

[1] In case you're interested, the preprocessing was done using the statistics software R; the script is available at http://mng.bz/lGg6. We'd like to thank Sandra Siegfried and Torsten Hothorn from the University of Zurich for providing us with help and the initial version of the R script.

The columns have the following meanings:

- *Wild*—The number of deer killed in road accidents in Bavaria.
- *Year*—The year (from 2002 to 2009 in the training set and from 2010 to 2011 for the test set).
- *Time*—The number of days to the event (starting with January 1, 2002, as zero). These numbers are measured in fractions of a day. The time resolution, 30 min, corresponds to a fraction of $1/48 = 0.020833$ (see the second row).
- *Daytime*—The time during the day with respect to sunset and sunrise. The following levels are included in the data set: night.am, pre.sunrise.am, post.sunrise.am, day.am, day.pm, pre.sunset.pm, post.sunset.pm, and night.pm, corresponding to the times night, before sunrise, after sunrise, morning, afternoon, and so on.
- *Weekday*—The weekday from Sunday to Saturday; holidays are coded as Sundays.

 HANDS-ON TIME   Open http://mng.bz/B2O0. The notebook contains all you need to load the data set for the deer accident case study.

- Use all you learned in this section to develop a probabilistic DL model for the target variable (*wild*). You should get an NLL of lower than 1.8 on the test set.
- A real challenge is an NLL lower than 1.6599, which is a value obtained with sophisticated statistical modeling (see the works from Sandra Siegfried and Torsten Hothorn at http://mng.bz/dygN).
- A solution is given in the notebook (try to do better than what's given). Compare your results with the solution.

Good hunting! If you get an NLL significantly below 1.65 on the test set, drop us a line, and we might do a paper together.

6.3   Go with the flow: Introduction to normalizing flows (NFs)

In section 6.1, you saw a flexible way to model complex distributions by providing a mixture of simple base distributions. This method works great when your distribution is in a low-dimensional space. In the case of PixelCNN++ and parallel WaveNet, the application tasks are regression problems, and the conditional outcome distribution is, therefore, one dimensional.

But how does one set up and fit a flexible high-dimensional distribution? Think, for example, of color images with $256 \times 256 \times 3 = 195{,}840$ pixels defining a 195,840-dimensional space where each image can be represented by one point. If you pick a random point in this space, then you'd most probably get an image that looks like noise. This means the distribution of realistic images like facial images only covers a sub-region, which might not be easy to define. How can you learn the 195,840-dimensional distribution from which facial images can be drawn? Use NFs! In a nutshell, an NF learns a transformation (flow) from a simple high-dimensional distribution to a complex one. In a valid distribution, probabilities need to sum up to 1 in the discrete case or the integral needs to be 1 in the continuous case, and these need to be normalized. The flows in NFs keep this normalizing property intact. Hence, the name normalizing flow or NF for short.

In this section, we explain how NFs work. You'll see that NFs are probabilistic models that you can fit with the same MaxLike approach that you've used throughout the last couple of chapters. You'll also be able to use a fitted distribution to generate realistic looking faces of people who don't even exist or to morph an image of your face with the image of Brad Pitt, for example.

NFs are especially useful in high-dimensional spaces. Because it's hard to imagine a space with more than three dimensions, we explain NFs in low dimensions. But don't worry, we get to the high-dimensional distribution of facial images at the end of this section.

What are NFs and what are they good for? The basic idea is that an NF can fit a complex distribution (like the one in figure 6.6) without picking in advance an appropriate distribution family or setting up a mixture of several distributions.

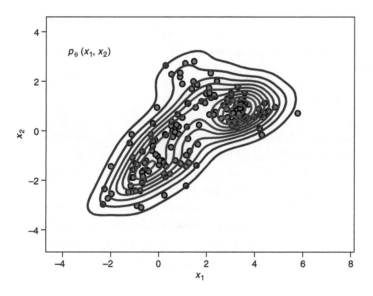

Figure 6.6 **Sketch of a parametric probability density estimation. Each point (x_1, x_2) is assigned a probability density. We chose the parameter θ to match the data points (dots).**

A probability density allows you to sample from that distribution. In the case of the facial image distribution, you can generate facial images from the distribution. The generated faces aren't the ones from the training data (or to be more precise, the chance to draw a training sample from the learned distribution is small).

NFs, therefore, fall under the class of generative models. Other well-known generative models are generative adversarial networks (GANs) and variational autoencoders (VAEs). GANs can generate quite impressive results when it comes to creating images of faces that don't exist. Visit http://mng.bz/rrNB to see such a generated image. If you want to learn more, the book *GANs in Action* by Jakub Langr and Vladimir Bok (Manning, 2019) gives an accessible and comprehensive introduction to GANs (see http://mng.bz/VgZP). But as you'll see later, NFs can also produce real-looking images.

In contrast to GANs and VAEs, NFs are probabilistic models that really learn the probability distribution and allow for each sample to determine the corresponding probability (likelihood). Say you've used NF to learn the distribution of facial images, and you have an image x, then you can ask the NF via $p(x)$ what's the probability of that image? This has quite useful applications, like novelty detection.

In novelty detection, you want to find out if a data point is from a certain distribution or if it's an original (novel) data point. For example, you've recorded data from a machine (let's say, a jet engine) under normal conditions. This can be quite high-dimensional data, like a vibrational spectra. You then train an NF for the "machine OK" distribution. While the machine is operating, you constantly check the probability of the data coming from the "machine OK" distribution. If this probability is low, you have an indication that the machine isn't working correctly and something is wrong. But before we come to high-dimensional data, let's start our journey into NFs with low-dimensional data.

6.3.1 *The principle idea of NFs*

In the left panel in figure 6.7, you see a one-dimensional data set. The data is a quite famous data set in statistics. It holds 272 waiting times between two eruptions of Old Faithful geyser in Yellowstone National Park. In the right panel of figure 6.7, you see a two-dimensional artificial data set. Imagine your statistics teacher asks you from which distribution does this data come. What would be your answer? Is it a Gaussian, a Weibull, a log normal? Even for the one-dimensional case on the left, none of the listed distributions fit. But because you're a good reader, you remember section 6.1 and come up with a mixture of, for example, two Gaussians. That works for quite simple distributions, such as the one shown in the left panel of figure 6.7, but for really high dimensional and complex distributions, this approach breaks down.

What to do? Remember the old saying, "If the mountain won't come to Mohammed, Mohammed must go to the mountain"? Figure 6.8 shows the main idea of an NF. Take data coming from a Gaussian and transform it so that at the end, the data looks like it's coming from a complicated distribution. This is done by a transformation function $g(z)$. On the other hand, the complicated function describing the data in x is transformed via the function $g^{-1}(x)$ to z.

The main task of the NFs is to find these transformations: $g(z)$ and $g^{-1}(x)$. We assume for a moment that we've found such a function pair: g and g^{-1}. We want two

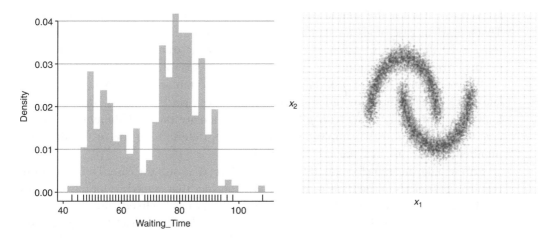

Figure 6.7 Two data sets: a real one on the left in 1D (waiting times between two geyser eruptions) and an artificial one on the right. Do you know a probability distribution that produces this kind of data? We don't.

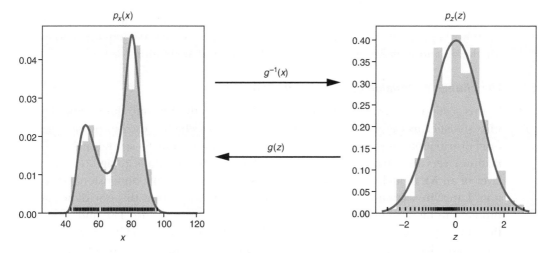

Figure 6.8 The NF principle. The complicated PDF $p_x(x)$ of the data x transformed to an easy Gaussian with the PDF $p_z(z) = N(z; 0, 1)$. The transformation function $x = g(z)$ transfers between the easy Gaussian in z and the complicated function in x.

things from it. First, it should enable us to sample from the complicated function $p_x(x)$, allowing for applications to generate new, realistic-looking images of faces. Second, it should allow us to calculate the probability $p_x(x)$ for a given x, allowing for applications like novelty detection.

Let's start with the first task and find out how we can use g to do the sampling of a new example x. Remember, you can't directly sample x from $p_x(x)$ because you don't know $p_x(x)$. But for the simple distribution $p_z(z)$, you know how to draw a sample. That's easy! In case of a Gaussian as the simple distribution, you can do it with TFP using `z=fd.Normal(0,1).sample()`. Then you apply the transformation function g to get the corresponding sample $x = g(z)$. So, the first task is solved.

What about the second task? How probable is a certain sample x? You can't calculate $p_x(x)$ directly, but you can transform x back to z via $z = g^{-1}(x)$ for which you know the probability $p_z(z)$. With $p_z(z)$, you can calculate the probability of x. In the case of a Gaussian as the simple distribution $p_z(z)$, determining the probability of a number z is easy: use `tfd.Normal(0,1).prob(z)`.

Can we take any transformation function g? Here, that isn't the case. To find out the required properties of the transformation, let's consider that we go in a loop from z to x and back. Let's take an example. What happens if we start with a fixed value of, say, $z = 4$? Then we'd use g to get the corresponding x value, $x = g(4)$, and go back from x to z again with $z = g^{-1}(x)$. You should again end up with the value $z = g^{-1}(x) = g^{-1}(g(4)) = 4$. This must apply for all values of z. That's why we call g^{-1} the inverse of g.

It's not possible for all functions g to find an inverse function g^{-1}. If a function g has an inverse function g^{-1}, then g is called *bijective*. Some functions such as $g(z) = z^2$ are only bijective on a limited range of data; here, for example, for positive values. (Can you tell what's the inverse function?) g has to be bijective. Additionally, we want the flows implemented efficiently. In the next sections, you learn about the mathematical details and their implications for an efficient implementation.

6.3.2   *The change of variable technique for probabilities*

In this section, you first learn how to use the NF method in one dimension. This is what statisticians call the *change of variable* technique, which is used to properly transform distributions. It's the core method of all NFs, where (usually) several such transformation layers are stacked to a deep NF model. To explain what's going on in a single layer of an NF model, we start with the transformation of a one-dimensional distribution. Later, in section 6.3.5, we'll generalize the findings from this one-dimensional problem to higher dimensions. To code such NF models, we use TFP and especially the TFP `bijector` package (for an example, see listing 6.3). All TFP `bijector` classes are about bijective transformations, which apply the change of variables technique to correctly transform probability distributions.

Let's start simple. Consider the transformation $x = g(z) = z^2$ and choose z to be uniformly distributed between 0 and 2. (We refer to this as the *simple example* in this section.) The function $g^{-1}(x) = \sqrt{x}$ satisfies $g^{-1}(g(x)) = \sqrt{z^2} = z$ for the picked range of z. By the way, that wouldn't be possible if z was chosen uniformly from –1 to 1 (a positive range is required). But now, if we work with the uniformly distributed z between 0 and 2, how does the distribution of $x = g(z) = z^2$ look? See if you can guess first.

A way of checking something in statistics is to always try it out with a simulation. To simulate 100,000 data points from a uniform distribution, you might use `tdf.Uniform (0,2).sample(1000)`. Take these values, square them, and plot a histogram (`plt.hist`).

The solution is given in the following notebook. But try it first to see if you can do it on your own.

HANDS-ON TIME Open http://mng.bz/xWVW. This notebook contains companion code for the change of variables/`TFP.bijectors` exercise in this chapter. Follow it while reading this section.

Probably this result is a bit contrary to your first intuition. Let's check what happens when you apply the square transformation to uniformly distributed samples. In figure 6.9, you see a plot of the square transformation function (the solid thick curve) and, on the horizontal axis, 100 samples (depicted by the ticks) drawn from a uniform distribution between 0 and 2. The corresponding histogram is shown above the plot. To square each sample (tick), you can go from the tick vertically up to the square function and where you hit it, then go horizontally left. The transformed values are the ticks drawn on the vertical axis. If you do that with all the z samples, you get a

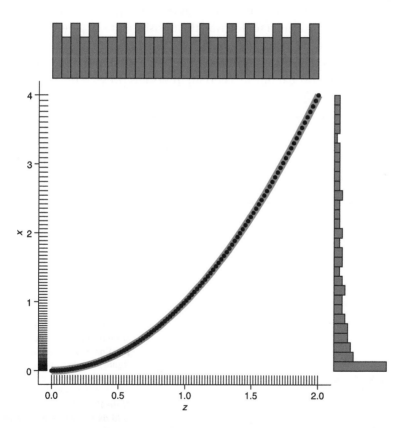

Figure 6.9   A square transformation function (solid thick curve) applied to 100 z samples drawn from a uniform distribution (ticks on the horizontal axis) yields transformed 100 x samples (ticks on the vertical axis). The histograms above and on the right of the plot show the distribution of the z and x samples, respectively.

distribution of the ticks on the vertical axis. Note that the ticks are denser in the region around 0 than those that are at around 4. The corresponding histogram is shown on the right. With this procedure, it becomes clear that a transformation function can squeeze samples together in regions where the transformation function is flat and move samples apart in regions where it's steep.

This intuition also implies that linear functions (with constant steepness but different offsets) don't change the shape of the distribution, only the values. Therefore, you need a non-linear transformation function if you want to go from a simple distribution to a distribution with a more complex shape.

Another important property of the transformation function g is that it needs to be monotone in order to be bijective.[2] This implies that the samples stay in the same order (no overtaking). For a transformation function that's monotone, increasing from $z_1 < z_2$ always follows $x_1 < x_2$ (see figure 6.9 for an example of a monotone increasing transformation). If the transformation function is monotone decreasing, then $z_1 < z_2$ always implies $x_1 > x_2$. This property also indicates that you always have the same number of samples between x_1 and x_2 as between $z_1 = g(x_1)$ and $z_2 = g(x_2)$.

For the NF, we need a formula to describe the transformation. Now that we've built our intuitive model of the transformation, let's do the final step needed and go from samples and histograms to probability densities. Instead of the number of samples in a certain interval, now the probability in a certain interval is preserved (see figure 6.10).

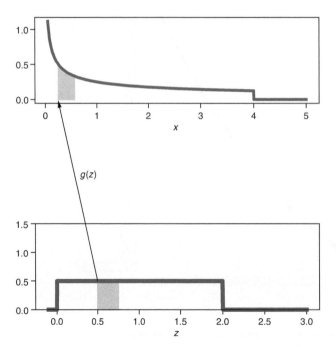

Figure 6.10 **Understanding transformations. The area** $p_z(z)|dz| = p_x(x)|dx|$ **(shaded in the figure) needs to be preserved. An animated version is available at https://youtu.be/fJ8YL2MaFHw. Note that strictly speaking, *dz* and *dx* should be infinitesimally small.**

---

[2] More precisely, it needs to be strictly monotone.

Strictly speaking (and we are quite sloppy in this book), $p_z(z)$ is a probability density. All probability densities are normalized, meaning the area under the density is 1. When using a transformation to go from one distribution to another distribution, this normalization is preserved; hence, the name "normalizing flow." You don't lose probability; it's like a conservation of mass principle. And this preserving property not only holds for the whole area under the density curve, but also for smaller intervals.

To come from a probability density value $p_x(x)$ to a real probability for values close to x, we have to look at an area under the density curve $p_x(x)$ within a small interval with the length dx. We get such a probability by multiplying $p_x(x)$ with dx: $p_x(x)dx$. The same is true for z, where $p_z(z)dz$ is a probability. These two probabilities need to be the same. In figure 6.10, you see the transformation. The shaded areas under the curve need to be the same.

From this we get the equation:[3]

$$p_z(z) \cdot |dz| = p_x(x) \cdot |dx|$$

This equation ensures that no probability is lost during the transformation (the mass is conserved). We can solve the equation to:

$$p_x(x) = p_z(z) \cdot |\frac{dz}{dx}|$$

$$p_x(x) = p_z(z) \cdot |\frac{dx}{dz}|^{-1}$$

Here we swapped the numerator dz and the denominator dx. It's OK and backed by stricter math.

$$p_x(x) = p_z(z) \cdot |\frac{dg(z)}{dz}|^{-1} \text{ where } x = g(z).$$

$$p_x(x) = p_z(z) \cdot |g'(z)|^{-1}$$

$$p_x(x) = p_z(g^{-1}(x)) \cdot |g'(g^{-1}(x))|^{-1} \text{ where } z = g^{-1}(x). \qquad \text{\textbf{Equation 6.2}}$$

Equation 6.2 is quite famous and has its own name: it's called the *change of variable* formula. The change of variable formula determines the probability density p_x of a transformed variable $x = g(z)$. You need to determine the derivative $\dfrac{dg(z)}{dz}$ and the inverse transformation function, and then you can use equation 6.2 to determine $p_x(x)$. The term $|\frac{dz}{dx}|$ describes the change of a length (the length of the interval on the horizontal axis in figure 6.10) when going from z to x. This ensures that the shaded area in fig-

---

[3] We take the absolute values ($|dz|$ and $|dx|$) because dz and dx could be negative.

ure 6.10 stays constant. We need the absolute value to cover cases where the transformation function is decreasing. In this case, $|\frac{dz}{dx}|$ would be negative. When going from x to z, the length scales the opposite way:

$$|\tfrac{dz}{dx}| = 1/|\tfrac{dx}{dz}|$$

Let's take a moment to recap what you've learned so far. If we have an invertible transformation $g(z)$ going from z to x, and the inverse function $g^{-1}(x)$ going from x to z, equation 6.2 tells us how the probability distribution changes under the transformation. Knowing the transformation $g(z)$ along with its derivative $g'(z)$ and $g^{-1}(x)$, we can apply the NF. We'll tackle the question of how to learn these flows, g and g^{-1}, in the next section. But first, let's apply the formula to the initial example and see how this can be done quite elegantly with TFP's `Bijector` class.

In the initial example, we assumed that z is uniformly distributed between 0 and 2 in this interval, $p_z(z) = \dfrac{1}{2}$, so that the distribution is normalized. Let's do the math for this example where $x = g(z) = z^2$. With $z = g^{-1}(x) = \sqrt{x}$ and $g'(g^{-1}(x)) = 2 \cdot g^{-1}(x)$, equation 6.2 becomes

$$p_x(x) = p_z(g^{-1}(x)) \cdot |g'(g^{-1}(x))|^{-1}$$

$$p_x(x) = \frac{1}{2} \cdot |2 \cdot \sqrt{x}|^{-1} = \frac{1}{4 \cdot \sqrt{x}}$$

This looks the same as the simulation (see figure 6.11).

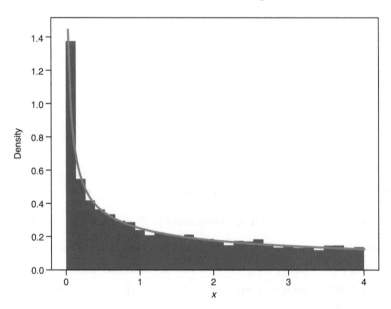

Figure 6.11 Comparing the densities of $x = z^2$ resulting from the simulation (histogram) and analytical derivation using equation 6.2 (curved solid line) when assuming a uniformly distributed z

It turns out that TFP has good support for transforming variables. At the heart of variable transformation is a bijective transformation function *g*. The package `tfp.bijector` is all about bijectors, which we introduced earlier in this section. Let's have a first look at a bijector in TFP (see the following listing and also the accompanying notebook http://mng.bz/xWVW).

Listing 6.3 A first bijector

```
tfb = tfp.bijectors
g = tfb.Square()
g.forward(2.0)
g.inverse(4.0)
```

This is a simple bijector, going from z → z**2.

Yields 4

Yields 2

In the listing, a bijector g transforms one distribution to another. The first (usually the simple) distribution is called the *base* distribution or the *source distribution* on which the bijector g is applied. The resulting distribution is called the *transformed* distribution or the *target distribution*. The next listing shows how our simple example can be implemented in TFP.

Listing 6.4 The simple example in TFP

The bijector; here a square function

```
g = tfb.Square()
db = tfd.Uniform(0.0,2.0)
mydist = tfd.TransformedDistribution(
    distribution=db, bijector=g)

xs = np.linspace(0.001, 5,1000)
px = mydist.prob(xs)
```

The base distribution; here a uniform distribution

Combining a base distribution and a bijector into a new distribution

TransformedDistribution behaves like a usual distribution.

Note that we didn't need to implement the change of variable formula ourselves. TFP is doing the work for us! If we'd like to create our own bijector, we'd need to implement the change of variable formula.

6.3.3 *Fitting an NF to data*

In this section, you learn the first step to use an NF for modeling complicated distributions and that this is quite easy using TFP bijectors. We restrict ourselves first to one-dimensional distributions. We do this by using only one flow, *g*. In the following section, we go deeper and chain several of those flows to allow for more flexibility to model complex distributions. Then in section 6.3.5, we'll use flows for higher dimensional distributions. In this section, you'll learn these flows, which are given by a parametric bijective function *g*.

> **SPOILER ALERT** You determine the parameters of a flow via the good old Max-Like principle.

How do we model a distribution via NFs? If your data x has the complicated unknown distribution $p_x(x)$, then use the bijective transformation function g to get x by transforming a variable z with a simple base distribution $x = g(z)$. If you know what transformation g to use, you're fine. You could apply it with the methods you just learned in section 6.3.2. The likelihood of $p_x(x)$ for each sample x is then given by the likelihood of the transformed value $p_x(x_i) = p_z(g^{-1}(x_i)) \cdot |g'(g^{-1}(x_i))|^{-1}$. But how do you know which bijective transformation g to use?

Solution number one: ask old-fashioned statisticians. They'll fire up EMACS and, in a first step, fit a simple model like a Gaussian to the data. Of course, a Gaussian isn't enough to fit a complicated distribution. The experienced statistician then stares at the difference between the model and the data and does some other magic only they and their priesthood understand in full detail. Finally, they mumble something like, "Apply a log transformation on your data, kid; then you can fit your data with a Gaussian." So off you go and implement a flow with `tfb.Exp()`. Meditate a second on why to use the exponential before you read on.

The answer is the statistician gave you the transformation on how to go from the complicated distribution to the simple Gauss distribution, $z = g^{-1}(x) = \log(x)$. Therefore, the flow g that goes from the simple to the complicated distribution is given by the inverse of the logarithm, which is the exponential $x = g(z) = \exp(z)$.

Solution number two: you realize that we live in the 21st century and have the computer power to find in a data-driven way the bijective transformation g that transforms a variable z with a simple base distribution $p_z(z)$ of your choice to the variable $x = g(z)$ of interest. Knowing the flow, g allows you to determine the complicated distribution $p_x(x) = p_z(z) \cdot |g'(z)|^{-1} = p_z(g^{-1}(x)) \cdot |g'(g^{-1}(x))|^{-1}$ (see equation 6.2).

The key idea for the data-driven approach is that you set up a flexible bijective transformation function g, which has learnable parameters θ. How to determine the values of these parameters? The usual way—with the MaxLike approach. You have training data x_i, and you can calculate the likelihood of a single training sample i by calculating $p_x(x_i) = p_z(g^{-1}(x_i)) \cdot |g'(g^{-1}(x_i))|^{-1}$ and the joint likelihood of all data points by multiplying all individual likelihood contributions $\prod_{i=1}^{n} p_x(x_i)$. In practice, you minimize the NLL $-\sum_{i=1}^{n} \log(p_x(x_i))$ in your training data. That's it!

Let's start with an extremely easy example. Our first learnable flow is linear and involves only two parameters: a and b $g(x) = a \cdot z + b$. In listing 6.5, you can see that we use an affine bijector. Just to get the term straight, an affine function $g(x) = a \cdot z + b$ is the linear function $g(x) = a \cdot z$ plus an offset b. In this book, we're a bit relaxed; we'll often say "linear" when we mean "affine." Of course, with such an easy flow, you can't do too much fancy stuff.

In the discussion of figure 6.9, we already pointed out that the shape of the distribution stays the same when using a linear transformation function. Now we want to learn the transformation from $z \sim N(0,1)$ to $x \sim N(5,0.2)$. Because both distributions are bell-shaped, an (affine) linear transformation can do the trick. The following listing shows the complete code, and it's also in the accompanying notebook.

> **Listing 6.5   A simple example in TFP**

```
a = tf.Variable(1.0)              Defines the variables
b = tf.Variable(0.0)
bijector = tfb.AffineScalar(shift=a, scale=b)       Sets up the flow
dist = tfd.TransformedDistribution(distribution=    using an affine
        tfd.Normal(loc=0,scale=1),bijector=bijector) transformation
                                                     defined by two
optimizer = tf.keras.optimizers.Adam(learning_rate=0.1)  variables

for i in range(1000):
    with tf.GradientTape() as tape:                    The NLL of the data
        loss = -tf.reduce_mean(dist.log_prob(X))
        gradients = tape.gradient(loss,               Calculates the
                    dist.trainable_variables)         gradients for the
    optimizer.apply_gradients(                        trainable variables
        zip(gradients, dist.trainable_variables))

                                                     Applies the gradients to
                                                     update the variables
```

Training for a few epochs results in $a \approx 0.2$ and $b \approx 5$ and so transforms the $N(0,1)$ distributed variable into an $N(5,0.2)$ distributed variable (see the notebook http://mng.bz/xWVW for the result). Of course, such a simple (affine) linear transformation is much too simple to transform a Gaussian into more complex distributions.

6.3.4   *Going deeper by chaining flows*

You saw in section 6.3.3 that a linear flow can only shift and stretch the base distribution, but it can't change the shape of the distribution. Therefore, the result of linearly transforming a Gaussian is, again, a Gaussian (with changed parameters). In this section, you learn a way to model a target distribution that has a very different shape compared to the base distribution. This lets you model complex real-world distributions such as the waiting time between two eruptions of Old Faithful geyser. You'll see that this is quite easy with TFP.

How do we create flows that can change the shape of a distribution? Remember the fool's rule of DL—stack more layers (as discussed in section 2.1.2). Also remember that between the layers in an NN, you use a non-linear activation function; otherwise, a deep stack of layers could be replaced by one layer. With respect to an NF, this rule tells you not to use just one but a series of flows (the non-linearities in between are important, and we come back to this point later). You start from z and go along a chain of k transformations to x: $z = z_0 \to z_1 \to z_2 \cdots \to z_k = x$. Figure 6.12 shows this transformation.

Let's look at a chain of two transformations from $z_0 \to z_1 \to z_2$ to understand the general formula. You know the probability distribution $p_{z_0}(z_0)$, but how can you

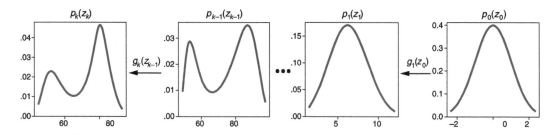

Figure 6.12 A chain of simple transformations makes it possible to create complex transformations needed to model complex distributions. From right to left, starting from a standard Gaussian distribution $z_0 \sim N(0,1)$ changes via successive transformations to a complex distribution with a bimodal shape (on the left).

determine the probability distribution $p_{z_2}(z_2)$? Let's do it step by step and, in each step, use the change of variable formula (equation 6.2).

First determine the probability distribution $p_{z_1}(z_1)$. You get z_1 by transforming z_0, $z_1 = g_1(z_0)$. To use the change of variable formula, you need to determine the derivative $g_1{}'$ and the inverted function g_1^{-1}. The distribution $p_{z_1}(z_1)$ can then be determined by equation 6.2 as $p_{z_1}(z_1) = p_{z_0}(z_0) \cdot |g_1{}'(z_0)|^{-1}$. Proceeding like that, you can determine the probability density p_{z_2} of the transformed variable $p_{z_2}(z_2) = p_{z_1}(z_1) \cdot |g_2{}'(z_1)|^{-1}$, where you can plug in the former formula for $p_{z_1}(z_1)$, yielding the chained flow:

$$p_{z_2}(z_2) = p_{z_0}(z_0) \cdot |g_1{}'(z_0)|^{-1} \cdot |g_2{}'(z_1)|^{-1}$$

Often, it's more convenient to operate on log probabilities instead of probabilities. Taking the log (and using the log rule $\log(a^p) = p \cdot \log(a)$ with $a = g_i{}'(z_i - 1)$ and $p = -1$) of the previous formula yields this:

$$\log(p_{z_2}(z_2)) = \log(p_{z_0}(z_0)) - \log(|g_1{}'(z_0)|) - \log(|g_2{}'(z_1)|)$$

For a complete flow (with $x = z_k$), this formula generalizes to:

$$\log(p_x(x)) = p_{z_0}(z_0) - \sum_{i=1}^{k} \log\left(\left|\frac{dg_i(z_{i-1})}{dz_{i-1}}\right|\right)$$

To calculate the probability $p_x(x)$, simply backup in the chain in figure 6.12 from $x = z_k \rightarrow z_{k-1} \cdots \rightarrow z_0$ and sum the $-\log(|g_i{}'(z_{i-1})|$ terms. Let's build such a chain in TFP.

It's quite convenient to create a chain of bijectors in TFP: simply use the class `Chain(bs)` from the `tfp.bijectors` package with a list of `Bijectors bs`. The result is again, a bijector. So, do we simply need to chain a few affine scalar bijectors or are we done? We're not quite done yet. An affine scalar transformation only shifts and scales a distribution. One way to think of this is that such an affine transformation is a straight line in figure 6.9. There isn't a possibility to change the shape of the distribution.

What do you need to do if you want to change the shape of the distribution? You could introduce some non-linear bijectors between the stacked linear flows, or you could use non-linear bijectors instead of the linear bijectors. Let's go for the first option.

You need to pick a non-linear parametric transformation function for which you can then find the parameter values via the MaxLike approach. There are many possible transformation functions (bijectors) to do so. Have a look at http://mng.bz/AApz. Many of the bijectors have either no parameters, like `softplus`, or limit the allowed range of z or x. The `SinhArcsinh` bijector has a complicated name but looks quite promising: it has two parameters, `skewness` and `tailweight`, and if `tailweight>0`, there are no restrictions on x and z. Figure 6.13 shows that bijector for some parameters. For `tailweight=1` and `skewness=1` it looks quite non-linear, and with these parameters, we do not need to restrict the range of x and y. We, therefore, use it to fit the Old Faithful data (see listing 6.6). Note that there might be other bijectors in the TFP package that fulfill the requirements as well.

Let's construct a chain and add `SinhArcsinh` bijectors between the `AffineScalar` bijectors. This is done in the following listing.

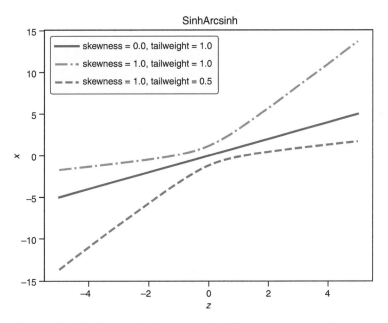

Figure 6.13 The bijector `SinhArcsinh` **for different parameter values**

Listing 6.6   The simple Old Faithful bijector example in TFP

```
num_bijectors = 5        ⟵┐  Number of layers
bs=[]
for i in range(num_bijectors):
```

```
sh = tf.Variable(0.0)                                        The AffineScalar
sc=tf.Variable(1.0)                                          transformation
bs.append(tfb.AffineScalar(shift=sh, scale=sc))      ←┘

skewness=tf.Variable(0.0)                                    The SinhArcsinh
tailweight=tf.Variable(1.0)                                  acting as non-
bs.append(tfb.SinhArcsinh(skewness,tailweight))      ←┘      linearity
```

Creates the chain of bijectors
from the list of bijectors

```
bijector = tfb.Chain(bs)                             ←┘
dist = tfd.TransformedDistribution(distribution=
        tfd.Normal(loc=0,scale=1),bijector=bijector)
```

Visit the notebook http://mng.bz/xWVW to see this chain of bijectors used for the Old Faithful geyser waiting times, which yields the histogram in figure 6.14. By the way, in figure 6.12, you see some of the steps from $N(0,1)$ to the distribution of the Old Faithful's waiting times.

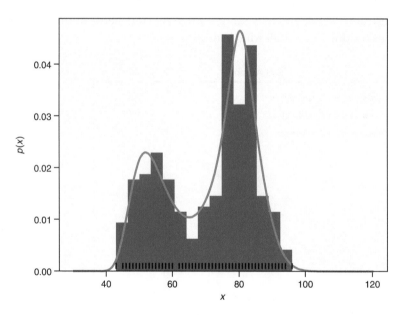

Figure 6.14 The histogram of the Old Faithful geyser waiting times (filled bars), along with the fitted density distribution (solid line). The histogram doesn't show the shape of a simple distribution like a Gaussian. A flow of five layers captures the characteristics of the data well (solid line).

So far, we've considered one-dimensional data, but does this method also work for higher dimensional data? Imagine, for example, image data where each image has the dimension 256 × 256 × 3 (height × width × channels). Again, we're interested in learning the distribution of this image data so that we can sample from it. It turns out that this flow method also works for higher dimensions. The only principle difference is that the bijectors are no longer one-dimensional functions but have as many dimensions as your data.

In the next two sections, we extend the NF method to higher dimensions. If you're more interested in the application of this method than in the mathematical twists, you can skip those sections and go directly to section 6.3.7. But if you want to know the details, keep reading!

6.3.5 *Transformation between higher dimensional spaces**

Let's formulate the task of modeling the distributions of high-dimensional data like images so that we can use the flow method to fit the distribution. First, we flatten the image data to receive (for each image) the vectors x with 196,608 entries. The resulting vectors live in a 196,608 space and have an unknown distribution of $p_x(x)$, which is probably complex. You can now pick a simple base distribution, $p_z(z)$, for a variable z, such as a Gaussian, for example. The task is to find a transformation $g(z)$ that transforms the vector z to the vector x. We need a bijective transformation g and, therefore, the dimensionality of x and z have to be the same. Let's see how such a transformation looks for a three-dimensional space, which means we deal with the data points $x = (x_1, x_2, x_3)$ and $z = (z_1, z_2, z_3)$. The transformation $x = g(z)$ looks like this:

$$g(z) = \begin{pmatrix} g_1(z_1, z_2, z_3) \\ g_2(z_1, z_2, z_3) \\ g_3(z_1, z_2, z_3) \end{pmatrix}$$

For the one-dimensional flow, the main formula was

$$p_x(x) = p_z(z) \cdot \left| \frac{dx}{dz} \right|^{-1} = p_z(z) \cdot \left| \frac{dg(z)}{dz} \right|^{-1} \qquad \textbf{Equation 6.3}$$

and the term $\left| \dfrac{dg(z)}{dz} \right|$ was identified as a change in length when going from z to x. In three dimensions, we need to take into account the change of a volume as well. For four and more dimensions, the change of the volume is now the change of a hypervolume of the transformation g. From now on we just call it a volume, regardless if we have a length or an area.

The scalar derivative $\left| \dfrac{dg(z)}{dz} \right|$ in the one-dimensional formula (equation 6.3) is replaced by a matrix of partial derivatives, which is called the Jacobi matrix. To understand the Jacobi matrix, we first recall what a partial derivative is. The partial derivative of a function $g(z_1, z_2, z_3)$ of three variables z_1, z_2, z_3 with respect to (w.r.t.) z_2 is written as $\dfrac{\partial g(z_1, z_2, z_3)}{\partial z_2}$. To make an easy example, what is $\dfrac{\partial g(z_1, z_2, z_3)}{\partial z_2}$ when

$g(z_1, z_2, z_3) = 42 \cdot z_2 + \sinh(\exp(z_1/z_3))$? Well you are lucky, it's 42. That was easy! The partial derivative w.r.t. z_1 and z_3 would have been much more complicated.

Instead of $g(z_1, z_2, z_3)$ just returning a single number, we consider the case in which g returns a vector, let's say, of three components. If you need an example, this function g could be a fully connected network (fcNN) with three input and output neurons. For this example, the Jacobi matrix looks as follows:

$$\frac{\partial g(z)}{\partial z} = \begin{pmatrix} \frac{\partial g_1(z_1,z_2,z_3)}{\partial z_1} & \frac{\partial g_1(z_1,z_2,z_3)}{\partial z_2} & \frac{\partial g_1(z_1,z_2,z_3)}{\partial z_3} \\ \frac{\partial g_2(z_1,z_2,z_3)}{\partial z_1} & \frac{\partial g_2(z_1,z_2,z_3)}{\partial z_2} & \frac{\partial g_2(z_1,z_2,z_3)}{\partial z_3} \\ \frac{\partial g_3(z_1,z_2,z_3)}{\partial z_1} & \frac{\partial g_3(z_1,z_2,z_3)}{\partial z_2} & \frac{\partial g_3(z_1,z_2,z_3)}{\partial z_3} \end{pmatrix}$$

In the one-dimensional case, you had to determine the absolute value of the derivative $|dg(z)/dz|$ in the change of variable formula (equation 6.3). In the higher dimensional case, it turns out that you have to replace this term by the absolute value of the determinant of the Jacobi matrix. The change for the variable formula for high-dimensional data looks like this:

$$p_x(x) = p_z(z) \cdot \left| \det \left(\frac{\partial g(z)}{\partial z} \right) \right|^{-1} \qquad \textbf{Equation 6.4}$$

You don't know what's a determinant or forgot about it? Don't worry. The only thing you need to know is that for a triangular matrix (like the one shown in equation 6.5), you can compute the determinant as a product of the diagonal elements. This is, of course, also true if some (or all) of the off-diagonal elements in the lower part of the triangular matrix are also zero. Anyway, you don't have to compute the determinant yourself.

Each TFP bijector implements the method `log_det_jacobian(z)`, and the flow or a chain of flows can be calculated as described previously. The calculation of a determinant is quite time-consuming. There's a nice trick, however, to speed up the calculation. If a matrix is a so-called triangular matrix, then the determinant is the product of the diagonal elements. How to get zeros in a Jacobi matrix? A partial derivative of a function g_k w.r.t. a variable z_i gets zero if the function g_k doesn't depend on variable z_i. If we build the flows so that $g_1(z_1, z_2, z_3)$ is independent of z_2, z_3 and $g_2(z_1, z_2, z_3)$ is independent of z_3, then the previous matrix becomes

$$\frac{\partial g(z)}{\partial z} = \begin{pmatrix} \frac{\partial g_1(z)}{\partial z_1} & 0 & 0 \\ \frac{\partial g_2(z)}{\partial z_1} & \frac{\partial g_2(z)}{\partial z_2} & 0 \\ \frac{\partial g_3(z)}{\partial z_1} & \frac{\partial g_3(z)}{\partial z_2} & \frac{\partial g_3(z)}{\partial z_3} \end{pmatrix} \qquad \textbf{Equation 6.5}$$

This matrix is a triangular matrix and, hence, you can obtain the determinant by the product of the diagonal elements. A nice property of a triangular Jacobi matrix is that you don't have to calculate the off-diagonal terms (shown in gray in equation 6.5) to determine the determinant. These off-diagonal terms play a role in the first term, $p_z(z) = p_z(g^{-1}(x))$ (equation 6.4), but not for the second term, $\left|\det\left(\frac{\partial g(z)}{\partial z}\right)\right|^{-1}$. To model complex distributions, it might be necessary to use complex functions for these off-diagonal terms. Fortunately, it's not a problem at all if these expressions are complicated because you don't have to calculate the derivatives of them. To get such a nice triangular Jacobi matrix, one simply has to ensure that $g_i(z)$ is independent of z_j with $j > i$.

We've seen that bijectors that lead to a triangular Jacobi matrix are convenient to handle. But are these also flexible enough to model all kinds of complex distributions? Fortunately, the answer is yes! In 2005, Bogachev and colleagues showed that for any D-dimensional distribution pair (a complicated distribution for x and a simple base distribution for z), you can find triangular bijectors that transform one distribution into the other.

6.3.6 *Using networks to control flows*

Now you're going to see the powerful combination of networks and NFs. The basic idea is to use NNs to model the components g_i of the D-dimensional bijector function $g(z) = (g_1(z_1, \ldots z_D), g_2(z_1, \ldots z_D), \ldots, g_D(z_1, \ldots z_D))$. The discussion in the last section gives us some guidelines on how to design the NNs used to model the different components g_i of the bijector g:

1. We want the bijector to have a triangular Jacobi matrix, which ensures that g_i is independent of z_j (where $j > i$), i.e., $g_i(z_1, z_2, \ldots, z_D) = g_i(z_1, \ldots, z_i)$.
2. We want the diagonal elements of the Jacobi matrix to be easy to compute: $\frac{\partial g_i(z_1, \ldots, z_i)}{\partial z_i}$.
3. For the off-diagonal elements in the lower triangular of the Jacobi matrix, there's no need to compute a partial derivative of these functions. They can be quite complicated.
4. Last, but not least, we need an invertible transformation.

Let's focus on the first item in the list and write the components of a triangular bijector function $g(z)$:

$$x_1 = g_1(z_1, z_2, \ldots, z_D) = g_1(z_1)$$
$$x_2 = g_2(z_1, z_2, \ldots, z_D) = g_2(z_1, z_2)$$

Equation 6.6

$$\ldots$$

$$x_D = g_D(z_1, z_2, \ldots, z_D) = g_D(z_1 \ldots, z_D)$$

The next question is which parametric functions do we use for the component g_i? Here the second and third guidelines in the preceding list come into play. You should design g_i such that the partial derivative $\dfrac{\partial g_i(z_1, \ldots, z_i)}{\partial z_i}$, corresponding to a diagonal element of the Jacobi matrix, is easy to compute. For a linear function, the derivative is easy to compute. Let's choose g_i to be linear in z_i:

$$x_i = g_i(z_1, z_2, \ldots, z_i) = b + a \cdot z_i$$

Note that g_i can be non-linear in $z_1, z_2, \ldots, z_i$. This means that the intercept b and the slope a can be complex functions of these z components: $b_i = b_i(z_1, z_2, \ldots, z_{i-1})$ and $a_i = a_i(z_1, z_2, \ldots, z_{i-1})$. This yields

$$x_i = g_i(z_1, z_2, \ldots, z_i) = b_i(z_1, z_2, \ldots, z_{i-1}) + a_i(z_1, z_2, \ldots, z_{i-1}) \cdot z_i$$

Because $b_i = b_i(z_1, z_2, \ldots, z_{i-1})$ and $a_i = a_i(z_1, z_2, \ldots, z_{i-1})$ can be complex functions, you can use NNs to model these. It's a known fact that NNs with at least one hidden layer are flexible enough to fit every function, and so a and b can depend in a complex manner on the provided z components. In one-dimensional cases, you need a monotone increasing or decreasing function to ensure bijectivity. This can be guaranteed by ensuring that the slope isn't zero. In multidimensional cases, instead of the slope, you now need to ensure that the determinant of the Jacobi matrix isn't zero. We do this by making sure that all entries of the diagonal are larger than zero. For this, you can use the same trick as in chapter 4 when modeling a positive standard deviation: you don't directly use the output $\alpha_i(z_1, z_2, \ldots, z_{i-1})$ of the NN as a slope, but you first pipe it through an exponential function. This yields $a_i = \exp(\alpha_i(z_1, z_2, \ldots, z_{i-1}))$ and, in this case, equation 6.6 becomes

$$x_i = g_i(z_1, z_2, \ldots, z_i) = b_i(z_1, z_2, \ldots, z_{i-1}) + \exp(\alpha_i(z_1, z_2, \ldots, z_{i-1})) \cdot z_i \quad \textbf{Equation 6.7}$$

Computing the determinant of the Jacobi matrix is easy. Just compute the product of the partial derivatives of g_i w.r.t. z_i:

$$\det\left(\frac{\partial g(z)}{\partial z}\right) = \prod_{i=1}^{D} \exp(\alpha_i(z_1, z_2, \ldots, z_{i-1}))$$

As you can see, the matrix is easy to calculate! The determinant is given by the product of positive terms and, thus, is also positive.

As discussed, models like the one in equation 6.6 allow for an efficient implementation of NF models. In the literature, these kinds of models are sometimes also called *inverse autoregressive models*. The name "autoregressive" indicates that the input of the regression model for the variable x_i depends only on previous observations of $x_1, \ldots, x_{j-1}$ from the same variable (hence the name, "auto"). You saw examples of the WaveNet and PixelCNN autoregressive models in section 6.1.1. But a flow model isn't autoregressive per se because $x_i = g_i(z_1, z_2, \ldots, z_i)$ is determined by the former (and current) values of z and not x. Still, there's a connection that gives rise to the name inverse autoregressive models. If you're interested in the details, you might want to look at the blog post http://mng.bz/Z26P.

To realize such an NF model with an fcNN, you need D different networks, each calculating a_i and b_i (see equation 6.7) from different inputs: $z_1, z_2, \ldots, z_i$ for $i \in \{1, 2, \ldots, D\}$. Having D networks would require many parameters, and further, the sampling from the D networks would also take quite some time. Why not take a single network that takes all $z_1, z_2, \ldots, z_D$ inputs and then outputs all a_i and b_i values from which you can calculate all $z_1, z_2, \ldots, z_D$ values in one go? Take a second to come up with an answer?

The answer is that an fcNN violates the requirement that g_i is independent of z_j with $j > i$: that's $g_i(z_1, z_2, \ldots, z_D) = g(z_1, \ldots, z_i)$ and thus doesn't yield a triangular Jacobian. But there's a solution. There are special networks, called autoregressive networks, that mask parts of the connections to ensure that the output nodes a_i don't depend on the input nodes z_j with $j > i$. Luckily, you can use TFP `tfp.bijectors.AutoregressiveNetwork`, which guarantees that property. This network was first described in a paper called "Masked Autoencoder for Distribution Estimation (MADE)" (see https://arxiv.org/abs/1502.03509).

Let's look at the training of such a network in $D = 4$ dimensions. In the training, we go from the observed four-dimensional x to a four-dimensional z, where we get the likelihood $p_x(x) = p_z(z) = p_z(g^{-1}(x))$. For this, we rely on

$$x_i = g_i(z_1, z_2, \ldots, z_i) = b_i(z_1, z_2, \ldots, z_{i-1}) + \exp(\alpha_i(z_1, z_2, \ldots, z_{i-1})) \cdot z_i$$

Equation 6.7 (repeated)

We then need to solve equation 6.7 for z_i, yielding:

$$z_1 = x_1$$
$$z_2 = \frac{x_2 - b_2(z_1)}{\exp(\alpha_2(z_1))}$$
$$z_3 = \frac{x_3 - b_3(z_1, z_2)}{\exp(\alpha_3(z_1, z_2))}$$
$$z_4 = \frac{x_4 - b_4(z_1, z_2, z_3)}{\exp(\alpha_4(z_1, z_2, z_3))}$$

This is a sequential process, and thus, training can't be parallelized and is rather slow. However, during the test phase, it's fast.[4]

Laurent Dinh, et al., introduced a somewhat different approach to build an invertible flow in a paper called "Density Estimation using Real NVP," which is available at https://arxiv.org/abs/1605.08803. In this paper, they proposed a flow called a real

---

[4] In fact, autoregressive flows also exist. With the different trade-offs, these nets are fast in training but slow in prediction. It turns out that WaveNet is such an autoregressive flow.

non-volume preserving flow or Real NVP. The name *non-volume preserving* states that this method (like the triangular flows) can have a Jacobian determinant unequal to one and can thus change the volume. Compared to the design in equation 6.6, their Real NVP design is much simpler (shown in figure 6.15). When comparing figure 6.15 to equation 6.6, you can see that the Real NVP architecture is a simplified and sparse version of the triangular flow. If you use a triangular flow and set the first d dimensions to $b = 0$ and $a = 0$ and then let the remaining dimensions a and b only depend on the first d components of z, then you end up with a Real NVP model. The Real NVP architecture isn't as flexible as a fully triangular bijector, but it allows for fast computations.

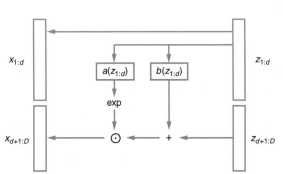

Figure 6.15   The architecture of a Real NVP model. The first d components, $z_1, z_2, \ldots, z_d$, stay untransformed, yielding $x_1 = z_1, x_2 = z_2, \ldots,$ $x_d = z_d$. The remaining components of x, $x_d + 1, \ldots, x$, depend only on the first d components of z, $z_1, z_2, \ldots, z_d$, and are transformed as $x_i = g_i(z_1, z_2, \ldots, z_i)$ $= b_i(z_1, z_2, \ldots, z_{i-1}) +$ $\exp(\alpha_i(z_1, z_2, \ldots, z_{i-1})) \cdot z_i$ for $i = d + 1, \ldots, D$; this multiplication is indicated by $\odot$.

In a Real NVP model, the first d components are passed through directly from z to x (see figure 6.15 and also the following example) and further used for training an NN, which outputs a_i and b_i for the remaining coordinates x_i for $i = d + 1, \ldots, D$.

The idea in Real NVP is to first choose a d between 1 and the dimensionality of your problem D (dimensionality of z and x). To make the discussion simpler, let's choose $D = 5$ and $d = 2$. But, of course, the results are also valid for a general case. The flow is going from z (following a simple distribution) to x (following a complex distribution). The first d components (here $d = 2$) are passed through directly from z to x (see the first two lines of equation 6.8). Now these d (here two), z_1 and z_2, are the input to an NN computing a_i and b_i (see equation 6.7), yielding the slope $a_i = \exp(\alpha_i)$ and the shift b of the linear transformation $x_i = b_i + a_i \cdot z_i$ for $i \in \{3, 4, 5\}$ (see lines 3–5 in equation 6.8). The NN has two heads as an outcome. Both have $D - d$ (here, $5 - 2 = 3$) nodes. One head is $b_1(z_1, z_2), b_2(z_1, z_2), b_3(z_1, z_2)$ and the other head is $a_1(z_1, z_2), a_2(z_1, z_2), a_3(z_1, z_2)$. The next three transformed variables are determined using the network via:

$$x_1 = g_1(z_1) = z_1$$

$$x_2 = g_2(z_2) = z_2$$

$$x_3 = g_3(z_1, z_2, z_3) = b_3(z_1, z_2) + \exp(\alpha_3(z_1, z_2)) \cdot z_3$$

$$x_4 = g_4(z_1, z_2, z_4) = b_4(z_1, z_2) + \exp(\alpha_4(z_1, z_2)) \cdot z_4$$

$$x_5 = g_5(z_1, z_2, z_5) = b_5(z_1, z_2) + \exp(\alpha_5(z_1, z_2)) \cdot z_5 \qquad \textbf{Equation 6.8}$$

It's an affine transformation like the one we used before, and the scale and shift terms are controlled by an NN, but this time, the NN only gets the first $d = 2$ components of z as input. Does this network fulfill the requirements to be bijective and triangular? Let's invert the flow and go from x to z. This yields

$$z_1 = x_1$$
$$z_2 = x_2$$
$$z_3 = \frac{x_3 - \mu_1(z_1, z_2)}{\exp(\alpha_3(z1, z2))}$$
$$z_4 = \frac{x_4 - \mu_2(z1, z2)}{\exp(\alpha_4(z1, z2))}$$
$$z_5 = \frac{x_5 - \mu_3(z1, z2)}{\exp(\alpha_5(z1, z2))}$$

Also, the Jacobi matrix has the desired triangular form, even if all off-diagonal elements in columns $> d$ are zero. You only need to compute the diagonal elements to determine the determinant, which is required for the NF method.

$$\frac{\partial g}{\partial z} = \begin{pmatrix} 1 & 0 & 0 & 0 & 0 \\ 0 & 1 & 0 & 0 & 0 \\ \frac{\partial g_3}{\partial z_1} & \frac{\partial g_3}{\partial z_2} & e^{\alpha_3} & 0 & 0 \\ \frac{\partial g_4}{\partial z_1} & \frac{\partial g_4}{\partial z_2} & 0 & e^{\alpha_4} & 0 \\ \frac{\partial g_5}{\partial z_1} & \frac{\partial g_5}{\partial z_2} & 0 & 0 & e^{\alpha_5} \end{pmatrix}$$

The non-zero, off-diagonal elements are gray-shaded in the equation because we don't need them. This part of the flow is called a *coupling layer*.

It's a bit strange in a Real NVP that the first d dimensions aren't affected by the flow. But we can bring them into play in additional layers. Because we want to stack more layers anyway, let's reshuffle the z_i components before we get to the next layer. Reshuffling is invertible, and the determinant of the Jacobi matrix is 1. We can use the TFP bijector `tfb.Permute()` to reshuffle. In listing 6.7, which shows the relevant code, we use five pairs of coupling layers and permutations (see also the following notebook).

HANDS-ON TIME   Open http://mng.bz/RArK. The notebook contains the code to show how to use a Real NVP flow of a banana-shaped, 2D distribution on a toy data set.

- Execute the code and try to understand it
- Play with the number of hidden layers

Listing 6.7   The simple example of a Real NVP TFP

```
bijectors=[]
    num_blocks = 5
    h = 32
    for i in range(num_blocks):
        net = tfb.real_nvp_default_template(
                   [h, h])
        bijectors.append(
            tfb.RealNVP(shift_and_log_scale_fn=net,
                      num_masked=num_masked))
        bijectors.append(tfb.Permute([1,0]))
        self.nets.append(net)
    bijector = tfb.Chain(list(reversed(bijectors[:-1])))

    self.flow = tfd.TransformedDistribution(
            distribution=tfd.MultivariateNormalDiag(loc=[0., 0.]),
            bijector=bijector)
```

Number of hidden layers in the NF model → `num_blocks = 5`

Size of the hidden layers → `h = 32`

Adds num_blocks of coupling permutations to the list of bijectors

Defines the network → `net = tfb.real_nvp_default_template([h, h])`

A shift and flow with parameters from the network

Permutation of coordinates

Distribution of z with two independent Gaussians → `self.flow = tfd.TransformedDistribution(...)`

So now you've seen how to construct flows using networks. The trick is to keep everything invertible and to construct the flows in a way that the determinant of the Jacobi matrix can be easily calculated. Finally, let's have a look at the Glow architecture and have some fun sampling real-looking facial images from a normalizing flow.

6.3.7   *Fun with flows: Sampling faces*

Now you come to the fun part. OpenAI did some great work in developing an NF model that they call the Glow model. You can use it to create realistic-looking faces and other images. The Glow model is similar to the Real NVP model with some tweaks. The main change is that the permutation is replaced by a 1×1 convolution.

In this section, we now work with image data. In the examples up to section 6.3.5, we worked with 1D scalar data. In section 6.3.5 and 6.3.6, we used D-dimensional data (for both z and x), but still the data were simple vectors. If we want to operate on images, we need to work with tensors to take their 2D structure into account. Therefore, we now have to operate on tensors x and z of shape (h, w, d), which define the height (h), width (w), and number of color channels (d) instead of vectors.

How do we apply a Real NVP-like flow on the tensors? Recall the Real NVP architecture for vectors (see figure 6.15 and equation 6.8). In the case of tensors, the first d channels (now d two-dimensional slices) aren't affected by the transformation but serve as input to a CNN. That CNN defines the transformations of the remaining channels of the input.

As in a regular CNN architecture, the height and width are reduced, and the number of channels is increased when going deeper into the network. The idea behind this is to find more abstract representations. But in an NF model, the input and output need to have the same dimensions. The number of channels is increased, therefore, by a factor of four if height and width are reduced by a factor of two.

In the output layer, the height and width are one, and the depth is given by the number of values of the input $h \cdot w \cdot d$. For more details, see the paper "Glow: Generative Flow with Invertible 1x1 Convolutions" by Kingma and Dhariwal, which you can find at https://arxiv.org/abs/1807.03039 or have a look at the official GitHub repository at https://github.com/openai/glow.

The bottom line is that an image z with dimensions (h, w, d), typically $(256,256,3)$, is transformed into a vector of length $h \cdot w \cdot d$, typically 196,608, where each dimension comes from an independent $N(0,1)$ distributed Gaussian. This vector can again be reshaped into a color image x of dimensions $(256 \times 256 \times 3)$.

The network has been trained on 30,000 images of celebrities. The training took quite some time, but fortunately one can download the pre-trained weights. Let's play with this. Open the following notebook and follow it while reading the text in this section.

 HANDS-ON TIME Open http://mng.bz/2XR0. The notebook contains code to download the weights of a pre-trained Glow model. It's highly recommended to use the Colab version because the weights are approximately 1 GB. Further, because the weights are stored in TensorFlow 1, we use a TF 1 version of Colab. With the notebook opened:

- Sample random faces
- Manipulate a face
- Morph between two faces
- Make Leonardo smile

First, sample a random face from the learned distribution of facial images. You can do this by sampling a vector **z** containing 196,608 independent Gaussian distributions and then transform this to a vector $x = g(z)$ that can be reshaped to a facial image. Doing so, one usually finds artifacts. To avoid this and get more realistic "normal" face images, one doesn't draw from $N(0,1)$ but from a Gaussian with reduced variance such as $N(0,0.7)$ to get closer to the center. This reduces the risk of getting unusual looking facial images.

Another interesting application is mixing faces. Figure 6.17 shows the basic idea. You start with the first image, say an image x_1 from Beyoncé. You then use the flow to calculate the corresponding vector $z_1 = g^{-1}(x_1)$. Then take a second image, say Leonardo DiCaprio, and calculate the corresponding z_2. Now let's mix the two vectors. We have a variable c in the range 0 to 1 that describes the DiCaprio content.

For $c = 1$, it's DiCaprio; for $c = 0$, it's Beyoncé. In the z space, the mixture is given by $z_c = c \cdot z_2 + (1 - c)z_1$. An alternative view on the formula is to rearrange it: $z_c = c \cdot z_2 + (1 - c)z_1 = z_1 + c(z_2 - z_1) = z_1 + c\Delta$. Then Δ is the difference between z_2 and z_1. See figure 6.16 for this interpretation.

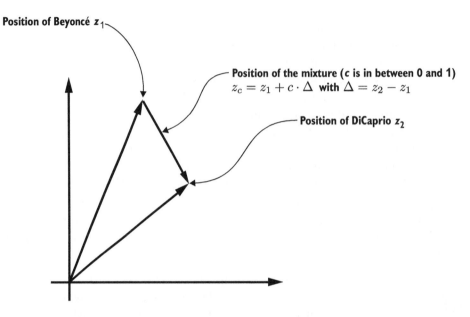

Figure 6.16   Schematic sketch of the mixture in the space z. Note that the z space is high-dimensional and not 2D as in the figure. We move in a linear interpolation from Beyoncé in the direction $\Delta = z_2 \cdot z_1$ toward DiCaprio.

We start from $c = 0$ (Beyoncé) and move from there in the direction Δ to DiCaprio. You then use the NF $x_c = g(z_c)$ to go from the z space to the x space. For some values of c, the resulting images, x_c, are shown in figure 6.17.

Figure 6.17   Morphing from Beyoncé to Leonardo DiCaprio. The values are from left to right, $c = 0$ (100% Beyoncé), $c = 0.25$, $c = 0.5$, $c = 0.75$, and $c = 1$ (100% DiCaprio). An animated version is available at https://youtu.be/JTtW_nhjIYA.

What's nice about figure 6.17 is that for all the intermediate x_c's, the faces do somewhat look realistic. The question is can we find other interesting directions in the high-dimensional space? It turns out, yes.

The CelebA data set is annotated with 40 categories, such as having a goatee, a big nose, a double chin, smiling, and so on. Could we use these to find a goatee direction? We take the average position of all images flagged as goatee and call it z_1, then we take the average of all images flagged as no goatee and call it z_2. Now let's hope that $\Delta = z_2 - z_1$ is indeed a direction having a goatee. These directions have been calculated by OpenAI, and we can use them in the notebook. Let's give it a try and grow DiCaprio a goatee. The result is shown in figure 6.18.

Figure 6.18 Growing Leonardo DiCaprio a goatee. The values are from left to right, $c = 0$ (original, no goatee), $c = 0.25$, $c = 0.5$, $c = 0.75$, and $c = 1$. You can find an animated version at https://youtu.be/OwMRY9MdCMc.

That's quite fascinating because the goatee information hasn't been used during the training of the flow. Only after the training happened was the direction of the goatee found in the latent space. Let's try to understand why moving in the latent z space produces valid images in the x space. Look at the example of morphing from Beyoncé to Leonardo DiCaprio. There are two points in the 196,608-dimensional x space. For a better understanding, let's take a look at the 2D example discussed in section 6.3.5. Feel free to open the notebook http://mng.bz/RArK again and scroll down to the cell, Understanding the Mixture. The z distribution in the 2D example is produced by two independent Gaussians (see the left side of figure 6.19), and the x distribution looks like a boomerang (see the right side of figure 6.19).

We start with two points in the x space: in the high-dimensional example, that's Beyoncé and DiCaprio. In our 2D examples, these are the points (0.6, 0.25) and (0.6, –0.25), labeled with stars in figure 6.19. We then use the inverse flow to determine the corresponding points z_1 and z_2 in the z space, labeled by stars on the left side of figure 6.19. In the z space, we then move along a straight line from z_1 to z_2. (This is what you saw in figure 6.16.) In figure 6.19, you can see that the line on the left is completely in the distribution. We don't move into regions where there's no training data (gray points). Now, we transform the line back to the x space of the real data. You can see on the right side of figure 6.19 that the resulting line is now curved and also stays in

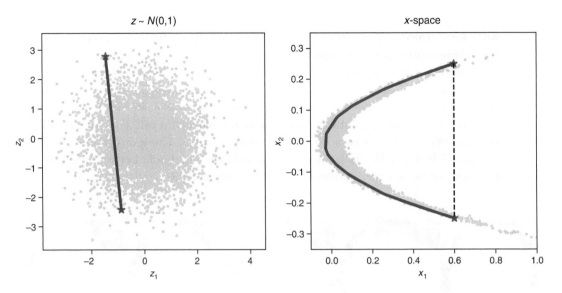

Figure 6.19   A synthetic 2D example of a complex *x* distribution (shown on the right) and the latent *z* distribution (on the left). A learned Real NVP flow transforms from latent space to *x* space. The straight line in the *z* space corresponds to moving along the curved line in the *x* space.

regions where there's data. The same happens in the high-dimensional space, which is the reason that all the points between Beyoncé and DiCaprio look like real faces.

What would happen if we connect the two points in the *x* space directly? We'd leave the region of known points (see the dashed line in figure 6.19). The same would happen in the high-dimensional space, producing images that wouldn't look like real images. How about the goatee? Again, we move along a straight direction in the latent space *z* without leaving the distribution. We start from a valid point (DiCaprio) and move along a certain direction (in our case, the goatee) without leaving the *z* distribution.

Summary

- Real-world data needs complex distributions.
- For categorical data, the multinomial distribution offers maximal flexibility with a drawback of having many parameters.
- For discrete data with many possible values (like count data), multinomial distributions are ineffective.
- For simple count data, Poisson distributions are fine.
- For complex discrete data including count data, mixtures of discretized logistic distributions are successfully used in the wild, like in PixelCNN++ and parallel WaveNet.

- Normalizing flows (NF) are an alternative approach to model complex distributions.
- NFs are based on learning a transformation function that leads from simple base distributions to the complex real-world distribution of interest.
- A powerful NF can be realized with an NN.
- You can use an NN-powered NF to model high-dimensional complex distributions like faces.
- You can also use NF models to sample data from the learned distribution.
- TFP offers the `bijector` package that's centered around an NF.
- As in chapters 4 and 5, the maximum likelihood (MaxLike) principle does the trick in learning NFs.

Bayesian approaches for probabilistic DL models

In part 3 of this book, you learn about Bayesian DL models. You'll see that Bayesian models become especially important when you encounter novel situations. Bayesian models are a special form of probabilistic models that add additional uncertainty.

In part 2 of this book, you learned how to set up non-Bayesian probabilistic NN models. These probabilistic models allowed you to describe the uncertainty inherent in data. You always need to deal with the inherent uncertainty in data if there's some randomness, meaning the observed outcome can't be determined completely by the input. This uncertainty is called *aleatoric uncertainty*.

But, as it turns out, there is also another kind of uncertainty inherent to the model. This uncertainty is called *epistemic uncertainty*. Epistemic uncertainty occurs because it's not possible to estimate the model parameters without any doubt. This is because we don't have unlimited training data. Usually, we only have training data that doesn't cover all possible situations. Think, for example, of a model that's trained to predict the reaction time of a person based on sex, age, coffee consumption, alcohol blood level, and temperature in the room. You collected data from student volunteers that you use to train your model. You evaluate the performance on a test set of students, and it works quite well. Now you want to apply your model to patients in a hospital. Do you expect your model to work? Not necessarily. But still, your model produces some predictions, even though these predictions might be just plain wrong. In this last part of the book, you learn how you can design your model so that you can recognize when the predictions of your model aren't reliable.

Bayesian learning 7

This chapter covers

- Identifying extrapolation as the Achilles heel of DL
- A gentle introduction to Bayesian modeling
- The concept of model uncertainty, which is called epistemic uncertainty
- The Bayesian approach as a state-of-the-art method to dealing with parameter uncertainty

This chapter introduces Bayesian models. Besides the likelihood approach, the Bayesian approach is the most important method to fit the parameters of a probabilistic model and to estimate the associated parameter uncertainty. The Bayesian modeling approach incorporates an additional kind of uncertainty, called *epistemic uncertainty*. You will see that incorporating epistemic uncertainty results in better prediction performance and, more appropriately, quantification of the uncertainty of the predicted outcome distribution. The epistemic uncertainty becomes especially important when applying prediction models to situations not seen during the training. In regression, this is known as *extrapolation*.

You'll see in this chapter that traditional non-Bayesian models don't express uncertainties if these are trained with few data or used for extrapolation. But Bayesian models do. Therefore, it's better to use Bayesian approaches when you have little training data or when you can't rule out that you'll encounter situations not seen in training—like an elephant in a room (see the figure at the beginning of this chapter). You'll also see that even state-of-the-art DL models like those that win the ImageNet challenge are usually great in classifying elephants, but these are not able to classify correctly an elephant in the room. Instead, a wrong class is predicted, often with a high probability. This inability to communicate uncertainty when dealing with new situations and so produce unreliable predictions are a serious deficit of non-Bayesian DL models. Bayesian DL models, on the other hand, have the ability to express uncertainty.

In this chapter, you'll learn the Bayesian modeling approach and apply it to simple models; for example, treating coin tosses in a Bayesian way as a Hello World-like example. Further, you'll also apply Bayesian modeling to linear regression. It turns out that more complex models like NNs need approximations to the Bayesian modeling approach. We'll cover these in chapter 8. This chapter is about understanding the principles of Bayesian modeling. Before diving into the Bayesian modeling approach, let's see what's wrong with the traditional, non-Bayesian NN models.

7.1   *What's wrong with non-Bayesian DL: The elephant in the room*

You'll see in this section that DL models can sometimes tell (with innocent and proud confidence) a completely wrong story. We show two examples, one from regression and one from classification, in which non-Bayesian DL fails. For regression, we provide you with a simple, one-dimensional toy example, and you'll immediately understand the reason why it fails. For classification, the example is the usual image classification, and thus, more complex, but the principle remains the same.

Usually, the predictions of traditional DL models are highly reliable when applied to the same data used in training, which somehow can lull you into a false sense of security. Bayesian modeling helps to alert you of potentially wrong predictions. Before addressing the weaknesses of traditional NN models, however, let's first recall the successes of DL.

Let's move back to a time when DL has not had its breakthrough. We are in the year 2012; the iPhone is just five years old. Here's what we're looking at:

- There's no possibility of text-to-speech with reasonable performance.
- Computers aren't good at recognizing your handwriting.
- A team of linguists is required to develop a translation program.
- Machines can't make sense of photos.

In figure 7.1, you see two examples that can be correctly classified by the VGG16 network. The VGG16 network, introduced in 2014, is an early network that started the DL revolution for image classification. You can use the following notebook to do the classifications yourself.

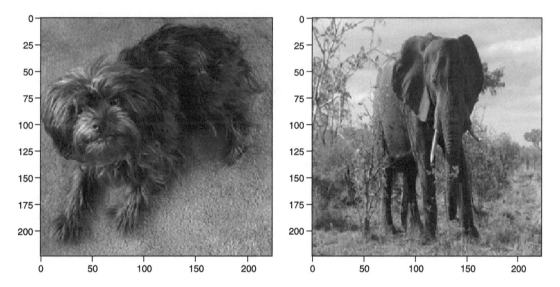

Figure 7.1 Good cases of DL. The left image shows a dog that's correctly classified as an Affenpinscher. The right image shows an elephant that's classified as a Tusker (an elephant species). The dog image is taken from http://mng.bz/PABn and the elephant image from http://mng.bz/JyWV.

HANDS-ON TIME Open http://mng.bz/1zZj and follow the notebook. It produces the figures in this chapter for this section. Try to understand what happened in the notebook.

All is done. There's no problem to fix in DL, and we're finished. Not quite. To get a feel for one important unmet challenge of DL, look at the left image in figure 7.2. The image clearly shows some kind of elephant. However, the same network that nicely classified the elephant in figure 7.1 as some elephant species completely fails for the image in figure 7.2—the DL model can't see the elephant in the room!

Why does the DL model fail to see the elephant? This is because in the training set used to fit the DL model, there were no pictures of elephants in rooms. Not surprisingly,

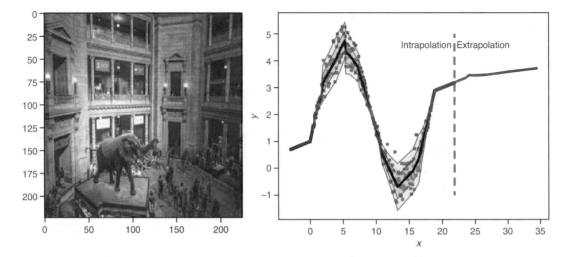

Figure 7.2   A bad case of DL. The high performant VGG16-CNN trained on ImageNet data fails to see the elephant in the room! The five highest-ranked class predictions of the objects in the image are horse_cart, shopping_cart, palace, streetcar, and gondola; the elephant is not found! This image is an extrapolation of the training set. In the regression problem on the right side of the dashed vertical line (extrapolation), there's zero uncertainty in the regions where there's no data.

the elephant images in the training set show these animals in their natural environment. This is a typical situation where a trained DL model fails: when presented with an instance of a novel class or situation not seen during the training phase. Not only DL models, but also traditional machine learning (ML) models get in trouble when the test data doesn't come from the same distribution as the training data. Exaggerating a bit, but DL crucially depends on the big lie:

$$P(\mathit{train}) = P(\mathit{test}) = \text{The "big lie"}$$

The condition $P(\mathit{train}) = P(\mathit{test})$ is always assumed; but in reality, the training and the test data don't often come from the same distribution. Imagine, for example, that you train an image classification model with images taken with your old camera, and you now want to classify images that you've taken with your new camera.

The dependence on this questionable assumption that there's no systematic difference between training and test data is a principal weakness of DL and ML in general. We, as humans, obviously learn differently. No child in the world would not see the elephant in figure 7.2 once he or she learned what an elephant looks like. There's speculation why this is the case. Judea Pearl, for example, suggested that the key to a more intelligent and robust DL would be to include causal structures. So far, DL can only exploit statistical correlations in the data. Currently, there is no clear answer to solve this problem.

Even if we only hope to exploit the statistical correlations in DL, we have a severe problem: the network doesn't tell us that it has a problem with the elephant in the room. It doesn't know when it doesn't know. It simply assigns the image with the elephant in the row to the wrong class, sometimes even with a high probability. Now, imagine yourself sitting in a self-driving car. Do you feel comfortable?

Looking at the right side of figure 7.2, we can see the reason for this lack of recognition. The network does a perfect job of assigning the uncertainty in the regions where there's ample data. The uncertainty is measured by the variance, which is modeled in addition to the mean. In chapter 5, we called this type of uncertainty *aleatoric uncertainty*. Now focus on the values x in the region indicated by extrapolation. While, for example, at $x = 20$, there's no spread in the data and the near-zero uncertainty is correct, the problem begins when we move to larger values and enter the region where there's no data (extrapolation). The network simply takes the last value of the uncertainty and *extrapolates* it to regions it hasn't seen, thus quoting the Star Trek motto: "To boldly go where no one has gone before." Well, maybe too boldly.

Similarly, the problem with the elephant can be seen as a problem of extrapolation. When we have only one variable x, we can draw it on a line and it's easy to see when we leave the regions where we have data. For the case of the elephant, it's less easy. Instead of a single real-valued quantity x, we now have the number of pixels squared (images of width 256 have 65,535 values). It's quite hard to see when you leave the space where you have data. But, there's a real need for that (again, imagine sitting in the self-driving car). We talk about this in section 7.2.

As another example, imagine you want to place a huge amount of your money in a certain investment and your DL model predicts a great reward. Wouldn't you want to know if your DL model is certain about its predicted outcome distribution? In another example, imagine a DL system that classifies medical histological samples. Here you'd also like to know how certain are the predicted class probabilities. (In case of uncertain predictions, you could get a medical doctor to look more carefully at the sample.)

How can the network tell us that it feels unsure? The solution is to introduce a new kind of uncertainty—epistemic uncertainty. *Epistemic* comes from the ancient Greek word "epistēmē," meaning knowledge. It reflects the uncertainty when you leave the regions with data. In practice, this uncertainty is modeled by the uncertainty in the parameters of the model, and is thus, sometimes also called *parameter* or *model uncertainty*. In section 7.2, we talk about a statistical way of thinking, called *Bayesian reasoning*. Bayesian reasoning makes it possible for us to model this kind of uncertainty.

7.2 *The first encounter with a Bayesian approach*

In this section, we try to understand the principle of Bayesian statistics by an intuitive example and then see how the Bayesian approach to the problem models the epistemic uncertainty.

- In section 7.2.1, we extend the standard linear regression model by allowing not just one solution, but a whole ensemble of solutions.
- In section 7.2.2, we take another look at the intuitive solution from section 7.2.1 and describe it in Bayesian terms to introduce Bayesian terminology.

7.2.1   *Bayesian model: The hacker's way*

To get an idea of what's meant by the epistemic uncertainty of a probabilistic prediction model, let's start with a simple example demonstrating the hacker's way to fit a Bayesian model. We fit a probabilistic linear regression model with the four points (see figure 7.3). In this model, we assume that the data has a constant spread, $\sigma = 3$, and so the model is

$$p(y|x, (a, b)) = N(y; \mu = a \cdot x + b, \sigma = 3)$$

Equation 7.1

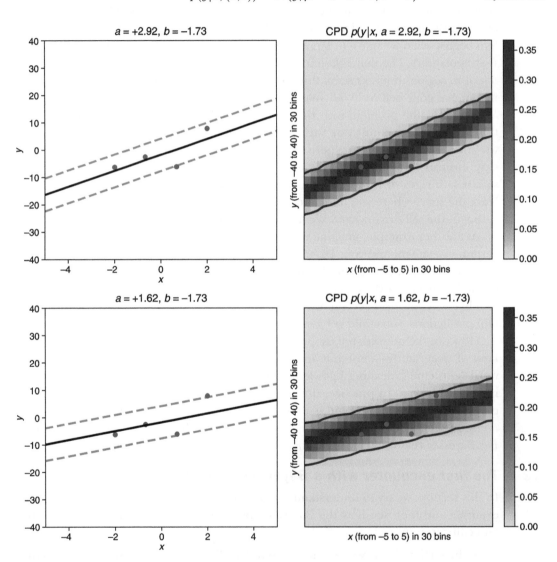

Figure 7.3   Linear regression and data. The left column shows the linear model for the indicated parameter values a and b, where the mean value is the solid line with the 2.5% and 97.5% percentiles. The right column shows the fitted conditional predictive distribution for the outcome $p(y|x, (a, b)) = N(y; \mu = a \cdot x + b, \sigma = 3)$, indicated with color coding. In the upper row, the parameter values correspond to the maximum likelihood (MaxLike) values a_{ml} and b_{ml}.

In figure 7.3, you see two examples of this linear regression model corresponding to two different parameter sets (a, b).

Looking at figure 7.3, let's first focus on the left part. In the upper left, we see the line fitted via the maximum likelihood (MaxLike) principle. As you may recall from the notebook http://mng.bz/wBrP, the MaxLike is 0.064, and the parameter values for which the MaxLike is maximized are $a = 2.92$ and $b = -1.73$. There's a second line in the lower part of the figure that's drawn with the parameter values $a = 1.62$ and $b = -1.73$ and has the likelihood of 0.056. When you're forced to come up with only one value for a and b, it makes absolute sense to use the value that maximized the likelihood (the upper part in the figure). But perhaps it's not a good idea to totally ignore the other parameters. Take those into account but don't trust those as much as you'd trust the best (MaxLike) solution.

What's a good measure of how much you can trust a set of parameters (a, b)? Why not take the likelihood $p(D|(a, b))$? The likelihood is proportional to the probability of observing the data D when assuming that our model parameters are given by the values a and b. Therefore, we want to weight each model (defined by certain values a and b) proportional to its likelihood. However, you should normalize the correct weights so that these sum up to 1. To achieve this, we use the normalized likelihoods $p_n(D|(a, b))$ as weights:

$$\sum_a \sum_b p_n(D|(a, b)) = 1$$

Practically, we calculate the sum of the likelihood $\sum_a \sum_b p(D|(a, b))$ and divide the

likelihood $p(D|(a, b))$ by that number to get a normalized version $p_n(D|(a, b))$. Figure 7.4 shows this normalized likelihood for different values of a and b.

HANDS-ON TIME   Open http://mng.bz/wBrP. This notebook, containing code for the method which we call Bayes the hacker's way, produces the figures in this chapter for this section. Follow the notebook while you're reading the main text until you reach the Go Back to the Main Text symbol before the analytical solution.

Now we come to the right side of figure 7.3. What's the quantity we're interested in? It's the probability to observe a y value for a given value of x with a model that's trained on some training data D $p(y|x, D)$. For this quantity, we take all possible values of $p(y|x, (a, b))$ into account. The upper right side of figure 7.3 shows an example with the MaxLike estimates for a and b. Another example with different values for a and b is shown in the lower right side. We now add thousands of those $p(y|x, (a, b))$ with different values for a and b together and weight them with the normalized likelihood $p_n(D|(a, b))$ to get the predicted distribution for y given x. Figure 7.5 shows this principle.

Likelihood (normalized)

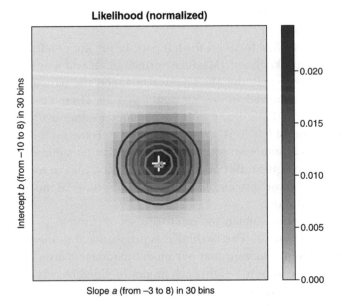

Figure 7.4   The normalized likelihood of the observed data for the true value $\sigma = 3$ and different parameter values for the slope (a) and the intercept (b). The likelihood $p_n(D|(a, b))$ is normalized, meaning that the sum over all pixels is 1.

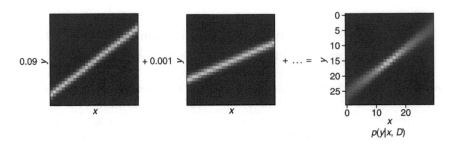

Figure 7.5   The images on the left of the equality sign show probabilistic regression models $p(y|x, (a, b))$, each corresponding to a different set of parameters (a, b). The factors to the left of the images indicate the normalized likelihood $p_n(D|(a, b))$ of the observed four data points D under the corresponding model. Adding up the different models $p(y|x, (a, b))$ and weighing them with the normalized likelihood $p_n(D|(a, b))$ results in the Bayesian prediction model shown on the right of the equality sign.

In more mathematical terms

$$p(y|x, D) = \sum_a \sum_b p(y|x, (a, b)) \cdot p_n(D|(a, b))$$

Equation 7.2

The sum goes over all possible values of the parameters a and b. Let's again look at the equation, maybe from a slightly different angle. The model $p(y|x, (a, b))$ is determined by the parameters and a and b. The data enters only to determine the normalized probability of having the specific parameter values a and b ($\sigma = 3$ is given). Because a and b are continuous quantities, we actually integrate over a and b. But we're even more sloppy; we just evaluate equation 7.2 at about 30 different values for a and b. Listing 7.1 provides the code corresponding to the equation, and figure 7.6 shows the resulting predictive distribution $p(y|x, D)$.[1]

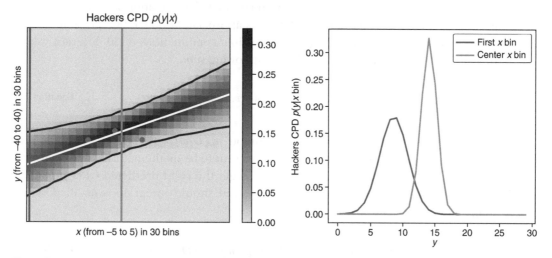

Figure 7.6 The predictive distribution for the Bayesian linear regression model trained with the four data points shown on the left side by the color coding and on the right by the conditional distribution at two different x positions (indicated with the lines on the right side). You can clearly see that the uncertainty gets larger when leaving the x regions where there's data.

Listing 7.1 The code corresponding to equation 7.2

```
pyx = np.zeros((nbins_c, nbins_c), dtype=np.float32)      ◁─┐  Starts with a
for a in np.linspace(amin, amax, nbins):          ◁─┐      │  blank canvas
    for b in np.linspace(bmin, bmax, nbins):             │
        p = getProb(a,b)       ┌─▷                        │  Loops over all
        pyx += pre_distribution(a,b) * getProb(a,b)       │  parameters a
```

Gets the probability for the parameters a and b given the data

---

[1] This might ring a bell for those of you who have some experience with statistical regression models looking at the waisted prediction band in figure 7.6. Indeed, you get a similar-looking result when computing a prediction interval that incorporates the confidence interval for the mean parameter of the conditional Normal distribution. Such a confidence interval for model parameters can be computed without Bayesian statistics, at least for models that are not too big and too complex. But for a DL model that is a complex non-linear model with millions of parameters, these non-Bayesian uncertainty measures require a resampling approach and many rounds of refitting the NN, which is too time-consuming to be feasible.

7.2.2   *What did we just do?*

You'll see in section 7.3 that the experiment we did in section 7.2.1 is actually well backed by a sound theory that's called Bayesian statistics. In section 7.2.1, you saw a hacker's way to fit a Bayesian model. It not only used a single MaxLike estimate for the weights, but it also used a whole distribution of possible weights. This distribution over w is given by the normalized likelihood $p_n(D|w) = C \cdot p(D|w)$, with C being a normalization constant.

When fitting a prediction model, you're mainly interested in the predictive distribution of the outcome y for the given input x. This is what we introduced in chapter 4 as CPD (conditional probability distribution): $p(y|x, D)$. Equation 7.2 tells you how to get this predictive distribution in a hacker's approach. You take 900 possible weight vectors $w_i = (a, b)$ corresponding to the possible combinations of 30 different values of a and b, respectively, and then take the following sum:

$$p(y|x, D) = \sum_{w_i} p(y|x, w_i) \cdot p_n(D|w_i)$$

Equation 7.3

For weights, we use the normalized likelihood $p_n(D|w) = C \cdot p(D|w)$. The parameters $w_i = (a, b)_i$ are continuous values. If you want to be mathematically more correct, you should use integrals instead of sums. To get the right predicted CPD $p(y|x, D)$ for continuous weights for the outcome y, you should integrate over all possible weights like this:

$$p(y|x, D) = \int_w p(y|x, w) \cdot p_n(D|w)dw$$

Equation 7.4

Let's try to nail down what changed compared to the previous probabilistic models in chapters 4 and 5, which resulted from the MaxLike approach.

First, a new thing is that you don't work with fixed weights in the trained NN but with a weight distribution $p_n(D|w)$. The weight distribution $p_n(D|w)$ is called *posterior distribution* in the Bayesian treatment because it's derived after (post) you've seen some data D. To emphasize that this is after seeing the data, we write $p(w|D)$ for the posterior. It's the probability of the weights w conditioned on the data D. We mathematically derive this equation in the next section. The name *posterior* somehow implies that there's also some *prior* distribution before seeing some data. You'll learn about prior distribution in the next section. But for now, note that we use a uniform prior in the preceding little experiment. In the next section, you'll also learn how to get from the prior parameter distribution to the posterior distribution.

Previous probabilistic models predict a CPD that only captures the aleatoric uncertainty of the data inherent variability. Bayesian models predict a CPD incorporating two kinds of uncertainties (see equation 7.3): the aleatoric uncertainty of the data inherent variability and the epistemic uncertainty of the parameter values that are captured by the probability distribution of the parameter $p(w|D)$. Later, you'll see that the epistemic uncertainty can, in principle, be reduced to zero (if you have an infinite number of training data that cover all possible future situations). You cannot decrease the aleatoric uncertainty with more data. You'll also see later that in the (rare) situation of a zero epistemic uncertainty, the outcome CPD, $p(y|x, D)$, is the same as the MaxLike CPD from chapters 4 and 5. But in our little example in section 7.2.1, we only have four data points and, therefore, the epistemic uncertainty isn't zero, and the MaxLike model (see figure 7.3) does look quite different from the Bayesian model (see figure 7.6). In the MaxLike method, the model predicts for each input x a CPD that has a constant width (also in x ranges where no data was available during training). In the Bayesian model, the predicted CPD gets broader when extrapolating to new x ranges. This is quite nice behavior. Your uncertainty should increase when leaving known grounds! We will come back to this point later in section 7.3.3 and compare for our simple example of linear regression the ML approach with the Bayesian approach. But first, let's have a closer look at the Bayesian approach.

7.3 *The Bayesian approach for probabilistic models*

The idea of setting up models that incorporate the uncertainty about its parameter values via a probability distribution is quite old. The Reverend Thomas Bayes (see figure 7.7) developed this approach in the 18th century. Nowadays, a whole branch in statistics is called Bayesian statistics.

The Bayesian approach is a well-established, clear, and thorough approach to fit probabilistic models that capture different kinds of uncertainties. It's an alternative way of doing statistics and interpreting probability. In mainstream statistics (the so-called *frequentist* statistics), probability is defined by analyzing repeated (frequent) measurements. More exactly, probability is defined as the theoretical limit of the relative

Figure 7.7   Thomas Bayes (1701-1761) was an English statistician, philosopher, and Presbyterian minister. The image is taken from Wikipedia (https://en.wikipedia.org/wiki/Thomas_Bayes) and is likely not showing Bayes. But because no other portrait is available, it's always used if an image of Bayes is needed.

frequency when doing an infinite number of repetitions. In Bayesian statistics, in contrast, probability is defined in terms of degree of belief. The more likely an outcome or a certain value of a parameter is, the higher the degree of belief in it. This seemingly loose idea also leads to a valid definition of a probability.

In the Bayesian approach, only the simplest problems can be tackled without the help of a computer. Therefore, this approach has languished away during the greater part of the 20th century. But now, with enough compute power, this approach is frequently used. It's a powerful approach, especially when you have some prior knowledge that you like to model.

In section 7.3.1, you learn how the fitting process works with the Bayesian approach. We give an overview of the most important terms and mathematical laws used in Bayesian statistics. In section 7.3.2, you use the learned skills to fit a Hello World Bayesian model.

7.3.1   *Training and prediction with a Bayesian model*

One of the most famous formulae of Bayesian statistics is called the *Bayes' theorem*. It even made its appearance on a neon sign that hangs in the Cambridge offices of the software company, HP Autonomy (see figure 7.8). Besides Einstein's $E = mc^2$, not many other mathematical formulas have achieved such popularity.

The Bayes' theorem links together four probabilities: the conditional probability of A given B, $P(A|B)$, the inverse of that conditional probability, the probability of B given A $P(A|B)$, and the unconditional probabilities of A, $P(A)$, and B, $P(B)$. In the sidebar at the end of this section, you'll see that the derivation of the Bayesian theorem is easy. But let's first use it to fit a Bayesian probabilistic model. For that, you write

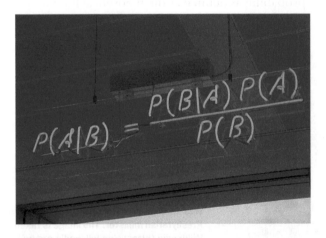

**Figure 7.8   The Bayesian theorem defines how to derive *P(A|B)*
from the inverse conditional probability *P(B|A)*, *P(A)*, and *P(B)*.
(This image is taken from http://mng.bz/7Xnv.)**

the parameter θ of the model instead of A, and you write D (which stands for the data) instead of B. This yields a more useful form of the Bayesian theorem:

$$p(\theta|D) = \frac{p(D|\theta)p(\theta)}{p(D)}$$

Equation 7.5

The quantities in equation 7.5 are so prominent that all of them have names:

- $p(\theta|D)$—The posterior (the probability of a certain value of a parameter θ given the data D)
- $p(D|\theta)$—The inverse (called the likelihood)
- $p(\theta)$—The prior
- $p(D)$—The quantity (also called the marginal likelihood or evidence)

Note that in the Bayesian interpretation, a certain value of a parameter θ isn't a sure thing but has an uncertainty described by the probability distribution $p(\theta)$. This distribution, $p(\theta)$, defines the probability of each parameter value θ. The probability of a certain parameter value $p(\theta)$ can be interpreted as a degree of belief for that certain value of the parameter.[2]

The Bayes' theorem is at the heart of fitting a Bayesian (or Bayes) model because it provides instruction on how to learn from the data the posterior distribution of the model parameter. This corresponds to finding the MaxLike parameter value θ_{maxLik}, given the training data D in non-Bayesian model fitting, but now we get a whole distribution $p(\theta|D)$. Knowing the posterior distribution of the parameter θ is all you need for a probabilistic Bayesian model. Now you can determine the predictive distribution:

$$p(y|x_{\text{test}}, D) = \int_{\theta} p(y|x_{\text{test}}, \theta) \cdot p(\theta|D)d\theta$$

Equation 7.6

We've approximated this predictive distribution in the last section in a brute-force approach, where we considered only some discrete values θ_i of the continuous parameter θ. In the previous regression example, the parameters are the slope and the intercept, $\theta_i = (a, b)_i$.

$$p(y|x_{\text{test}}, D) = \sum_{i} p(y|x_{\text{test}}, \theta_i) \cdot p(\theta_i|D)$$

Equation 7.7

To interpret the formula of the predictive distribution, it helps to remember the predictive distribution in the MaxLike model:

$$p(y|x_{\text{test}}, D) = p(y|x_{\text{test}}, \theta_{\text{maxLik}})$$

---

[2] In this book, we're a bit relaxed when it comes to mathematical notation. If the parameter θ is a continuous quantity, we should call it probability density instead of a probability, but we don't do this here and in the rest of the book.

We picked a distribution for the CPD with parameter θ and then used the data to determine θ_{maxLik}. Given θ_{maxLik}, all possible outcomes y follow the CPD $p(y|x_{\text{test}}, \theta_{\text{maxLik}})$, so you can forget about the data after you compute θ_{maxLik}. With the Bayes approach, you don't work with a CPD that corresponds to a single (optimized) parameter value, but you do a weighted average (with weight $p(\theta_i|D)$) over many CPDs, $(p(y|x_{\text{test}}, \theta_i))$, with different parameter values θ_i to get the predictive distribution (see, for example, figure 7.5).

To gain better insight, imagine the following example. You run an actively managed fund, and you need a probabilistic forecast for the future value of a certain stock, so you want $p(y|x_{\text{stock}})$. You have several experts on your team. Each expert i provides a slightly different probabilistic prediction $p(y|x_{\text{stock}}, \theta_i)$. The best you can do to get one forecast out of this is to average the predicted CPDs and give each $p(y|x_{\text{stock}}, \theta_i)$ an appropriate weight. This weight should be proportional to the performance of the expert's model on past data D of the given stock (the likelihood $p(D|\theta_i)$). Further, you add your subjective judgment of the models coming from these experts in general (the prior $p(\theta_i)$). Alternatively, not willing to judge the experts, you might as well give each expert the same subjective *a priori* judgment (the prior is constant). This gives you the unnormalized posterior distribution (see equation 7.5). After normalizing, this tells you to use the posterior $p(\theta_i|D)$ as weights, yielding:

$$p(y|x_{\text{stock}}, D) = \sum_i p(y|x_{\text{stock}}, \theta_i) \cdot p(\theta_i|D)$$

In this view, a Bayesian model is a weighted ensemble model—we use the wisdom of the crowd but weight the contributions of the individual experts. To get the terms for the different distributions straight, we've collected those in table 7.1 along with the corresponding formulas and some explanations.

Table 7.1 Probability distributions used in this chapter

Name	Formula	Notes/Examples
Likelihood	$p(D|\theta)$	D is for the data that might be single quantities (as in a coin toss) or that consists of pairs (as in linear regression or in typical DL settings).
		y_i is the specific value of the outcome taken in example i.
		Coin toss: data D is the outcome heads ($y = 1$) or tails ($y = 0$) of different throws. The likelihood for a single toss $p(y_i|\theta)$ is determined from a Bernoulli distribution: θ is the likelihood for heads and $1 - \theta$ is the likelihood for tails.
		Linear regression: data D are now pairs (x_i, y_i). The parameter θ consists of the slope a and the intercept b. The likelihood for a single example is given by $p(y_i|x_i, a, b)$, which is determined from a Normal distribution $(y_i|x_i) \sim N(a \cdot x_i + b, \sigma)$.

Table 7.1   Probability distributions used in this chapter (*continued*)

Name	Formula	Notes/Examples
Prior	$p(\theta)$	In the Bayes setting, parameters are distributed according to the prior distribution. This distribution needs to be defined before you see the data. There is some degree of subjectivity in stating your prior beliefs. Some examples include: Coin toss: $p(\theta) = U(\theta; 0, 1)$. (You don't trust anybody. The probability θ for heads is uniformly distributed.) Regression: $p(a) = N(a; 0, 1)$. Bayesian networks: $p(w) = N(w; 0, 1)$ (the weights are *a priori* standard normal distributed).
Posterior	$p(\theta \vert D)$	The parameter distribution is learned from the data using the Bayes formula. Mantra: The posterior is proportional to the likelihood times the prior $p(\theta \vert D) \propto P(D \vert \theta) \cdot P(\theta)$. The normalization constant can be determined from the condition that $\int P(\theta \vert D) d\theta = 1$ (for continuous parameters) or from $\sum_i p(\theta_i \vert D) = 1$ (for discrete parameters).
Predictive distribution in the MaxLike setting A.k.a CPD (conditional probability distribution) for the outcome *y* Or unconditional outcome probability distribution (if it's not predicted from *x*)	$p(y \vert \theta_{\text{maxLik}}, x)$ $p(y \vert \theta_{\text{maxLik}})$	*y* is now a variable and not a fixed value. Linear regression: $p(y \vert x) = \frac{1}{\sqrt{2\pi\sigma^2}} e^{-(a \cdot x + b - y)^2 / 2\sigma^2}$ $= N(y; a \cdot x + b, \sigma)$ with *a* and *b* estimated from the training data *D*. Here and in typical DL settings, this distribution is conditioned on *x* (a.k.a CPD). Coin toss: Bernoulli $p(y = 1) = \theta$, $p(y = 0) = 1 - \theta$ with θ estimated from the data via MaxLike.
Predictive distribution in a Bayesian setting (also posterior predictive distribution) A.k.a CPD (conditional probability distribution) Or unconditional outcome probability distribution (if it's not predicted from *x*)	$p(y \vert x, D)$ $p(y)$	*y* is a variable and not a fixed value. Its distribution is conditioned on the input *x* and *D*. Typically, this is calculated via the posterior $p(\theta \vert D)$ via $p(y \vert x, D) = \int p(y \vert x, \theta) \cdot p(\theta \vert D) d\theta$ Note that $p(y \vert x, \theta)$ is the predictive distribution for the outcome comprising contributions from a distribution of parameter values θ (not only a single value θ_{maxLik} as in the MaxLike approach). We integrate over all values of θ and weight them given their posterior probability $p(\theta \vert D)$.

NOTE A small hint on how to read the formulas in table 7.1. What's on the right side of the pipe symbol (|) is the "from" part. What's on the left of the pipe symbol is the "to" part. You read those terms from right to left. Sometimes it helps to draw an arrow below the formulae in our minds to make it clear. So, $p(D|\theta)$ is the probability that from the parameter θ, you get the data D. If there are mathematicians in the room, say, "$p(D|\theta)$ is the probability of the data D given the parameters θ." But thoughts are free and think what you prefer.

The Bayesian theorem (equation 7.5) allows you to learn about the parameter distribution $P(\theta|D)$ of θ when you have some data D. The quantity $P(\theta|D)$ is therefore called posterior because you determine it after you've seen the data (the name *posterior* comes from the Latin *post* meaning *after*). But how can you derive $P(\theta|D)$? You need to determine the likelihood of the observed data $P(D|\theta)$ under the model with parameter θ. In addition, you need to know the prior $P(\theta)$ and the evidence $P(D)$. Because your training data D is fixed, $P(D)$ is a constant. Realizing that $P(D)$ is a constant leads you to the fact that the posterior distribution is proportional to the likelihood times the prior: $p(\theta|D) \propto P(D|\theta) \cdot P(\theta)$, which is also called the Bayesian mantra.

THE BAYESIAN MANTRA The posterior is proportional to the likelihood times the prior.

This shows that the evidence $P(D)$ is just there so that posterior probability sums up (or integrates) to 1. It's mathematically often more convenient to use the Bayesian mantra and calculate the proportionality afterward by the requirement that:

$$\int P(\theta|D)d\theta = 1$$

Fixing $P(D)$ was easy, but how to choose the prior $P(\theta)$? If you have no prior knowledge about the parameter values, you can, for example, use a uniform distribution giving each parameter value the same probability. This means you pick the following prior: $P(\theta) = \text{const}$. In this special case, the posterior distribution $P(\theta|D)$ is proportional to the likelihood. Why? Because $P(\theta|D)$ is a probability distribution; hence, it must integrate to 1, and therefore, it holds that the posterior $P(\theta|D)$ is given by the normalized likelihood if the prior is constant. This is exactly what was used in the hacker's example where we used the different normalized likelihoods for different parameter values to weight the contributing CPDs in equation 7.2. Here it is again:

$$p(y|x, D) = \sum_a \sum_b p(y|x, (a, b)) \cdot p_n(D|(a, b)) \qquad \textbf{Equation 7.2 (repeated)}$$

In Bayesian regression problems (and later deep Bayesian NNs), we want to predict for each input its CPD $p(y|x)$. But before we come to that, let's first try to fit a single (unconditional) distribution $p(y)$.

Derivation of the Bayes theorem

The Bayesian theorem can be derived from the product rule as follows:

$$P(A, B) = P(A|B) \cdot P(B)$$

In a few words, the product rule says the joint probability that both events *A* and *B* occur, given by *P(A, B)*, is the same as the probability *P(A)*, where the (first) event *A* occurs, times the probability that when *A* occurs, then *B* or *P(B|A)* occurs. Read those equations from left to right: *P(B|A)* is from *A* to *B* or, in general, $P(\text{to}|\text{from})$. Makes sense! Think for example about the probability that during a beach stroll you find an oyster, $P(\text{oyster}) = 0.2$. The probability that an oyster contains a pearl is $P(\text{pearl}|\text{oyster}) = 0.01$. From this you can compute the probability that you find an oyster that contains a pearl by $P(\text{oyster.with.pearl}) = P(\text{oyster}) \cdot P(\text{pearl}|\text{oyster}) = 0.2 \cdot 0.001 = 0.0002$. Let's derive the Bayes formula.

$$p(\theta|D) = \frac{p(D|\theta) \cdot p(\theta)}{p(D)}$$

You need to use the product rule in the previous equation and realize that you can sweep *A* and *B*. Doing so yields this equation:

$$P(B) \cdot P(A|B) = P(B, A) = P(A, B) = P(A) \cdot P(B|A)$$

Dividing both sides by *P(B)* gives us the Bayesian theorem:

$$P(A|B) = \frac{P(A) \cdot P(B|A)}{P(B)}$$

That was easy! Given the power of the Bayes theorem, the derivation is a piece of cake. The derivation of the other powerful formula, $E = mc^2$, however, is a bit harder.

7.3.2 *A coin toss as a Hello World example for Bayesian models*

Let's use the learned concepts of Bayesian statistics from section 7.3.1 to fit your first Bayesian model. To keep it simple, let's assume that you want to predict the outcome of a coin toss experiment. The two possible outcomes are heads ($y = 1$) and tails ($y = 0$). You want to determine the predictive distribution $p(y)$ for the two possible outcomes.

Note that in most other examples in this book, you have some input, and you've estimated the outcome distribution conditioned on the input values. In these kinds of examples, you estimate a CPD for the outcome. In this coin toss example, you have no input variables. The probability for getting heads doesn't depend on any external variables; you always toss the same coin. Therefore, you only need to estimate an unconditional probability distribution for the outcome.

Predicting the (unconditional) outcome distribution for the coin toss example is easy if you know that it's a fair coin. For a fair coin, the predictive distribution assigns a probability of 0.5 to heads and a probability of 0.5 to tails. This probabilistic outcome captures the aleatoric uncertainty inherent in a coin toss experiment—

you just don't know whether you'll get heads or tails. The epistemic uncertainty on the other hand is zero. You know for sure that the probability for heads is 0.5; after all, it's a fair coin.

In terms of probabilistic models, you describe the predictive distribution as a Bernoulli distribution with a binary outcome y (heads: $y = 1$, tails: $y = 0$). It has only one parameter, θ, which corresponds to the probability of getting heads, so $\theta = P(y = 1)$. If you have a fair coin, the parameter θ is $\theta = 0.5$. But θ can take other values. The left side of figure 7.9 shows the predictive distribution for a fixed θ.

Let's assume that the coin comes from a suspicious gambler, and you can't assume that it's a fair coin. You also can't tell the exact value of θ. This means you need to estimate the probability for heads: $\theta = P(y = 1)$.

To generate some training data, you throw the coin three times and observe heads all three times: $D = (1, 1, 1)$. Uh-oh, the first impression is that you've got an unfair coin. But how sure can you be after three throws? We'll come to the Bayes treatment in a second, but first, let's find out what you get with a non-Bayesian approach.

THE MAXLIKE APPROACH FOR THE COIN TOSS EXAMPLE

Let's use the traditional non-Bayesian MaxLike approach to fit the Bernoulli model to the results of the coin toss experiment. To fit the model, you use your training data: $D = (y_1 = 1, y_2 = 1, y_3 = 1)$. Based on this data, what's the best value of the parameter θ in the Bernoulli model (see figure 7.9)?

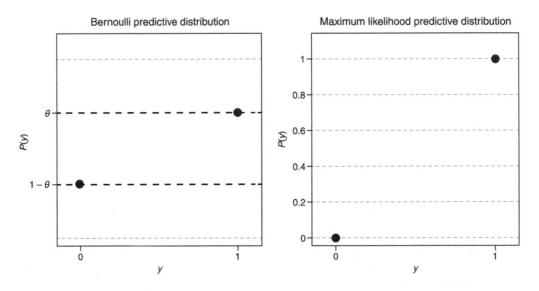

Figure 7.9   The Bernoulli distribution of a binary variable Y with a parameter θ (left). On the right, you see the predictive distribution for the outcome derived by a MaxLike approach after observing heads three times in a row.

The MaxLike estimate for the probability for heads ($y = 1$) is computed by the number of observed heads (n_1) divided by the number of throws (n): $\theta_{\text{maxLik}} = \dfrac{n_1}{n} = \dfrac{3}{3} = 1$. The standard deviation is given by $sd(\theta_{\text{maxLik}}) = \theta_{\text{maxLik}} \cdot (1 - \theta_{\text{maxLik}}) = 1 \cdot 0 = 0$. (To check out the derivation of the formula for the standard deviation, see http://mng.bz/mB9a.) This means the MaxLike estimate assigns the probability of one and an aleatoric uncertainty of zero ($sd(\theta_{\text{maxLik}}) = 0$) to the outcome, heads. In this case, the predictive distribution (see figure 7.9 on the right side) doesn't contain any uncertainty. The resulting model says that the coin toss always shows heads. That's quite a risky statement after seeing only three throws!

BAYESIAN APPROACH FOR THE COIN TOSS EXAMPLE

Let's take the Bayesian approach to fit the Bernoulli model to the outcome of the results of the coin toss experiment. You assume that you need to allow for some uncertainty about the parameter θ. After all, you only have training data of three points! Instead of estimating a single (optimal) value for the parameter θ, your aim is to determine the posterior distribution for the parameter. Look at the Bayes formula (equation 7.5) again:

$$p(\theta|D) = \frac{p(D|\theta)p(\theta)}{p(D)} \qquad \textbf{Equation 7.5 (repeated)}$$

where $p(\theta|D)$ is the posterior, $p(D|\theta)$ is the likelihood, $p(\theta)$ is the prior, and $p(D)$ is the marginal likelihood (for normalization). This tells you that you need to determine the joint likelihood $p(D|\theta)$ and that the prior $p(\theta)$ and $p(D)$ serve as normalization constants. What's the joint likelihood? You multiply the likelihoods of all three observations, which yields the joint likelihood:

$$P(D|\theta) = P(y = 1) \cdot P(y = 1) \cdot P(y = 1) = \theta \cdot \theta \cdot \theta = \theta^3$$

Now, what to choose for the prior? You know that the parameter θ must be a number between zero and one because it's the probability to get heads for each toss. Let's assume that all values of θ between zero and one are equally likely and take a uniform distribution. Because θ can take any value between zero and one, $p(\theta)$ is a continuous probability distribution, which needs to integrate to one (see the upper panel in figure 7.11).

But before dealing with continuous distributions and integrals to derive the analytical solution, let's again use the brute-force approach. For this, we recommend that you follow the code in the notebook and do the exercises.

SOLVING THE BAYES SOLUTION OF THE COIN TOSS EXAMPLE VIA BRUTE-FORCE APPROXIMATION

HANDS-ON TIME Open http://mng.bz/5a6O. This notebook shows how to fit a Bernoulli distribution in the Bayesian way by taking the brute-force approach.

- Do the coin toss experiment with the brute-force approach assuming a uniform prior.

- Investigate the development of the parameter's posterior shape in case of a large training data set.

To use brute force, we sample the prior $p(\theta)$ at 19 grid points ($\theta_1 = 0.05, \theta_2 = 0.1,$ $\theta_3 = 0.15, \ldots, \theta_{19} = 0.95$). In this brute-force approach, we only have a bunch of discrete values for θ_1, and we can therefore work with sums instead of integrals and probabilities instead of probability densities. That's because we assume that all 19 values of prior $P(\theta)$ have the same probability: $P(\theta) = \dfrac{1}{19} \approx 0.052632$ (see the upper left panel in figure 7.10).

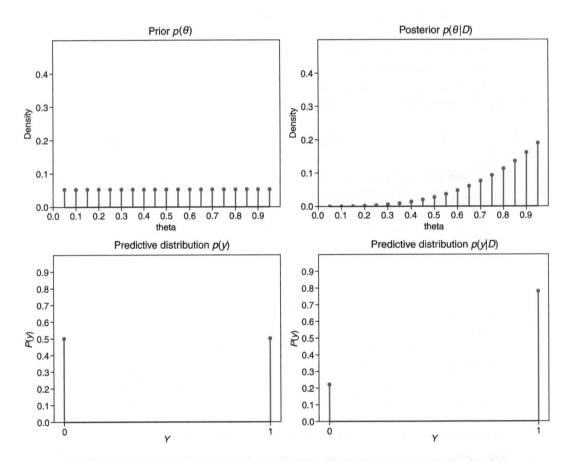

Figure 7.10 **Prior distribution (upper left panel) and posterior distribution (upper right panel). The lower panels show the CPDs for the outcome (1 for heads and 0 for tails). The plots were created using the brute-force approach to the coin toss experiment.**

Before computing the posterior parameter distribution, let's check out how the predictive distribution for the outcome looks before we see any data. Because the prior is giving the same probability for all θ_i values, you expect to get heads and tails with equal probabilities. Let's check our intuition and derive the predictive distribution using this equation:

$$p(y|x, D) = \sum_i p(y|x, w_i) \cdot p(w_i|D) \qquad \textbf{Equation 7.8}$$

In the coin toss example, we called the model parameter θ instead of w, and we have no input x, which yields:

$$P(y = 1) = \sum_i P(y = 1|\theta_i) \cdot p(\theta_i)$$

Plugging in $P(y = 1|\theta_i) = \theta_i$ (the likelihood for heads) and $P(\theta) = \dfrac{1}{19} \approx 0.052632$ (the prior) yields $P(y = 1) = 0.5$ and, accordingly, $P(y = 0) = 1 - P(y = 1) = 0.5$. This is exactly what we expected: a 50:50 chance for heads or tails (see the lower left plot in figure 7.10). You can determine the unnormalized likelihood by using the Bayesian mantra given here:

THE BAYESIAN MANTRA The posterior is proportional to the likelihood times the prior.

Let's compute the unnormalized posterior at each of the 19 grid points θ_i (see table 7.2):

$$\text{unnorm\_post}_i \propto \text{jointlik}_i \cdot \text{prior}_i = \theta_i{}^3 \cdot \frac{1}{19}$$

To get the normalized posterior values, you divide each unnormalized posterior by the sum over all values:

$$p(\theta_i|D) = \frac{\text{unnorm\_post}_i}{\sum_{i=1}^{19} \text{unnorm\_post}_i}$$

For the resulting values, look at the upper right plot in figure 7.10. As expected, after seeing heads three times, the posterior favors a θ_i that's close to one. But the posterior still gives some probability to θ values smaller than one, allowing for a coin that doesn't deterministically yield heads for each toss. Now you have all the ingredients to determine the predictive distribution based on the posterior:

$$p(y = 1|D) = \sum_i p(y = 1|\theta_i) \cdot p(\theta_i|D)$$

Table 7.2   **Brute-force results collected in a table. Each row corresponds to one grid point. The columns hold the parameter values (theta), joint likelihood (jointlik), prior, unnormalized posterior (unnorm_post), and post.**

	theta	jointlik	prior	unnorm_post	post
0	0.05	0.000125	0.052632	0.000007	0.000028
1	0.10	0.001000	0.052632	0.000053	0.000222
2	0.15	0.003375	0.052632	0.000178	0.000748
3	0.20	0.008000	0.052632	0.000421	0.001773
4	0.25	0.015625	0.052632	0.000822	0.003463
5	0.30	0.027000	0.052632	0.001421	0.005983
6	0.35	0.042875	0.052632	0.002257	0.009501
7	0.40	0.064000	0.052632	0.003368	0.014183
8	0.45	0.091125	0.052632	0.004796	0.020194
9	0.50	0.125000	0.052632	0.006579	0.027701
10	0.55	0.166375	0.052632	0.008757	0.036870
11	0.60	0.216000	0.052632	0.011368	0.047867
12	0.65	0.274625	0.052632	0.014454	0.060859
13	0.70	0.343000	0.052632	0.018053	0.076011
14	0.75	0.421875	0.052632	0.022204	0.093490
15	0.80	0.512000	0.052632	0.026947	0.113463
16	0.85	0.614125	0.052632	0.032322	0.136094
17	0.90	0.729000	0.052632	0.038368	0.161551
18	0.95	0.857375	0.052632	0.045125	0.190000

Plugging in $P(y = 1|\theta_i) = \theta_i$ (the likelihood for heads) and $p_i(\theta|D)$ (posterior from the last column in table 7.2) yields

$$p(y = 1|D) = 0.78$$

and

$$p(y = 0|D) = 1 - p(y = 1|D) = 0.22$$

According to this predictive distribution based on the posterior, you can expect heads with a 78% chance and tails with a 22% probability (see the lower right plot in figure 7.10).

SOLVING THE BAYES SOLUTION OF THE COIN TOSS EXAMPLE ANALYTICALLY

Fitting a Bayesian Bernoulli model for the coin toss example is such an easy problem that you can solve it exactly. Let's see how it works though.

For the prior, you again use a uniform distribution, giving each possible θ the same *a priori* probability. Because we want $p(\theta)$ to be a valid probability distribution, $p(\theta)$ needs to integrate to one. The prior parameter distribution is therefore $p(\theta) = 1$ for θ between zero and one. To derive the prior predictive distribution under the continuous prior, you can start with equation 7.6:

$$P(Y = 1) = \int_0^1 P(Y = 1|\theta) \cdot p(\theta)d\theta \qquad \text{Equation 7.6 (repeated)}$$

But here you have no input feature x and you are in a situation before seeing data, meaning you also have no data D and you need to use the prior $p(\theta)$, instead of the posterior $p(\theta|D)$, yielding:

$$p(y) = \int_\theta p(y|\theta) \cdot p_n(\theta)\, d\theta$$

Variant of equation 7.6 for the unconditional case before seeing data

Accordingly, the predicted probability for the outcome $Y = 1$ before seeing data can be determined as follows:

$$P(Y = 1) = \int_0^1 P(Y = 1|\theta) \cdot p(\theta)d\theta \quad \text{(We use equation 7.4.)}$$

$$P(Y = 1) = \int_0^1 \theta \cdot 1 d\theta = \frac{1}{2} \cdot \theta^2 \Big|_0^1 \quad \text{(We do the integration and get the antiderivative}$$

$$\frac{1}{2}\theta^2 \text{ of } \theta.)$$

$$P(Y = 1) = \frac{1}{2} \cdot 1 - \frac{1}{2} \cdot 0 = 0.5 \qquad \text{(We put in the numbers.)}$$

$$P(Y = 0) = 1 - P(Y = 1) = 0.5 \qquad \text{(We use the counter probability to calculate } P(Y = 0).)$$

Uff! That worked out, and you got the same prior predictive distribution as in the brute-force approach (see the lower left panel in figure 7.11). To determine the posterior, you'll again use the Bayes formula:

$$p(\theta|D) = \frac{p(D|\theta)p(\theta)}{p(D)}$$

The terms in this formula have the following names:

- $p(\theta|D)$ is the posterior.
- $p(D|\theta)$ is the likelihood.

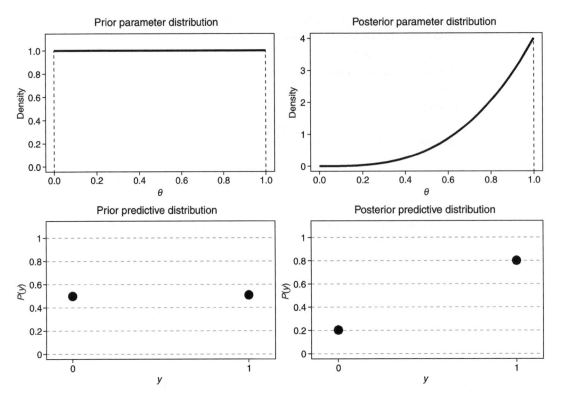

Figure 7.11   **Prior and posterior distributions (upper panel) and corresponding and predictive distributions (lower panel) for the analytical approach to the coin toss experiment.**

- $p(\theta)$ is the prior.
- $p(D)$ is the marginal likelihood (for normalization).

This formula tells you that you need to determine the joint likelihood $p(D|\theta)$ and the prior $p(\theta)$, if you want to determine the unnormalized posterior. You already have the prior $p(\theta) = 1$. What is the joint likelihood? The same as in the brute-force approach. Let's recap. You've got three observations (three times heads) yielding the joint likelihood:

$$P(D|\theta) = P(y=1) \cdot P(y=1) \cdot P(y=1) = \theta \cdot \theta \cdot \theta = \theta^3$$

Now you have everything you need to calculate the posterior of the parameter distribution. To help with that, you can use the Bayesian mantra: the posterior is proportional to the likelihood times the prior. We'll fix the normalization constant C next.

$$p(\theta|D) = \text{posterior} = C \cdot \text{likelihood} \cdot \text{prior} = C \cdot \theta^3 \cdot 1$$

Let's derive the normalization constant C that ensures that the posterior integrates to one:

$$\int_0^1 p(\theta|D)d\theta = \int_0^1 C \cdot \theta^3 d\theta = \left[\frac{C}{4} \cdot \theta^4\right]_0^1 = \frac{C}{4} = 1 \Rightarrow C = 4$$

Plugging $C = 4$ into the formula for the posterior, which you derived above, yields the posterior $p(\theta|D) = 4 \cdot \theta^3$. Let's enjoy your derived posterior (see figure 7.11, upper right panel). The shape looks similar to what you got with the brute-force approach, favoring θ values close to one. It's worth noting that the posterior still captures some uncertainty; it doesn't claim that the coin always falls on heads. In this case, the posterior would look like a sharp peak at 1 in figure 7.11.

Let's derive the predictive distribution under the posterior. Considering the posterior parameter distribution, you'd expect that it assigns a much higher probability to heads ($y = 1$) than to tails ($y = 0$). You derive the posterior predictive distribution by using a version of equation 7.6, but here we have no x and the equation looks like this:

$$p(y|D) = \int_\theta p(y|\theta) \cdot p(\theta|D)d\theta$$

Equation 7.6 for an unconditional setting (where we have no x)

In the coin toss example, that yields to

$$P(Y = 1|D) = \int_0^1 P(Y = 1|\theta) \cdot P(\theta|D)d\theta$$

When plugging in $\int_0^1 P(Y = 1|\theta) = \int_0^1 \theta \cdot 4 \cdot \theta^3 d\theta$ and $p(\theta|D) = 4 \cdot \theta^3$, you get

$P(Y = 1|D) = \int_0^1 P(Y = 1|\theta) \cdot P(\theta|D)d\theta$ (We use equation 7.4.)

$P(Y = 1|D) = \int_0^1 \theta \cdot 4 \cdot \theta^3 d\theta = \frac{4}{5} \cdot \theta^5 \big|_0^1$ (We do the integration, getting the antiderivative $\frac{4}{5}\theta^5$ of $4\theta^4$.)

$P(Y = 1|D) = \frac{4}{5} \cdot 1^5 - \frac{4}{5} \cdot 0^5 = 0.8$ (We put in the numbers.)

$P(Y = 0) = 1 - P(Y = 1) = 0.2$ (We use the counter probability to calculate $P(Y = 0)$.)

Again, you get a similar (but more exact) result as with the brute-force approximation. The Bayesian predictive distribution leaves some uncertainty about the outcome and gives us a 20% probability to observe tails (see figure 7.11, lower right panel). This seems reasonable after observing only three throws. In this case, the Bayesian model seems to be preferable to the MaxLike model, which yields a predictive distribution that predicts heads with a probability of one (see figure 7.9, the right panel).

THE TAKE-HOME MESSAGES FROM THE COIN TOSS EXAMPLE AND THE EXERCISES IN THE NOTEBOOK

- An analytical derivation of the posterior and the predictive distribution is possible in simple models like the Bernoulli model. With the brute-force method, you can approximate the analytical solutions. Brute force has the advantage that it still works when integration gets difficult. Note that the brute-force method isn't the silver bullet either. It's not possible to use it for complex problems like NNs.
- Compared to the prior, the posterior gives more mass (probability) to parameter values that lead to higher likelihoods for the observed data.
- Unlike the MaxLike approach, in the Bayes approach you don't pick only one parameter value with the highest probability to derive the predicted distribution. Instead, you average over all possible predicted distributions weighted with the posterior probabilities of the corresponding parameter values. The larger the training data set, the smaller the spread of the posterior (shown in the notebook http://mng.bz/5a6O).
- The larger the training set, the smaller the influence of the prior (shown in the notebook).
- For large training data sets, the posterior is a narrow (Gaussian) distribution around the MaxLike parameter estimate.

Some (fun) facts about the choice of priors

You saw in the regression and in the coin toss examples how to train a simple Bayesian model. In chapter 8, you'll see how to train Bayesian DL models. But before doing so, let's try to gain some confidence in the Bayesian approach and dissipate concerns on the usage of a prior. In Bayesian modeling, not only do you need to pick a distribution for the outcome's CPD, but you also have to pick a distribution for the prior $p(\theta)$ before you see any data.

After getting some training data, you can determine the posterior $p(\theta|D)$ by using the Bayes theorem (equation 7.5). Still the prior distribution has some influence because you use it to determine the posterior. This Bayesian training procedure sparked a big discussion among the usually introverted statistician folks. The main arguments of the anti-Bayes camp are

- Working with a prior introduces subjectivity. With the prior you can give a high probability to certain parameter ranges. As a consequence, you pull the posterior towards this range.
- It's more scientific to "let the data speak."

On the other hand, the Bayes camp argues that

- All reasonable priors lead to similar models, which all converge for large data sets toward the model received with the MaxLike approach.
- The prior's effect of "shrinkage towards the prior" helps to avoid false positive results.

As a catchy example to support their second argument, Bayesians picked an empirical study (published in a scientific biology journal) that was analyzed in a non-Bayesian way and came to the conclusion that good-looking parents get more daughters than sons (the *p*-value was 0.015).[a] This result was interpreted as an evolutionary effect because, for women, it'd be more beneficial to be good looking than for men. The results made it to the public media, such as "Daily Mail," where you can find nice pictures of famous and beautiful parents with their firstborn baby, a girl (see http://mng.bz/6Qoe. The link might not work if you have ad blockers activated).

The data came from a British study where teachers were asked to rate the attractiveness of their pupils. Forty years later, the grown-up pupils were asked about the gender of their children. The non-Bayesian analysis found a significantly higher percentage of daughters among the good-looking parents compared to the not-so-good-looking parents. Andrew Gelman, a famous Bayesian, re-analyzed the data by using a prior, which gave high probabilities on small effects of the parent's attractiveness to their offspring's gender. He justified his prior choice by the fact that all other known influential factors on the offspring's gender (such as, for example, the stress of the parents during pregnancy) were also small. His analysis led to the conclusion that the attractiveness of the parents doesn't impact the likelihood of getting a baby girl.

To support the usage of priors, Gelman did a simulation study with small, true effect sizes and quite small sample sizes. Analyzing these data in a non-Bayesian manner led in most simulation runs to non-significant findings. But due to its random nature, some runs led to significant results. Among those significant results, 40% of the reported effects pointed in the wrong direction! And if the result was catchy, it got published. Therefore, Gelman reasoned, it's more reasonable to perform a Bayesian analysis with a conservative prior serving as a regularization method.

Is it reasonable for DL models to regularize the weights by using a prior that prefers small weight values? We think yes, and we give you some reasons:

- Experience shows that trained NNs often have small weights.
- Smaller weights lead to less extreme outputs (in classification, less extreme probabilities), which is desirable for an untrained model.
- It's a known property of prediction models that adding a component to the loss function, which prefers small weights, often helps to get a higher prediction performance. This approach is also known as *regularization* or *weights decay* in non-Bayesian NNs.

---

a The *p* value estimates the probability that an observed effect (or a stronger effect) is found due to pure chance. Usually a finding with a *p* value below 0.05 is called statistically significant.

7.3.3   *Revisiting the Bayesian linear regression model*

In the beginning of this chapter, you saw how to do Bayesian linear regression the hacker's way. In the hacker's way, we used a Bayes model with an infinitely large prior for the two parameters *a* and *b*. The resulting model had a nice property to get more uncertainty in the extrapolation range where no training data is available (see the right side of figure 7.12). This isn't the case for a traditional model fitted via the Max-Like approach (see the left side of figure 7.12).

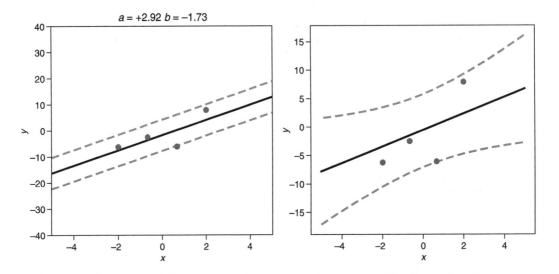

Figure 7.12   Four data points fitted with a probabilistic linear regression model when assuming a known data spread, $\sigma = 3$. On the left, you see the MaxLike model; on the right, the Bayesian model with an infinitely large prior. The solid line represents the mean of the predicted outcome distribution, and the dashed lines show the 2.5% and 97.5% percentiles of the CPD.

Because only a Bayesian model can express an enhanced uncertainty when leaving known grounds, it seems that fitting a Bayesian model is the better choice than fitting a traditional MaxLike-based model. This is visible in the two fits in figure 7.12. When looking at the width of the predicted CPD, the Bayes model predicts a much broader CPD when leaving the range in which there's data. But, also, in the interpolation range of the training data, the Bayes model has a higher uncertainty than the MaxLike model. Because the model fit relies on only four data points, the higher uncertainty of the Bayes model might be more realistic, which would then also support our vote for the Bayesian model. On the other hand, the large spread could also only be due to the broad prior (a uniform distribution), which was used for the model parameters (slope and intercept). To investigate if the Bayesian model yields more realistic predictions for the conditional outcome distribution, let's perform some experiments to answer the following questions:

- How does the predictive distribution depend on the prior and the amount of training data?
- Has a Bayesian model a better prediction performance than a traditional MaxLike-based model?

To answer these two questions, you can perform the following experiments:

1 Simulate from a linear data generating process (with $\sigma = 3$) several training data sets with different sizes (for example, with 2, 4, 20, and 100 data points). Then fit for all training sets the MaxLike model and three Bayesian models: one with a uniform prior, one with a standard Normal prior, and one with a mean-centered Normal with a scale of 0.1. Check how the resulting CPD changes with the width of the prior. Check also that the width of the Bayesian CPD decreases with growing training data and gets more similar to the CPD of the MaxLike model.

2 Investigate for different training set sizes if the prediction performance is better for the Bayesian or the MaxLike-based model. Sample a training set and a test set that has *x* values in the range of the training set. Then fit a Bayesian and the MaxLike model and determine the test negative log likelihood (NLL). (The model with the better prediction performance yields a lower test NLL.) To get reliable results, you should use large test data sets and repeat the whole procedure several times, so that you can compare the resulting distributions and means of the obtained test NLLs.

Before getting started with these experiments, you need to make sure that you can conduct them in a reasonable amount of time. Unfortunately, the brute-force method for Bayesian fitting is much too slow. We could speed up the fitting procedure a lot if we knew the analytical solution. You saw in the coin toss example in section 7.3.2 that determining the analytical Bayes solution requires solving some integrals. You were able to solve these integrals in the coin toss example because you only had one model parameter and an easy likelihood and prior distribution. But in a more complex model with many parameters, these integrals get quickly complicated. It turns out that Bayes usually can't be solved analytically, and one has to resort to simulations or approximations. This is also the reason that Bayes models weren't popular before massive computation power became available. You'll learn more about those approximations in chapter 8.

But for a simple linear regression model, such as the hacker's example, it's still possible to derive the Bayes solution. For that you need to assume that the data variance σ^2 is known (like we did in the hacker's example). Further, you need to use a Gaussian prior for the model parameter's slope and intercept. But already then, the derivations are quite lengthy. Therefore, you can skip the math and directly implement the resulting analytical formulas to compute the posterior and predictive distribution (see the last notebook in this chapter). A complete treatment and derivation of the formulas used is given in Christopher M. Bishop's, *Pattern Recognition and Machine Learning*, which you can access via http://mng.bz/oPWZ.

Using an analytical expression, you can check that you can reproduce the results of the Bayes hacker's example in section 7.2. In the hacker's example, we worked with a uniform prior. This can be achieved by setting in the analytical solution the scale parameter of the Gaussian prior to infinity (or something very large). If you want to convince yourself, we recommend you go to the last part of the Bayes the Hacker's Way notebook from the beginning of this chapter (see http://mng.bz/qMEr). Now, that you have the fast, analytical Bayes solution in hand, you can do the two suggested experiments in the following notebook.

HANDS-ON TIME   Open http://mng.bz/nPj5. This notebook produces the plots in figure 7.13 and answers the following questions:

- How does the predictive distribution depend on the prior and the amount of training data?
- Has a Bayesian model a better prediction performance than a traditional MaxLike-based model?

Using this notebook, you can investigate these two questions. Let's look at the first question: How does the predictive distribution depend on the prior and the amount of training data? The short answer is that the choice of the prior distribution isn't critical if it's not extremely narrow. The larger the training data, the closer the Bayes model gets to the MaxLike model. In the notebook, you can work this out step by step.

In the Gaussian prior of the analytical solution, you can set the mean and the standard deviation. As the mean of the prior, you pick zero because you don't know if the intercept or slope are positive or negative numbers. The main tuning parameter is the scale, σ_0, of the prior. Setting it to a large number like $\sigma_0 = 10000$ is equivalent to a flat prior, and setting it to a small number like $\sigma_0 = 0.1$ results in a peaky prior around the mean at zero. In figure 7.13, you can see that a prior with $\sigma_0 = 0.1$ yields a predictive distribution with a slope close to 1 and a relatively small width that doesn't change over the displayed x range. A prior with $\sigma_0 = 1$, on the other hand, yields a CPD that's quite similar to the CPD corresponding to a flat prior with $\sigma_0 = 10000$. This indicates that a Gaussian prior with a 0 mean and a standard deviation of 1 doesn't impose a large bias on the resulting fit. These statements are valid for all sizes of the training data set (see the upper and lower rows in figure 7.13). The main effect of the training data size is the reduced epistemic uncertainty of the Bayes model when working with a larger training data set. In the limits of a large training data set, the uncertainty is purely aleatoric and a Bayes model yields the same CPD as a MaxLike-based model (see the rightmost column in figure 7.13).

Let's turn to the second question: Has a Bayesian model a better prediction performance than a traditional MaxLike-based model? The short answer is yes! As discussed in chapter 5, the test NLL is the proper measure to quantify and compare the prediction performance of different models: the lower, the better. To investigate the test NLL difference of the Bayes and MaxLike models beyond random variations, you average the test NLL over 100 models, each working with newly generated data. Figure 7.14 shows

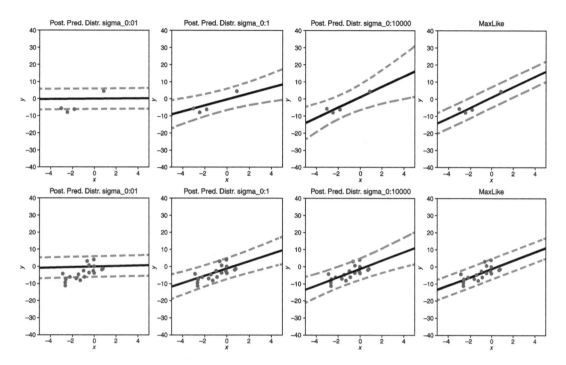

Figure 7.13 Influence of the prior's scale, σ_0, on the resulting predicted CPD in a Bayesian linear model (first three columns) and the corresponding CPD of a MaxLike-based linear model (rightmost column). The Bayesian models work with a given data standard deviation of 3 and a Gaussian prior for the slope and intercept with a mean 0 and a standard deviation of 0.1, 1, and 10,000, respectively (see the titles of the plots). In the upper row, the training data contained 4 data points; in the lower row, 20 data points.

the results. You can see that the Bayes model outperforms the MaxLike-based model. The smaller the training data set, the more you gain in prediction performance when using a Bayesian model instead of a traditional MaxLike-based model.

Is there an intuitive explanation why the Bayesian method outperforms the MaxLike method? Remember the example of financial experts in section 7.3.1? The Bayes approach uses the wisdom of many, while the MaxLike method relies on the expertise of the single best expert. If there is little data, it makes sense to listen to many experts.

Before turning to Bayesian NN in the next chapter, let's summarize what you should take away from this introduction to Bayesian modeling. Bayesian models can capture epistemic uncertainty about its parameter values via probability distributions. To take a Bayesian approach, you need to pick a prior for the parameter distribution. The prior can be a constant (uniformly distributed) or bell-shaped (normal distributed, often with a mean of zero), designed to incorporate *a priori* knowledge or to regularize the model. When training a Bayesian model, the posterior is determined. The more data used for training, the smaller is the spread (variance) of the posterior, indicating a decreased parameter (epistemic) uncertainty. If you have a large training data set, your Bayesian model yields similar results as a MaxLike model.

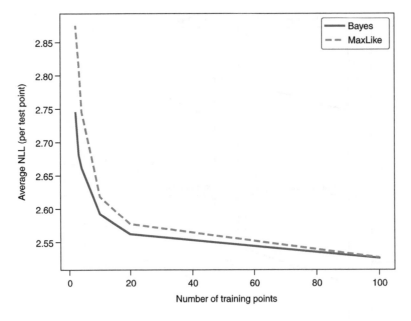

Figure 7.14   Prediction performance comparison of a Bayes model and MaxLike-based linear model via a test NLL (the lower, the better). Both models work with a given data variance. The Bayes model works for slope and intercept with a Gaussian with a mean of 0 and a scale of 1.

Summary

- The inherent uncertainty in the data, called aleatoric uncertainty, can be modeled with the probabilistic approach introduced in chapters 4 to 6.
- In addition, Bayesian probabilistic models also capture the epistemic uncertainty.
- The epistemic uncertainty is caused by the uncertainty to the model parameter.
- Non-Bayesian models fail to express uncertainty when leaving known grounds. (These can't talk about the elephant in the room.)
- Bayesian models can express uncertainty when doing predictions in the extrapolation regime or in the case of insufficient training data.
- In Bayesian models, each parameter is replaced by a distribution.
- Before fitting a Bayesian model, you need to pick a prior distribution.
- The Bayes mantra is, "The posterior is the prior times the likelihood." It is a consequence of the Bayes theorem.
- As opposed to the aleatoric data inherent uncertainty, you can reduce the epistemic model parameter uncertainty by extending the training data, resulting in a posterior with lower variance.
- A Bayesian model shows a better prediction performance than non-Bayesian variants if the training data is limited.

Bayesian neural networks

This chapter covers

- Two approaches to fit Bayesian neural networks (BNNs)
- The variational inference (VI) approximation for BNNs
- The Monte Carlo (MC) dropout approximation for BNNs
- TensorFlow Probability (TFP) variational layers to build VI-based BNNs
- Using Keras to implement MC dropout in BNNs

In this chapter, you learn about two efficient approximation methods that allow you to use a Bayesian approach for probabilistic DL models: variational inference (VI) and Monte Carlo dropout (also known as MC dropout). When setting up a Bayesian DL model, you combine Bayesian statistics with DL. (In the figure at the beginning of this chapter, you see a combination portrait of Reverend Thomas Bayes, the founder of Bayesian Statistics, and Geoffrey Hinton, the leader and one of the godfathers of DL.) With these approximation methods, fitting Bayesian DL models with many parameters becomes feasible. As discussed in chapter 7, the Bayesian method also takes care of the epistemic uncertainty that's not included in non-Bayesian probabilistic DL models.

In chapters 4, 5, and 6, you worked with deep probabilistic classification and regression models. These models capture the data-inherent (aleatoric) uncertainty by predicting a whole distribution for the outcome. In chapter 7, you learned about an additional uncertainty, called *epistemic uncertainty*, that captures the parameter uncertainty of the outcome distribution. This epistemic uncertainty becomes essential when you use a DL model to make predictions in new situations (recall the elephant in the room). If you can't see the elephant, you'd like to know at least that something is wrong.

You also saw in the last chapter that the fitting of Bayesian probabilistic models lets you quantify parameter uncertainty and, moreover, gives better predictions (lower negative log-likelihood, or NLL), especially in situations with few training data. Unfortunately, the Bayesian approach soon becomes slow and, essentially, impossible if you turn from small toy examples to real-world DL tasks.

In this chapter, you'll learn some approximation methods that allow fitting Bayesian variants of probabilistic DL models. This gives you a tool to detect if the predicted outcome distributions are uncertain. Bayesian DL models have the advantage that they can detect novel situations by expressing a larger epistemic uncertainty, which leads to a larger outcome uncertainty. You'll see that Bayesian DL regression models report greater uncertainties in extrapolation regimes, and Bayesian DL classification models raise the uncertainty flag for novel classes, indicating that their predictions aren't reliable.

8.1   *Bayesian neural networks (BNNs)*

Let's apply the Bayesian approach described in chapter 7 to neural networks (NNs). Figure 8.1 (on the left) shows the mother of all Bayesian networks: Bayesian linear regression. Compared to standard probabilistic linear regression, the weights aren't fixed but follow a distribution $P(\theta|D)$. There's absolutely no reason that we can't continue to use distributions instead of single weights for an NN. Figure 8.1 (on the right) also shows such a simple BNN. It turns out that solving a deep BNN isn't so easy, but TensorFlow Probability (TFP) provides you with the right tools.

In section 7.3, we used an analytical solution to solve a simple linear regression problem. This solution was only possible with the further restriction that the parameter σ_x, describing the spread of the data, doesn't depend on x, but must be known in

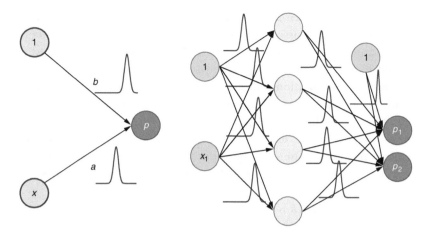

Figure 8.1   A graphical representation of a Bayesian simple linear regression problem by a simple NN without a hidden layer and only one output node. This provides an estimate for the expected value of the outcome (on the left). In a Bayesian variant of the NN for linear regression, distributions replace the slope (*a*) and intercept (*b*). This is also possible for deep networks, yielding a Bayesian neural network (BNN). A simple example of such a network is shown on the right.

advance. This analytical approach isn't applicable for BNNs with hidden layers because those are too complex. You might wonder if we should again revert to the Bayes for hacker's approach from chapter 7 (section 7.2). In principle, that approach also works for deeper BNNs. However, again speed is the problem: it would take too long if we'd go straight from Bayesian linear regression with two parameters to NNs with 50 million weights.

To see this, recall that for the brute-force approach in chapter 7, we evaluated the variable *a* at *nbins* = 30 values. We also evaluated the variable *b* at *nbins* = 30 values. All together, we evaluated the variables *a* and *b* at $nbins^2 = 900$ different combinations. A brute-force approach for a network with 50 million parameters would need to evaluate the posterior at `nbins^50 million` different combinations. Let's be satisfied with only `nbins` = 10. Then we have $10^{50,000,000}$ evaluations. If you could do one billion evaluations per second, that would still take you $10^{50,000,000}/10^9 = 10^{49,999,991}$ seconds. Even for a small network with 100 weights, that would take $10^{100}/10^9 = 10^{91}$ seconds (see the following fun fact).

FUN FACT Go to https://www.wolframalpha.com/ and type 10^{91} seconds into the search field. Solution: It takes $3.169 \cdot 10^{83}$ years to evaluate all grid points— about 10 billion times longer than the age of the universe!

Neither analytical methods nor the brute-force approach does the trick for BNNs. What's next? There's an approach called Markov Chain Monte Carlo (MCMC for short). This approach samples parameter values more efficiently compared to the brute-force method. The first MCMC algorithm was the Metropolis-Hastings algorithm developed in the 1950s and 1970s. The world's largest technical professional organization, the prestigious IEEE (Institute for Electrical and Electronic Engineers), ranks this approach among the ten most influential algorithms for science and engineering developed in the 20th century (see http://mng.bz/vxdp). It has the advantage that, given enough computations, it's exact. It also works for small problems, say 10 to 100 variables (or weights in our language), but not for larger networks such as DL models with typically millions of weights.

Can we do something else to get a reasonable time to obtain an approximation for the normalized posterior? There are two approaches: one is the variational inference (VI) Bayes; the other is Monte Carlo (MC) dropout. The variational Bayes approach is welded into TFP, providing Keras layers to do the VI. MC dropout is a simple approach that can be done in Keras as well.

8.2   Variational inference (VI) as an approximative Bayes approach

In situations where you can't determine the analytical solution for a Bayesian NN or use the MCMC methods, you need to use techniques to approximate the Bayesian model. In this section, you learn about such an approximation method—variational inference (VI). In section 8.2.1, we give a detailed derivation of the VI approximation. In section 8.2.2, we use the VI approximation for a simple linear regression example. Because we have the analytical solution for this example (see section 7.3.3), we can judge the quality of the VI approximation.

You can use the VI approximation approach for all kinds of DL models. In section 8.5, you use it for two case studies: one for a regression problem and one for a classification problem. To understand the basic ideas of this approach and to be able to compare it with some exact methods, we demonstrate the approach on the same simple linear regression problem from chapter 7. You're encouraged to follow the notebook while reading the text.

 HANDS-ON TIME Open http://mng.bz/4A5R and follow the notebook as you read the text. This notebook is about linear regression in the Bayesian way. It shows the analytical approach, VI, and also how to use TFP. Try to understand what happens in the notebook.

The main idea of the Bayes approach in DL is that with BNNs, each weight is replaced by a distribution. Normally, this is quite a complicated distribution, and this distribution isn't independent among different weights. The idea behind the VI Bayes method is that the complicated posterior distributions of the weights are approximated by a simple distribution called *variational distribution*.

Often one uses Gaussians as parametric distributions; this is also done by default when using TFP. The Gaussian variational distribution is defined by two parameters: the mean and the variance. Instead of learning a single weight value w, the network has to learn the two parameters of weight distribution: w_μ for the mean of the Gauss and w_σ for the spread of the Gauss (see figure 8.2). Besides the type of the variational distribution that is used to approximate the posterior, we also need to define a prior distribution. A common choice is to use the standard normal, $N(0, 1)$, as the prior.

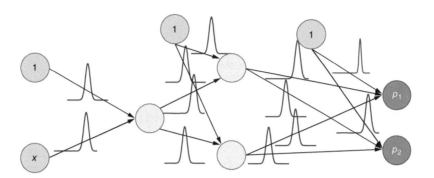

Figure 8.2 A Bayesian network with two hidden layers. Instead of fixed weights, the weights now follow a distribution.

Sections 8.2.1 and 8.2.2 are somewhat involved but give you some insights into the derivation of the VI approximation. You can skip those sections if you're not interested in the derivations. In section 8.3, you learn how to use the TFP implementation of the VI method.

8.2.1 Looking under the hood of VI*

VI has been used in DL since the invention of the variational autoencoder in late 2013 by Kingma and Welling from Amsterdam University. The implementation of VI as we use it here (referred to as the Bayes by Backprop algorithm) was introduced in the paper, "Weight Uncertainty in Neural Networks," from the Google DeepMind scientists Blundell and colleagues (https://arxiv.org/abs/1505.05424). TFP effectively integrates this approach as you'll see later. But let's understand the inner mechanics of the VI principle first. In figure 8.3, you see a sketch of that principle.

The actual normalized posterior distribution, $p(\theta|D)$, is inaccessible. The reason is that the integral, which needs to be solved to ensure that the posterior is normalized (see section 7.3.2), is high-dimensional. As discussed in section 8.1, we can't use the brute-force approximation because it's far too slow. Further, such high-dimensional integrals are also too complex to be solved analytically.

To get a feeling for the meaning of the different parameters in figure 8.3, let's assume a deep BNN. The parameter θ replaces the weights of the non-Bayesian variant of the NN. The parameter θ in a Bayesian network isn't fixed but follows a distribution. The left panel in figure 8.3 shows the abstract space of possible distributions, and the dot in the upper left represents the posterior $p(\theta|D)$. Instead of determining the

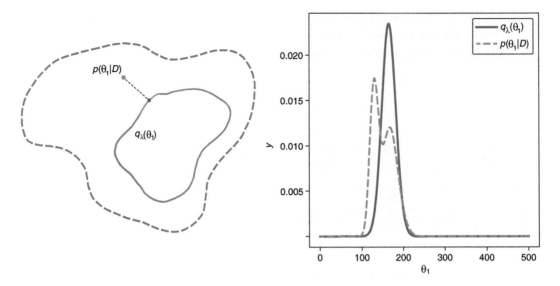

Figure 8.3 The principle idea of variational inference (VI). The larger region on the left depicts the space of all possible distributions, and the dot in the upper left represents the posterior $p(\theta_1|D)$, corresponding to the dotted density in the right panel. In the left panel, the inner region depicts the space of possible variational distributions $q_\lambda(\theta_1)$. The optimized variational distribution $q_\lambda(\theta_1)$, illustrated by the point in the inner loop, corresponds to the solid density displayed in the right panel, which has the smallest distance to the posterior as shown by the dotted line.

posterior directly, we approximate it with a simple, variational distribution, $q_\lambda(\theta)$ such as a Gaussian (see the bell-shaped density in the right panel of figure 8.3). There are infinitely many Gaussians out there, but these make up only a subgroup of all possible distributions. (In the left panel of figure 8.3, it's marked as the small region labeled with $q_\lambda(\theta)$.) The job of VI is to tune the variational parameter λ so that $q_\lambda(\theta)$ gets as close as possible to the true posterior $p(\theta|D)$. The right side of the figure shows this situation again for a single θ_1. The 1D posterior distribution is approximated by a 1D Gaussian variational distribution. For each Gaussian, you have two parameters: $\lambda = (\mu, \sigma)$. These are called *variational parameters*.

You want the variational distribution to be as close to the real posterior as possible, or in more mathematical terms: minimize the distance between the nice distribution and the real one. You can fiddle with the shape of the nice distribution by manipulating the variational parameters $\lambda = (\mu, \sigma)$.

It might be a good idea to recap all the terms. Table 8.1 gives the important terms for VI. You should know all, except for the one in the last row. We introduce the parameter w in the last row in section 8.2.2.

But what measure can you use to describe the similarity or divergence between two distributions? And, maybe even more important, how can you measure the divergence to a posterior that you don't know? Well, the Kullback–Leibler (KL) divergence is the

Table 8.1   **Different terms used in VI**

Term	In the simple example	Name	Remarks
θ	$\theta = (a, b) = $ (slope, intercept)	Parameters	θ (theta) isn't fixed but follows a distribution.
			In the non-Bayes case, θ is fixed and is identical to the tunable parameters w of the network.
$p(\theta\|D)$	$p(a\|D)$	Posterior distribution	Usually not tractable.
$q_\lambda(\theta)$	$N(a; \mu_a, \sigma_a)$ $N(b; \mu_b, \sigma_b)$	Variational approximation	Tractable functions, such as an independent Gaussian for each θ_i.
λ	$\lambda = (\mu_a, \sigma_a, \mu_b, \sigma_b)$	Variational parameters	Parameters of the variational distribution that approximate the posterior distribution.
w	$w = (w_0, w_1, w_2, w_3)$ $\lambda = (w_0, sp(w_1), w_2, sp(w_3))$	Tunable parameters	Optimized parameters in the Bayesian network. The shortcut $sp(w_1)$ is for the `softplus` function, resulting in positive parameters as needed for the standard deviation of a Gaussian.

answer to both questions. You already encountered KL divergence in section 4.2. Let's use it and write the formula for the KL divergence between $p(\theta|D)$ and $q_\lambda(\theta)$. If you remember section 4.2, the KL divergence isn't symmetrical. If you're lucky and choose the right order, $\text{KL}[q_\lambda(\theta)\|p(\theta|D)]$, the unknown posterior drops out, and the following expression is all you need to optimize:

$$\lambda^* = \text{argmin}\{\text{KL}[q_\lambda(\theta)\|p(\theta)] - E_{\theta \sim q_\lambda}[\log(p(D|\theta)]\} \qquad \textbf{Equation 8.1}$$

If you did it differently and started with $\text{KL}[p(\theta|D)\|q_\lambda(\theta)]$, you won't get a usable expression for equation 8.1. (In the sidebar, you'll find the derivation of the expression for equation 8.1). This equation looks a bit scarier than it actually is. Let's have a closer look at the two terms in equation 8.1.

Derivation of the optimization equation

Let's derive equation 8.1. It's a bit of calculus, so feel free to skip this if it isn't your cup of tea. On the other hand, it could be fun, so let's get started.

We start with the KL divergence between the variational approximation $q_\lambda(\theta)$ and the true posterior $p(\theta|D)$. The strange thing is that we don't know the true posterior. But, as it turns out in a few lines, if we calculate $\text{KL}[q_\lambda(\theta)\|p(\theta|D)]$ and not $\text{KL}[p(\theta|D)\|q_\lambda(\theta)]$, the true posterior drops out and only the KL divergence you need to compute is between the variational distribution and the prior distribution that's known.

(continued)

Let's write the definition of the KL divergence and indicate the data with D. If you can't remember how to write the KL divergence of, say, two functions f and g, maybe this rule of thumb will help: it's "back alone down," meaning that the second function g in $\mathrm{KL}[f(\theta)\|g(\theta)]$ will be alone and in the denominator. The following definition of the KL divergence shouldn't surprise you too much:

$$\mathrm{KL}[q_\lambda(\theta)\|p(\theta|D)] = \int q_\lambda(\theta)\log\frac{q_\lambda(\theta)}{p(\theta|D)}d\theta$$

$p(\theta|D)$ is the second function ("in the back") and, thus, only appears once ("alone") in the integral and, further, it is in the denominator ("down"). (You could also look up the definition of the KL divergence.) Now, there are some algebraic manipulations ahead. Feel free to follow the steps using a pen and paper. The first thing we do is to use the definition of the conditional probability, $p(\theta|D) = p(\theta, D)/p(D)$:

$$\mathrm{KL}[q_\lambda(\theta)\|p(\theta|D)] = \int q_\lambda(\theta)\log\frac{q_\lambda(\theta)}{p(\theta, D)/p(D)}d\theta$$

Then we use the calculation rules of the logarithm $\log(A \cdot B) = \log(A) + \log(B)$ and $\log(B/A) = -\log(A/B)$ to split the integral into two parts:

$$\mathrm{KL}[q_\lambda(\theta)\|p(\theta|D)] = \int q_\lambda(\theta)\log p(D)d\theta - \int q_\lambda(\theta)\log\frac{p(\theta, D)}{q_\lambda(\theta)}d\theta$$

Because $\log p(D)$ doesn't depend on θ, we can put it before the integral:

$$\mathrm{KL}[q_\lambda(\theta)\|p(\theta|D)] = \log p(D) \cdot \int q_\lambda(\theta)d\theta - \int q_\lambda(\theta)\log\frac{p(\theta, D)}{q_\lambda(\theta)}d\theta$$

And because $q_\lambda(\theta)$ is a probability density and for all probability densities the integral is one, we have $\int q_\lambda(\theta)d\theta = 1$:

$$\mathrm{KL}[q_\lambda(\theta)\|p(\theta|D)] = \log p(D) - \int q_\lambda(\theta)\log\frac{p(\theta, D)}{q_\lambda(\theta)}d\theta$$

The first term doesn't depend on the variational parameter λ; therefore, all you need to minimize is $-\int q_\lambda(\theta)\log\frac{p(\theta, D)}{q_\lambda(\theta)}d\theta$. The optimal value λ is thus:

$$\lambda^* = \mathrm{argmin}\left\{-\int q_\lambda(\theta)\log\frac{p(\theta, D)}{q_\lambda(\theta)}d\theta\right\}$$

Now, let's arrange it into the form of equation 8.1 with $p(\theta, D) = p(\theta|D) \cdot p(\theta)$

$$\lambda^* = \mathrm{argmin}\left\{-\int q_\lambda(\theta)\log\frac{p(D|\theta) \cdot p(\theta)}{q_\lambda(\theta)}d\theta\right\}$$

and with the calculus rules for the logarithm:

$$\lambda^* = \operatorname{argmin}\left\{\int q_\lambda(\theta)\log\frac{q_\lambda(\theta)}{p(\theta)}d\theta - \int q_\lambda(\theta)\cdot\log p(D|\theta)d\theta\right\}$$

The first term is the definition of the KL divergence between the variational and the prior distribution: $\mathrm{KL}[q_\lambda(\theta)\|p(\theta)]$ (remember "back alone down"). The second term is the definition of the expectation of the function $\log p(D|\theta)$. So finally, we have

$$\lambda^* = \operatorname{argmin}\left\{\mathrm{KL}[q_\lambda(\theta)\|p(\theta)] - E_{\theta\sim q_\lambda}[\log(p(D|\theta))]\right\}$$

and are done with deriving the expression in equation 8.1. Wasn't so hard, was it?

Because we want to minimize the equation 8.1, the first term needs to get as small as possible. It's again a KL divergence, but this time, it's between the variational approximation $q_\lambda(\theta)$ and the prior $p(\theta)$. Because the KL divergence is (kind of) a distance, this term wants the approximate distribution $q_\lambda(\theta)$ to be as close to the prior distribution $p(\theta)$ as possible. In BNN, the prior is usually chosen to be around zero, so this term ensures that the distribution $q_\lambda(\theta)$ is centered at small values. For this reason, we also call the first term a *regularizer*. It favors θ distributions that are centered at zero. Choosing a narrow prior around values far away from zero might lead to poor performance.

The second term, $E_{\theta\sim q_\lambda}[\log(p(D|\theta))]$, is an old friend. It calculates the expected value of $\log(p(D|\theta))$, given the parameter θ. The parameter θ is distributed according to the approximative variational distribution λ, which is determined by the variational parameter λ. But after all, $E_{\theta\sim q_\lambda}[\log(p(D|\theta))]$ is an expectation over $\log(p(D|\theta))$. Do you recognize this dear friend? Well, maybe, look closer. The expectation is the same as the mean if the number of draws goes to infinity. But the mean is sometimes easier to understand than the expectation, so we go with the mean and sample the parameter θ from q_λ for the network.

Now, look at the right side of figure 8.3. If you draw from the distribution (for example, for θ_1), you get $\theta_1 = 2$. Or, in our linear regression example, you randomly pick a and b from $q_\lambda((a, b))$. Then, given $\theta = (a, b)$, you calculate the log probability that we observe in the data D. In the linear regression example, where we assumed that the data is distributed like a Gaussian around the mean $\mu = a \cdot x + b$ with fixed standard deviation σ, you get

$$\log(p(D|(a, b))) = \sum_{i=1}^{n}\log(N(y_i; a \cdot x_i + b, \sigma))$$

Oh, hello. Welcome back, my dear friend log-likelihood! How did I not see you in the first place! Let's nail it down. The second term (including the minus), $-E_{\theta\sim q_\lambda}[\log(p(D|\theta))]$, is the averaged NLL, which we as always like to minimize. The average is taken over different values of θ, which are drawn from $q_\lambda(\theta)$.

To wrap up, in equation 8.1, we want the NLL averaged according to the probability of θ to be minimal, with the restriction that the variational distribution of the parameter θ isn't too far away from the prior $p(\theta)$.

8.2.2   Applying VI to the toy problem*

Congratulations on not skipping to section 8.3! We still have a bit of math to digest in this section. We now apply the VI approach to our toy problem with Bayesian regression. You already saw applications of Bayesian regression in section 7.2.1 (solved via the hacker's approach and brute force) and section 7.3.3 (solved analytically). As a reminder, the Bayesian variant of a probabilistic model for simple linear regression is given by $p(y|x,(a,b)) = N(y; \mu = a \cdot x + b, \sigma = 3)$. We assume, as before, that the standard deviation σ, capturing the aleatoric uncertainty, is known. Don't bend your head as to why we set $\sigma = 3$; we just choose it so that the plot looks nice.

In the Bayesian variant, we first need to define our priors for the two model parameters ($\theta = (a, b)$) with the slope a and the intercept b. As before, we choose the normally distributed $N(0, 1)$. Then, we define the variational distribution $q_\lambda(\theta)$, which is tuned to approximate the posterior $p(\theta|D)$. In principle, the variational distribution could be a complex object, but here we keep things simple and choose two independent Gaussians.

The slope parameter a ($a \sim N(\mu_a, \sigma_a)$) is drawn from the first Gaussian, and the parameter b ($b \sim N(\mu_b, \sigma_b)$) is drawn from the second. This leaves us with four variational parameters, $\lambda = (\mu_a, \sigma_a, \mu_b, \sigma_b)$, that we determine via optimization. We use stochastic gradient descent to optimize the vector $w = (\mu_a, w_1, \mu_b, w_3)$. The scale parameters, σ_a and σ_b, need to be positive, and we don't want to restrict the values of w_1 and w_3. Therefore, we feed w_1 and w_3 through a softplus function as we did in section 5.3.2. In listing 8.1, you can see the corresponding code: sigma_a = tf.math.softplus(w[1]) and sigma_b = tf.math.softplus(w[3]).

Figure 8.4 shows the network. It's a small network because we want to compare it with the brute-force method in section 7.2.1.

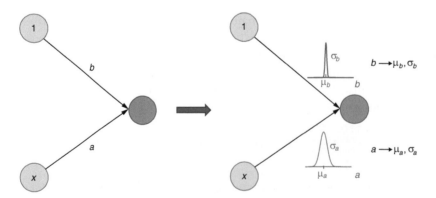

Figure 8.4   The simple linear regression model. On the left is a non-Bayesian NN and on the right, a Bayesian model with variational inference (VI) approximation. The weights, a and b, in the VI model are replaced by Gaussian distributions, parameterized by the variational parameters $\lambda = (\mu_a, \sigma_a, \mu_b, \sigma_b)$.

The task is to tune the variational parameters to minimize equation 8.1. We determine the parameters $w = (\mu_a, w_1, \mu_b, w_3)$ by using gradient descent. But before we start coding and minimizing equation 8.1, let's take a closer look at the loss function in this equation to get a better understanding of what's going on during minimization:

$$\text{loss}_{\text{VI}} = \text{loss}_{\text{KL}} + \text{loss}_{\text{NLL}} = \text{KL}[q_\lambda(\theta)\|p(\theta)] - E_{\theta \sim q_\lambda}[\log(p(D|\theta))] \quad \textbf{Equation 8.2}$$

Because we use Gaussians for the variational approximations $q_\lambda(a)$ and $q_\lambda(b)$ and also a standard normal $N(0, 1)$ Gaussian for the prior, the KL divergence between a variational Gaussian $N(\mu, \sigma)$ and the prior $N(0, 1)$ can be calculated analytically. (We skip the derivation because it's quite tedious without adding much insight.) From this, we get

$$\text{loss}_{\text{KL}} = \text{KL}[q_\lambda(w)\|p(w)] = \text{KL}[N(\mu, \sigma)\|N(0, 1) = -\frac{1}{2}(1 + \log(\sigma^2) - \mu^2 - \sigma^2)$$

Equation 8.3

Don't trust this? Have a look at the notebook after the VI section, where you can verify this numerically.

For the second loss_{NLL} term in equation 8.2, we need to calculate the expectation of the NLL: $E_{\theta \sim q_\lambda}[\log(p(D|\theta))]$. This time we aren't so lucky. It's not possible to calculate this term in closed form. We therefore approximate the expected value with the empirical mean by averaging over $-\log(p(D|\theta))$ for a different θ, which we can sample from $\theta \sim q_\lambda$. But how many samples of θ are required? Well, it turns out that a single sample is usually enough (we'll come back to this point later).

To digest it a bit, let's look at the code in listing 8.1 and imagine a forward pass through the NN shown in figure 8.4, including the evaluation of the loss in the training set. Let's start with a vector w that holds the four fixed values: $w = (\mu_a, w_1, \mu_b, w_3)$. These values control the variational parameters (see the calculations of `sigma_a`, `mu_a`, `sigma_sig`, and `mu_sig` in listing 8.1) via $\lambda = (\mu_a, sp(w_1), \mu_b, sp(w_3))$, where sp is the softplus. The variational distributions $N(\mu_a, \sigma_a)$ and $N(\mu_b, \sigma_b)$ are now fixed, and we can calculate the regularizing loss component (see the first component in equation 8.2) via equation 8.3. As a starting point, we choose for all four parameters 0.1, yielding `loss_kl = -0.5` (see listing 8.1). Next, we calculate the NLL part of the loss function:

$$\log(p(D|(a, b)) = \sum_{i=1}^{n} \log(N(y_i; a \cdot x_i + b, \sigma))$$

where $N(y; \mu, \sigma)$ is the density function of a Normal distribution. To approximate this NLL term, we sample a single value for a, b. Using this sample, we're now fixed in a non-Bayesian NN, and you can calculate the NLL as usual (see listing 8.1). First, you choose the appropriate TFP distribution for the outcome:

```
y_prob = tfd.Normal(loc = x · a + b, scale = sigma)
```

Then, having the correct distribution, you calculate the NLL by summing overall training examples via:

```
loss_nll = -tf.reduce_sum(y_prob.log_prob(ytensor))
```

We add the two loss components (`loss_kl` and `loss_nll`) together to get the final loss. Are we done? Almost. We have the power of TensorFlow and can calculate the derivations of the loss with respect to (w.r.t.) $w = (\mu_a, w_1, \mu_b, w_3)$ and update these. But reality bites, and there's a subtle problem.

Let's say we want to calculate the derivative of the loss w.r.t. the weight $\mu_a = w[0]$, which gives the mean of the distribution of the slope $a \sim N(\mu_a, \sigma_a)$. In figure 8.5, on the left, you see the relevant part of the computational graph for sampling the slope parameter a from its variational distribution $N(\mu_a, \sigma_a)$. The part of the graph for the parameter b is analog. You remember from chapter 3 that you have to calculate the local gradient of the output w.r.t. the input. Easy. Just calculate the derivative of the density of $N(\mu_a, \sigma_a)$ w.r.t. μ_a. Wait—a is sampled from a Gaussian. How do we calculate the derivative through a sampled variable? This isn't possible because the value of a is random and we don't know at which position to take the derivative of the normal density.

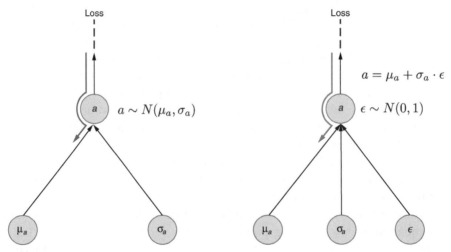

Figure 8.5 The reparameterization trick. Because backpropagation (here shown for $\dfrac{\partial}{\partial \mu_a}$) doesn't work through a random variable such as $a \sim N(\mu_a, \sigma_a)$ (left plot), we use the reparameterization trick (right plot). Instead of sampling a from $a \sim N(\mu_a, \sigma_a)$, we calculate a as $a = \mu_a + \sigma_a \cdot \epsilon$ with ϵ sampled from a standard Normal distribution $\epsilon \sim N(0, 1)$ that has no tunable parameters. In the end, when using the reparameterization trick (right), a is again Normal distributed according to $a \sim N(\mu_a, \sigma_a)$, but we can backpropagate through to get $\dfrac{\partial}{\partial \mu_a}$ and $\dfrac{\partial}{\partial \sigma_a}$ because the random variable $\epsilon \sim N(0, 1)$ doesn't need to be updated.

We can't calculate the derivative of $a \sim N(\mu_a, \sigma_a)$ w.r.t. σ_a or μ_a. Is all lost? In 2013, Kingma and Welling found the solution for that dilemma, but many others independently found that solution as well. Instead of sampling $a \sim N(\mu_a, \sigma_a)$, you can calculate $a_{\text{rep}} = \mu_a + \sigma_a \cdot \epsilon$ and then sample $\epsilon \sim N(0, 1)$. You can check in the notebook http://mng.bz/4A5R that $a_{\text{rep}} \sim N(\mu_a, \sigma_a)$ and reparameterization works! The good thing about reparameterization is that you can backpropagate through it w.r.t. σ_a or μ_a. (We do not need a backpropagation w.r.t. ε.) Figure 8.5 shows the reparameterization on the right. Now we're done, and we have a working solution to calculate the gradients. This listing shows the complete code.

Listing 8.1 Using VI for the simple linear regression example (full code)

The initial condition of the vector w ▷
```
w_0=(1.,1.,1.,1.)
log = tf.math.log
w = tf.Variable(w_0)
e = tfd.Normal(loc=0., scale=1.)          ◄── The noise term, needed for the variational trick
ytensor = y.reshape([len(y),1])
for i in range(epochs):
    with tf.GradientTape() as tape:
```

Controls the center of parameter a ▷
```
        mu_a = w[0]
        sig_a = tf.math.softplus(w[1])     ◄── Controls the spread of parameter a

        mu_b = w[2]                          ◄── Controls the center of parameter b
```
Controls the spread of parameter b ▷
```
        sig_b = tf.math.softplus(w[3])

        l_kl = -0.5*(1.0 +
            log(sig_a**2) - sig_a**2 - mu_a**2 +     KL divergence with Gaussian priors
            1.0 + log(sig_b**2) - sig_b**2 - mu_b**2)
```

Samples b ~ N(mu_b, sigma_b) ▷
```
        a =  mu_a + sig_a * e.sample()      ◄── Samples a ~ N(mu_a, sigma_a) with the reparameterization trick
        b =  mu_b + sig_b * e.sample()

        y_prob = tfd.Normal(loc=x*a+b, scale=sigma)
        l_nll = \
            -tf.reduce_sum(y_prob.log_prob(ytensor))     ◄── Calculates the NLL

        loss = l_nll + l_kl
    grads = tape.gradient(loss, w)
    logger.log(i, i, w, grads, loss, loss_kl, loss_nll)      Gradient descent
    w = tf.Variable(w - lr*grads)          ◄──
```

In figure 8.6, you can see how the parameters μ_a and μ_b converge during the training of the Bayesian model via the approximation VI method to the same values that we got analytically without using approximations (see section 7.3.3).

Let's recap how the estimation of the variational parameters was done in our simple regression example. The estimation minimized the loss that was derived for the VI method expression (equation 8.2, shown here again):

$$\text{loss}_{\text{VI}} = \text{loss}_{\text{KL}} + \text{loss}_{\text{NLL}} = \text{KL}[q_\lambda(\theta) \| p(\theta)] - E_{\theta \sim q_\lambda}[\log(p(D|\theta))]$$

Equation 8.2 (repeated)

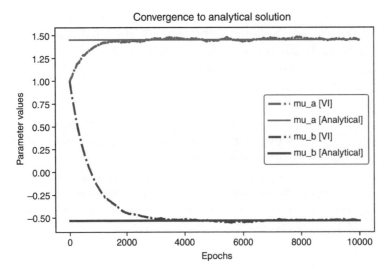

Figure 8.6 The variational parameters μ_a (upper curve) and μ_b (lower curve) during several epochs converging close to the analytical solution

We used gradient descent to optimize the variational parameters $\lambda = (\mu_a, sp(w_1),$ $\mu_b, sp(w_3))$. The expectation $E_{\theta \sim q_\lambda}[\log(p(D|\theta))]$ can be approximated by the average of different $\log(p(D|\theta))$ values, each corresponding to a different θ sampled from q_λ. In principle, an infinite number of different θ's must be drawn from the distribution q_λ and averaged to perfectly reproduce the expectation. This is the law of large numbers. However, in a practical sense, only a single draw of θ is done; the resulting $\log(p(D|\theta))$ is then taken as an approximation for $E_{\theta \sim q_\lambda}[\log(p(D|\theta))]$.

In our example, we drew a single realization $\theta = (a, b)$. Then we took the gradient of equation 8.1 w.r.t. the variational parameters (location, μ_a, μ_b, and scale, σ_a, σ_b, of the distributions $a \sim N(\mu_a, \sigma_a)$ and $b \sim N(\mu_b, \sigma_b)$). The gradient didn't point to the right direction of the steepest descent. Only the average of an infinite number of gradients would do so. Does this algorithm make sense? Let's see if a single draw still makes sense.

To recap, for our example, we have four variational parameters: μ_a, σ_a, μ_b, σ_b. We focused on the location parameters of the distribution μ_a and μ_b, and we started with $\mu_a = 1$ and $\mu_b = 1$. Then we calculated the gradient w.r.t. μ_a and μ_b, which were -3.09940 and 2.2454. Taking one gradient step with the learning rate = 0.001, we arrived at $\mu_a = 1 + 0.001 \cdot 3.09940 = 1.0031$ and $\mu_b = 1 - 0.001 \cdot 2.2354 = 0.9975$. Then we repeated the gradient descent one step after another (see figure 8.7).

Although the gradient is noisy, it still finds its way to the minimum. Calculating a more accurate gradient by summing over many iterations isn't necessary and would be a waste of computations. The direction would be more accurate, however, having less fluctuation in the arrow (figure 8.7 and go watch the animation), but a rough and fast estimate is also fine and much quicker to calculate. The trick of replacing the

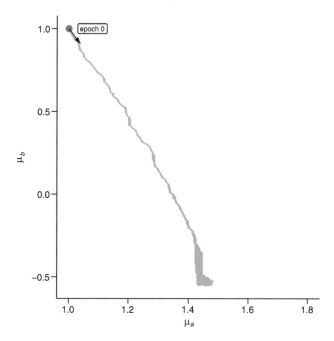

Figure 8.7 Training the variational parameters. To train a BNN means to learn the distributions for $\theta = (a, b)$. The simplest BNN (shown in figure 8.4) has only two parameters, *a* and *b*, for which with VI, a Gaussian distribution is assumed: $a \sim N(\mu_a, \sigma_a)$, $b \sim N(\mu_b, \sigma_b)$. Here the location parameters μ_a and μ_b are shown during several training epochs. The dot is the current value of the variational parameters (μ_a, μ_b) at a given epoch. Also shown is the negative gradient (the line pointing away from the dot). https://youtu.be/MC_5Ne3Dj6g provides an animated version.

expectation with only one evaluation is also used for different occasions in DL research like reinforcement learning or variational autoencoders.

8.3 *Variational inference with TensorFlow Probability*

TFP has several methods to build VI BNNs, so let's first see how simple it is to build a VI network in TFP. There is a class, `tfp.layers.DenseReparameterization`, that you can use like a standard Keras layer, stacking one layer after another to build a fully connected Bayesian network. Listing 8.2 shows the code for the network shown in figure 8.2. Can you guess how many parameters this Bayesian network has? Note that the bias terms have no variational distribution and, thus, only one weight.

Listing 8.2 Setting up a VI network with three layers

```
model = tf.keras.Sequential([
  tfp.layers.DenseReparameterization(1, input_shape=(None,1)),
  tfp.layers.DenseReparameterization(2),
  tfp.layers.DenseReparameterization(3)
])
```

In the default setting, `DenseReparameterization` includes the bias as a fixed parameter and not as a distribution. Therefore, the bias (edge from 1 to the output in figure 8.4) carries only one parameter. The node from *x* to the output is modeled with a Gaussian requiring two parameters (one for the center and one for the scale), so the first layer has three parameters to learn. Similarly, the second layer has two bias terms and two edges resulting in $2 + 2 \cdot 2 = 6$ parameters. Finally, the last layer has three biases and six edges resulting in $3 + 2 \cdot 6 = 15$ parameters. In total, this network has 24 parameters. Going Bayesian roughly requires two times the number of parameters compared to a standard NN. As a little exercise, copy the code to a notebook and call it model.summary().

TFP is also quite flexible. Let's rebuild the linear regression problem from section 7.3.3, in which we replace the slope *a* and intercept by distributions, and σ is assumed to be known. To be compatible with TFP, we need to translate the model into a variational Bayes network (see figure 8.4). To fully define our network, we also need to state our priors for the two variables *a* and *b*. We choose the normally distributed $N(0,1)$.

You'll find the code for the network in listing 8.3. In contrast to TFP's default setting, we want the bias to also be a distribution. We thus need to overwrite it by setting `bias_prior_fn=normal` and `bias_posterior_fn=normal` in the constructor of the `DenseReparameterization` layer. Further, there is currently the following oddity (not to call it a bug) in TFP layers. This loss (shown in equation 8.1) consists of the usual NLL and an additional term called KL divergence. Normally, you take KL divergence and the NLL using the sum of overall training data (see listing 8.3). In DL, however, it's quite common to calculate the mean NLL per training example (the summed NLL divided by the number of training examples). This is fine. We just need the minimum of the loss function, which doesn't change if we divide the loss by a constant. (We also did this in all examples up to now.) But now, the KL divergence needs to be transformed to the mean per our training example as well, and this is currently not the case in TFP. Digging deeper into TFP's documentation, you find the somewhat cryptic statement in `DenseReparameterization` (http://mng.bz/Qyd6) and also in the corresponding convolutional layers (`Convolution1DReparameterization`, `Convolution2D-Reparameterization`, and `Convolution3DReparameterization`):

> *When doing minibatch stochastic optimization, make sure to scale this loss such that it is applied just once per epoch (e.g., if kl is the sum of losses for each element of the batch, you should pass kl / num_examples_per_epoch to your optimizer).*

To address this, one needs to also divide the KL term by the number of training data (num). This can be done via the following lines of code (the next listing shows this fix):

```
kernel_divergence_fn=lambda q, p, _: tfp.distributions.kl_divergence(q, p) /
    (num · 1.0)
```

Listing 8.3 Coding our simple network from figure 8.4

```
def NLL(y, distr):
    return -distr.log_prob(y)

def my_dist(mu):
    return tfd.Normal(loc=mu[:,0:1], scale=sigma)


kl = tfp.distributions.kl_divergence
divergence_fn=lambda q, p, _: kl(q, p) / (num * 1.0)


model = tf.keras.Sequential([
    tfp.layers.DenseReparameterization(1,
        kernel_divergence_fn=divergence_fn,
        bias_divergence_fn=divergence_fn,
        bias_prior_fn= \
    tfp.layers.util.default_multivariate_normal_fn,
        bias_posterior_fn= \
    tfp.layers.util.default_mean_field_normal_fn()
                                    ),
    tfp.layers.DistributionLambda(my_dist)
])



sgd = tf.keras.optimizers.SGD(lr=.005)
model.compile(loss=NLL, optimizer=sgd)
```

◁ The usual NLL loss for a Gaussian distribution with fixed variance

◁ Rescales KL divergence term (kind of a bug fix for TFP)

◁ TFP usually doesn't assume distributions on the bias; we overwrite this here.

TFP also offers layers to build convolutional BNNs using VI. For the usual 2D convolutions, these layers are called `Convolution2DReparameterization`. There are also 1D and 3D variants named `Convolution1DReparameterization` and `Convolution3D-Reparameterization`. Further, for the dense and convolutional BNNs, there are some special classes and some advanced VI methods in TFP. Most notably, `DenseFlipout` can be used as a drop-in replacement for `DenseReparameterization`. `DenseFlipout` uses a trick that speeds up learning. The flip-out trick is also available for convolutions (see, for example, `Convolution2DFlipout`). The flip-out method is described in detail in the paper by Y. Wen, P. Vicol, et al., at https://arxiv.org/abs/1803.04386. In the notebook http://mng.bz/MdmQ, you use these layers to build a BNN for the CIFAR-10 data set (see figure 8.9).

8.4 *MC dropout as an approximate Bayes approach*

In section 8.3, you took a first glimpse at a BNN approximated by VI. VI allows you to fit a Bayesian DL model by learning an approximative posterior distribution for each weight. The default in TFP is to approximate the posterior by a Gaussian. These BNNs have twice as many parameters compared to their non-Bayesian versions, because each weight is replaced by a Gaussian weight distribution that's defined by two parameters (mean and standard deviation). It's great that VI lets us fit a BNN despite its huge number of parameters. But it would be even nicer if the number of parameters

wouldn't double when going from a non-Bayesian NN to its Bayesian variant. Fortunately, that's possible with an easy method called MC dropout. (MC stands for Monte
Carlo and insinuates that a random process is involved as in a Monte Carlo casino.) In
2015, a PhD student, Yarin Gal, was able to show that the dropout method was similar
to VI, allowing us to approximate a BNN. But before turning to a dropout as a Bayesian method, let's see how the dropout was introduced.

8.4.1   *Classical dropout used during training*

Dropout during training was introduced as a simple way to prevent an NN from overfitting. (This was even the title of the paper when Srivastava et al., presented the
method in 2014.) How does it work? When doing dropout during training, you set
some randomly picked neurons in the NN to zero. You do that in each update run.
Because you actually drop neurons, the weights of all connections that start from the
dropped neuron are simultaneously dropped (see figure 8.8).

In Keras, this can easily be done by adding a dropout layer after a weight layer and
giving the dropout the probability $p*$ (here we use $p*$ to indicate that this is an MC
drop probability, which sets the weight to zero) as an argument (see the following listing). During training, the dropout is often only used in the fully connected layers.

Listing 8.4   Defining and training a classification CNN with dropout layers

```
model = Sequential()
model.add(Convolution2D(16,kernel_size,padding='same',\
input_shape=input_shape))
model.add(Activation('relu'))
model.add(Convolution2D(16,kernel_size,padding='same'))
model.add(Activation('relu'))
model.add(MaxPooling2D(pool_size=pool_size))
model.add(Convolution2D(32,kernel_size,padding='same'))
model.add(Activation('relu'))
model.add(Convolution2D(32,kernel_size,padding='same'))
model.add(Activation('relu'))
model.add(MaxPooling2D(pool_size=pool_size))

model.add(Flatten())
model.add(Dense(100))
model.add(Activation('relu'))
model.add(Dropout(0.5))           ◁┐    Dropout layer that sets each
model.add(Dense(100))             │     neuron of the former weight layer
model.add(Activation('relu'))     │     to 0 with a probability of 0.5
model.add(Dropout(0.5))           ◁┘
model.add(Dense(nb_classes))
model.add(Activation('softmax'))

model.compile(loss='categorical_crossentropy',optimizer='adam',\
metrics=['accuracy'])
```

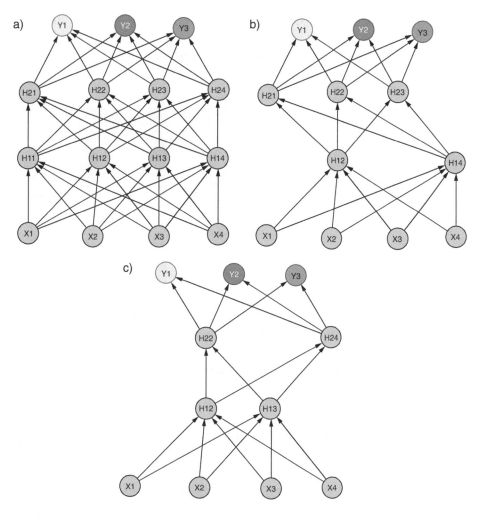

Figure 8.8 Three NNs: a) shows the full NN with all neurons, and b) and c) show two versions of a thinned NN where some neurons are dropped. Dropping neurons is the same as setting all connections that start from these neurons to zero.

Before we discuss the dropout method in more detail, you can easily convince yourself that dropout successfully fights overfitting by working through the following notebook. In the notebook, you develop a classification convolutional neural network (CNN) for the CIFAR-10 data set that has 50,000 images and 10 classes (see figure 8.9).

HANDS-ON TIME Open http://mng.bz/XP29. This notebook uses (classical) dropout to fight overfitting while training a DL model for the CIFAR-10 classification.

- Check that the loss curves of the training data are valid with and without dropout
- Check the accuracy with and without dropout

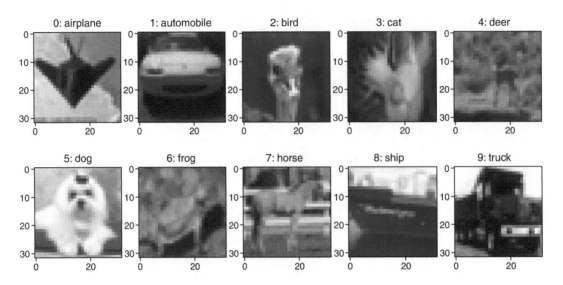

Figure 8.9 Example images for the ten classes in the CIFAR-10 data set

In the notebook http://mng.bz/4A5R, you saw that the dropout during training prevents overfitting and even improves the accuracy. For this exercise, see figure 8.10, where the results of the notebook are displayed.

Let's see how dropout during training works. In each training loop, you apply dropout and get another thinned version of the NN (see figure 8.10). Why does dropout help to prevent overfitting? One reason is that you train many thinned NN versions, which have fewer parameters than the full NN. In each step, you only update the weights that weren't dropped. Overall, you train not just a single version of the network but an ensemble of thinned versions of the NN that share weights. Another reason is that fewer complex features are learned when using dropout. Because dropout forces the NN to cope with missing information, it yields more robust and independent features.

How do you use a dropout-trained NN during testing? It's simple. You go back to the full NN with fixed weights. There's only one detail: you need to downweigh the learned weight values to $w^* = p^* \cdot w$. This downweighting accounts for the fact that during training each neuron gets, on average, p^* less inputs than in the full NN. The connections are, thus, stronger than these would be if no dropout is applied. During the application phase, there's no dropout and, hence, you downweigh the too strong weights by multiplying those with p^*. Fortunately, you don't have to adjust the weights

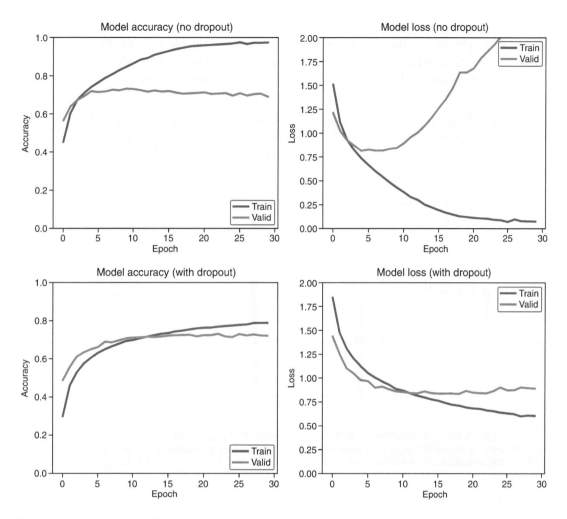

Figure 8.10   CIFAR-10 results achieved with and without using dropout during training. During testing, the weights are fixed (no MC dropout). When using dropout, the accuracy on the validation data is higher (left panel), and the distance between validation and trained loss is much smaller (right panel). This indicates that dropout prevents overfitting.

manually; Keras takes care of that. When using a dropout-trained NN during testing and applying the predict command on new input, Keras does the correct thing.

8.4.2   *MC dropout used during train and test times*

As you saw in section 8.4.1, dropout during training can easily enhance the prediction performance. For this reason, it quickly became popular in the DL community and is still widely used. But dropout has even more to offer. Turn on dropout during testing and you can use it as a BNN! Let's see how this works.

In a BNN, a distribution of weights replaces each weight. With VI, you used a Gaussian weight distribution with two parameters (mean and standard deviation). When using dropout, you also have a weight distribution, but now the weight distribution is simpler and essentially consists of only two values: 0 or w (see figure 8.11).

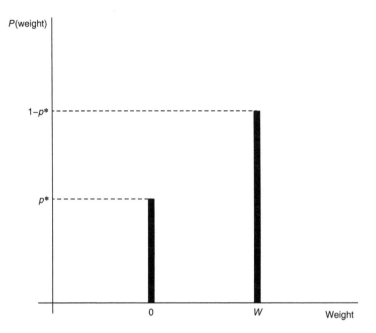

Figure 8.11 The (simplified) weight distribution with MC dropout. The dropout probability p^* is fixed when defining the NN. The only parameter in this distribution is the value of w.

The dropout probability p^* isn't a parameter but is fixed when you define the NN (for example, $p^* = 0.3$). The dropout probability is a tuning parameter: if you don't get good results when using $p^* = 0.3$, you can try it with another dropout rate. The only parameter of the weight distribution in the MC dropout method is the value w (see figure 8.11 and, for details, see the MC dropout paper by Yarin Gal and Zoubin Ghahramani at https://arxiv.org/abs/1506.02157). Learning the parameter w works as usual. You turn on dropout during training and use the usual NLL loss function, which you minimize by tuning the weights via stochastic gradient descent (SGD).

As a side remark, in Gal's dropout paper, the loss consists of the NLL and an additional regularization term that penalizes large weights. We'll skip this regularization term as most practitioners in the field do. It's simply not needed in practice. In Gal's framework, dropout is similar to the VI inference fitting a BNN method from section 8.2, but this time, the distribution from figure 8.11 is taken instead of the Gaussian usually used in the VI method. By updating the w values, you actually learn the weight distributions that approximate the weight posteriors (see figure 8.11).

How do you use the dropout-trained NN as a BNN? As for all Bayesian models, you get the predictive distribution by averaging over the weight distribution (see equation 7.6).

$$p(y|x_{\text{test}}, D) = \sum_i p(y|x_{\text{test}}, w_i) \cdot p(w_i|D) \qquad \textbf{Equation 8.4}$$

To get the predictive distribution in a dropout-trained NN, you turn on dropout also during test time. Then, with the same input, you can make several predictions where each prediction results from another dropout variant of the NN. The predictions you get in this manner approximate the predictive distribution in equation 8.4 as you will see in the next couple of lines. More precisely, you predict for the same input x_{test} T-times a conditional probability distribution (CPD) $p(y|x_{\text{test}}, w_i)$. For each prediction, you get different CPDs, $(p(y|x, w_i))$, corresponding to a sampled weight constellation w_i (see the following case studies). It's called MC dropout because for each prediction, you make a forward pass through another thinned version of the NN, resulting from randomly dropping neurons. You then can combine the dropout predictions to a Bayesian predictive distribution:

$$p(y|x_{\text{test}}, D) = \frac{1}{T} \sum_{t=1}^{T} p(y|x_{\text{test}}, w_t)$$

This is an empirical approximation to equation 8.4. The resulting predictive distribution captures the epistemic and the aleatoric uncertainties.

To use MC dropout in Keras, there are two options. In the first option, you simply create your network by setting the training phase to true in the model definition. A more elegant way is to make it choosable, if dropout is used during test time or not. The next listing shows how to do so in Keras (and see the notebook http://mng.bz/MdmQ).

Listing 8.5   Getting MC dropout predictions

Defines a function using the model input and learning phase as input and returning the model output. What's important is the learning phase. When set to 0, all weights are fixed and adjusted by the dropout p* during test time; when set to 1, dropout is used at test time.

```
import  tensorflow.keras.backend as K
model_mc_pred = K.function([model_mc.input, K.learning_phase()],
    [model_mc.output])
T= 5
for i in range(0,T):
  print(model_mc_pred([x_train[0:1],0])[0])

for i in range(0,T):
  print(model_mc_pred([x_train[0:1],1])[0])
```

Defines the number of dropout predictions

Each of the T predictions

Each of the T predictions for the same input are different because they're determined from a different thinned NN version, corresponding to a different dropout run.

8.5   Case studies

Let's return to our original problem that led us to BNNs. Recall the example in section 7.1, where we couldn't find the elephant in the room because such images were not part of the training set. Let's see if Bayesian modeling can help to express appropriate uncertainties when encountering new situations that aren't present in the training data (see figure 8.12, which we repeat from chapter 7 here).

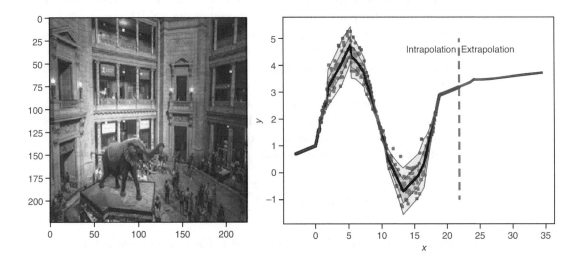

Figure 8.12   Bad cases of DL. The elephant isn't seen by the high performant VGG16 CNN trained on ImageNet data. The five highest ranked class predictions are horse_cart, shopping_cart, palace, streetcar, and gondola— the elephant isn't found! In the regression problem, there's zero uncertainty in the regions where there's no data (see under Extrapolation on the right and also figure 4.18).

8.5.1   Regression case study on extrapolation

Let's first tackle the regression task in a case study (see the right side of figure 8.12) and compare the two methods: the VI network from section 8.4 and the Monte Carlo approximation from the last section. We also include a non-Bayesian approach in the example. You can use the same synthetic sinus data that you used in sections 4.3.2 and 4.3.3 to fit a non-linear regression model with a flexible variance. To do it yourself, work through the following notebook.

HANDS-ON TIME Open http://mng.bz/yyxp. In this notebook, you investigate the advantages BNNs can offer in a regression task for extrapolation. You use synthetic data to fit different probabilistic NN:

- You fit a non-Bayesian NN.
- You fit two Bayesian NN, one via VI and one via dropout.
- You investigate the uncertainties expressed by the NN.

As validation data, you use 400 examples with x values ranging between –10 and 30 that are spaced in steps of 0.1. This range doesn't only cover the range of training data, where you expect the model to estimate the parameters with low uncertainty, but also covers a range beyond the training data, where you expect a higher epistemic uncertainty. After setting up the case study in this manner, you can check whether the models are able to express an increased uncertainty when getting into the extrapolation range (lower than –3 or larger than 30). The different probabilistic NN models yield quite different results as you'll see.

For comparing the three approaches, let's look at the predictive distribution for the outcome. You saw in section 7.3 that you can compute the predictive distribution for a Bayesian model via equation 8.5. (This is the same formula as found in equation 7.6, but we call the parameters in NNs usually w instead of θ.)

$$p(y|x_{\text{test}}, D) = \int_\theta p(y|x_{\text{test}}, \theta) \cdot p(\theta|D)d\theta \qquad \textbf{Equation 8.5}$$

This equation tells us to average overall possible weight configurations w of a network. We approximate this integral by taking the samples $y \sim p(y|x_{\text{test}}, D)$ for the different configurations (w) of the network. Note that, with sampling, you don't need to care for the weighting with the posterior $p(\theta|D)$. The reason is that you automatically sample more often those w that have higher posterior probabilities $p(\theta|D)$.

Let's take a closer look at how to determine the outcome distribution of $p(y|x_i, D)$ for a given input x_i. To investigate the outcome distribution, we need to look at the trained models and draw T samples from the networks. You'll see that there are some differences in the three different probabilistic NN models.

In the non-Bayesian NN, you have a fixed weight at each connection c. To be consistent with the Bayesian terminology, we call this value θ_c. We want to represent this by a probability distribution and so we assign the probability 1 to the fixed weight θ_c (see the upper left plot in figure 8.13). Sampling from these probability distributions (you have one distribution per connection) always yields identical NNs (see the first row, first through third columns in figure 8.13). Therefore, the NN yields in each of the T runs for the same input x, the same parameters for the Gaussian $N(y; \mu_{x,w_t}, \sigma_{x,w_t}) = N(y; \mu_{x,w}, \sigma_{x,w})$ (see table 8.2). To get the empirical outcome distribution, you can sample from this Gaussian: $y \sim N(\mu_{x,w}, \sigma_{x,w})$. In table 8.2, because the quantities $\mu_{x,w}$ and $\sigma_{x,w}$ are the same in all rows, the predicted outcome distribution at position x is in all runs $p(y|x, w) = N(y; \mu_x, \sigma_x)$. In this case, we know that the outcome distribution is $N(y; \mu_x, \sigma_x)$. To do the same as for the Bayesian approaches, we still sample one value per run and so get T values from the outcome distribution for each x position (see the left plot in the upper panel in figure 8.14).

A Bayesian VI NN replaces the fixed weight θ_c with a Gaussian distribution with the mean μ_c and a standard deviation σ_c (see the middle row, in the rightmost column, in figure 8.13). During test time, you sample T-times from these weight distributions, always getting slightly different values for the connections (see the second row, first to

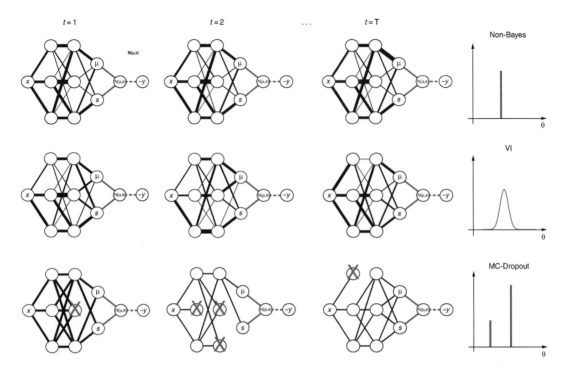

Figure 8.13 Sketch of the sampling procedure of three models used in the regression case study. In the last column (on the right), one edge of the network is picked, showing its distribution. The remaining columns show realizations of different networks for *T* different runs. In each run, the input x_i is the same, and the values of the edges are sampled according to their distributions. In the upper row, you see the non-Bayesian approach, where all realized NN are the same. In the middle, you see the VI-Bayesian approach, where the values of the edges are sampled from Gaussians. On the bottom right, the MC dropout approach, where the values of edges come from binary distributions. For animated versions, see https://youtu.be/mQrUcUoT2k4 (for VI); https://youtu.be/0-oyDeR9HrE (for MC dropout); and https://youtu.be/FO5avm3XT4g (for non-Bayesian).

Table 8.2 Predicted conditional probability distributions (CPDs) from a Bayesian NN that was trained via VI for the sinus regression task. Each row corresponds to one out of *T* predictions, yielding for all 400 *x* values, a Gaussian CPD of $N(\mu_x, \sigma_x)$ from which it's possible to sample.

predict_no	$x_1 = -10$	$x_2 = -9.9$	$\ldots$	$x_{400} = 30$
1	$y \sim N(\mu_{x_1,w_1}, \sigma_{x_1,w_1})$	$y \sim N(\mu_{x_2,w_1}, \sigma_{x_2,w_1})$	$\cdots$	$y \sim N(\mu_{x_{400},w_1}, \sigma_{x_{400},w_1})$
2	$y \sim N(\mu_{x_1,w_2}, \sigma_{x_1,w_2})$	$y \sim N(\mu_{x_2,w_2}, \sigma_{x_2,w_2})$	$\cdots$	$y \sim N(\mu_{x_{400},w_2}, \sigma_{x_{400},w_2})$
$\ldots$	$\ldots$	$\ldots$	$\cdots$	$\ldots$
T	$y \sim N(\mu_{x_1,w_T}, \sigma_{x_1,w_T})$	$y \sim N(\mu_{x_2,w_T}, \sigma_{x_2,w_T})$	$\cdots$	$y \sim N(\mu_{x_{400},w_T}, \sigma_{x_{400},w_T})$

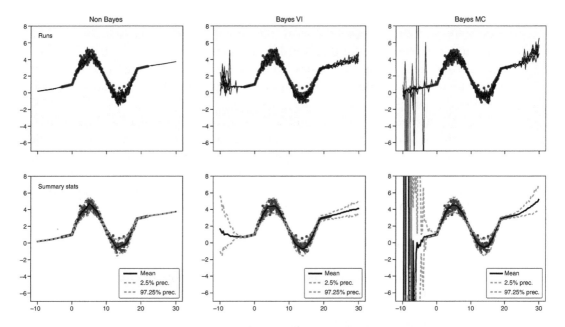

Figure 8.14 Predictive distributions. The solid lines in the top row show five samples from the outcome distribution for the three models (classic NN, VI Bayes NN, and dropout Bayes NN). The second row shows summary statistics: the solid line represents the mean, and the lower and upper dashed lines depict the upper and lower borders of the 95% prediction interval.

third columns in figure 8.13, where the thickness of the connections indicate whether the sampled value is larger or smaller than the mean of the weight distribution). The NN, therefore, yields in each of the T runs slightly different parameters of the Gaussian $N(\mu_{x,w_t}, \sigma_{x,w_t})$, which we collect in the T rows of table 8.2. To get the empirical outcome distribution, you can sample from all of these determined Gaussians: $y \sim N(\mu_{x,w_t}, \sigma_{x,w_t})$. If you sample one value per run, you get T outcome values at each x position (see figure 8.14, middle plot in the upper panel).

The Bayesian MC dropout NN replaces each fixed weight θ_c with a binary distribution (see the third row in the last column of figure 8.13). During test time, you sample T-times from these weight distributions, always getting either zero or the value w_c for a connection (see the third row, first through third column of figure 8.13). To get the empirical outcome distribution, you can sample from all of these determined Gaussians: $y \sim N(\mu_{x,w}, \sigma_{x,w})$ (see figure 8.14, right plot in the upper panel).

Let's use the results from the T predictions to first explore the outcome uncertainty for all three models. Figure 8.14 displays the results for the different methods. In the first row of figure 8.14, for the first 5 of the T rows in table 8.2, a line is drawn to connect the different sampled outcome values y at the different x positions. In the second row, all the T results are summarized by the mean value (solid line) and the 95% prediction interval (dashed lines). The lower dashed line corresponds to the 2.5%

percentile and the upper to the 97.5% percentile. For the non-Bayesian approach, you sample always from the same Gaussian $N(\mu_x, \sigma_x)$. Therefore, you could, in principle, compute the dashed lines for this Gaussian distribution as $y = \mu_x \pm 1.96 \cdot \sigma_x$. This isn't the case for the Bayesian approaches, where we don't know the analytical form of the outcome distribution and, therefore, have to sample and then calculate the percentiles from the samples.

To wrap up, let's take a final look at the last row of figure 8.14 and compare the Bayes with the non-Bayes approaches. The central line indicates the mean position of your value *y* given the data. In all approaches, it follows the data. The dashed line indicates the regions in which we expect 95% of the data. In the region where we have training data, all approaches yield similar results. The uncertainty captured by the spread of the CPD is large in regions where the data spread is also large. All models are, thus, able to model the aleatoric uncertainty. When we leave the region where we have data and go into the extrapolation region, the non-Bayesian approach fails. It assumes 95% of the data in an unrealistically narrow region. Total disaster, so sad! The Bayesian approaches, however, know when they don't know and express their uncertainties when leaving known grounds.

8.5.2   *Classification case study with novel classes*

Let's revisit the elephant in the room problem, where you face a classification task. When presenting a new input image to a trained classification NN, you get for each class seen during training a predicted probability. To predict the elephant image (see figure 8.12), we used the VGG16 CNN trained on ImageNet in section 7.1. ImageNet has 1,000 classes including different kinds of elephants. But the VGG16 network wasn't able to find the elephant in the room, meaning the elephant wasn't among the top five classes. A plausible explanation is that elephant images in the training data set never included an elephant in a room. With such an image (see figure 8.12, left panel), we ask the NN model to leave known grounds and to do extrapolation. Would it help to use a BNN? A BNN would probably not see the elephant either, but it should be better able to express its uncertainty. Unfortunately, you can't give it a go because the ImageNet data set is huge, and you need several days on a strong GPU machine to train a Bayesian version of the VGG16 CNN.

Let's do it in a smaller way so that you can do the experiment yourself in notebook http://mng.bz/MdmQ. You can work with the CIFAR-10 data set that has only 50,000 images and 10 classes (see figure 8.15).

You can use a part of the CIFAR-10 data set to train a Bayesian CNN and do some experiments with it. But how do you design an experiment that recognizes if the NN model expresses uncertainty when leaving known grounds? Let's go to the extreme and see what happens when you provide a trained CNN with an image from a class that isn't part of the training data. For that, you can train a CNN on only nine classes; for example, without the class *horse* (remove all images showing horses from the training data). When presenting a horse image to the trained NN, it estimates probabilities

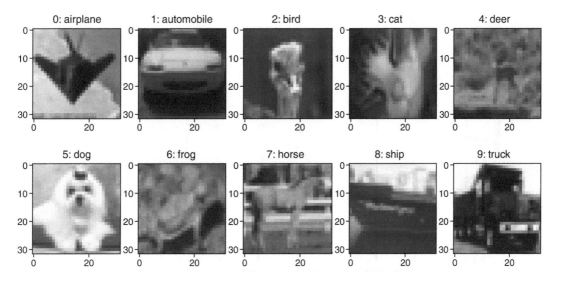

Figure 8.15 **Example images for the ten classes in the CIFAR-10 data set (same as figure 8.9)**

for the classes on which it was trained. All of these classes are wrong, but the NN still can't assign a zero probability to all classes because the output needs to add up to one, which is enforced using the softmax layer. Is it possible to find out if you can trust the classification based on the predicted distribution using a Bayesian approach? You can do the experiment yourself in the following notebook.

HANDS-ON TIME Open http://mng.bz/MdmQ. In this classification case study with novel classes notebook, you investigate the advantages BNNs can offer in a classification task. You use training data from 9 of the 10 classes in the CIFAR-10 data set to fit different probabilistic NNs:

- You fit a non-Bayesian NN.
- You fit two BNNs, one via VI and one via MC dropout.
- You compare the performance achieved with the different NNs.
- You investigate the uncertainties expressed by the NNs.
- You use the uncertainties to detect novel classes.

During test time, a traditional probabilistic CNN for classification yields for each input image a multinomial probability distribution (*MN* in the equations). In our case, one that's fitted with nine outcome classes (see figure 8.16). The probabilities of the k classes provide the parameters for this multinomial distribution: $\mathrm{MN}(p_1, p_2, \cdots, p_k)$.

As in the regression case, let's look at the predicted CPDs of three different probabilistic NN models first. In the non-Bayesian NN, you have fixed weights, and for one input image, you get one multinomial CPD: $p(y|x, w) = \mathrm{MN}(p_1(x, w), \ldots, p_9(x, w))$

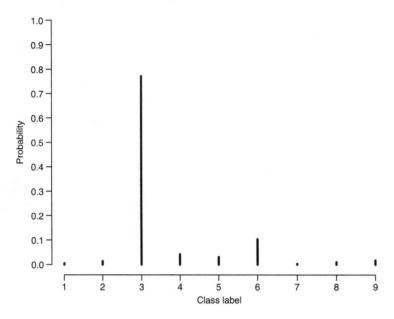

Figure 8.16   Multinomial distribution with nine classes:
$\mathrm{MN}(p_1, p_2, p_3, p_4, p_5, p_6, p_7, p_8, p_9)$

(see table 8.3). If you predict the same image T times, you always get the same results. All rows of the corresponding table 8.3 are the same.

Table 8.3   Predictive distribution of a probabilistic CNN for the CIFAR-10 classification task trained with 9 out of 10 classes. Each prediction is a multinomial CPD with 9 parameters (probability for class 1, 2, . . ., 9).

predict_no	Image x_1 with known class	Image x_2 with unknown class
1	$y \sim \mathrm{MN}(p_1(x_1, w_1), \ldots, p_9(x_1, w_1))$	$y \sim \mathrm{MN}(p_1(x_2, w_1), \ldots, p_9(x_2, w_1))$
2	$y \sim \mathrm{MN}(p_1(x_1, w_2), \ldots, p_9(x_1, w_2))$	$y \sim \mathrm{MN}(p_1(x_2, w_2), \ldots, p_9(x_2, w_2))$
. . .	. . .	. . .
T	$y \sim \mathrm{MN}(p_1(x_1, w_T), \ldots, p_9(x_1, w_T))$	$y \sim \mathrm{MN}(p_1(x_2, w_T), \ldots, p_9(x_2, w_T))$

In a BNN fitted with VI, the fixed weights are replaced with Gaussian distributions. During test time, you sample from these weighted distributions by predicting the same input image not only once, but T times. For each prediction, you get one multinomial CPD: $p(y|x, w_t) = \mathrm{MN}(p_1(x, w_t), \ldots, p_9(x, w_t))$. Each time you predict the image, you get a different CPD ($p(y|x, w_t)$), corresponding to the sampled weight constellation w_t. This means all rows of the corresponding table 8.3 are different.

In the BNN fitted with MC dropout, you replace the fixed weights with binary distributions. From here on this reads like the VI case. For each prediction, you get one multinomial CPD: $p(y|x, w) = \text{MN}(p_1(x, w), \dots, p_9(x, w))$. Each time you predict the image, you get a different CPD ($p(y|x, w_t)$) corresponding to the sampled weight constellation w_i. Meaning all rows of the corresponding table 8.3 are different.

SUMMARIZING AND VISUALIZING UNCERTAINTY IN CLASSIFICATION MODELS

Plotting the predicted probabilities of one row in table 8.3 (parameters of the multinomial CPD) yields the plots in the second, third, and fourth rows of figure 8.17. The aleatoric uncertainty is expressed in the distribution across the classes, which is zero if one class gets a probability of one. The epistemic uncertainty is expressed in the spread of the predicted probabilities of one class, which is zero if the spread is zero. The non-Bayesian NN can't express epistemic uncertainty (you can't get different predictions for the same image), but the BNN can.

Let's look at the results of the network on a known class for two examples first. In the left panel of figure 8.17, you can see that all networks correctly classify the image of an airplane. In the two BNNs, you can see little variation in the plots, indicating that the classification is quite certain. The MC dropout Bayesian CNN shows a little more uncertainty than the VI CNN and also assigns some probability to the class *bird*. This is understandable when looking at the image.

If we go to the unknown class, all predictions in figure 8.17 are wrong. But you can see that the BNNs can better express their uncertainty. Of course, the Bayesian networks also predict a wrong class in all of their T runs. But what we see for each of the T runs is that the distributions vary quite a bit. When comparing the VI and MC dropout methods, again MC dropout shows more variation. Also, the shapes of the predicted probability distribution look different for MC dropout and VI. In the case of VI, the distributions look quite bell-shaped. This might be due to the Gaussian weight distributions used in VI. MC dropout, relying on Bernoulli distributed weights, yields richer predictive distribution shapes. Let's now try to use a 9-dimensional predictive distribution to quantify the uncertainty of the prediction (see table 8.3 and figure 8.17).

UNCERTAINTY MEASURES IN A NON-BAYESIAN CLASSIFICATION NN

In the case of a traditional, non-Bayesian NN, you get for one image, one CPD (see the second row in figure 8.17). You classify the image to the class with the highest probability: $p_{\text{pred}} = \max(p_k)$. The CPD only expresses the aleatoric uncertainty, which would be zero if one class gets a probability of one and all other classes get a probability of zero. You can use p_{pred} as a measure for certainty or $-\log(p_{\text{pred}})$ as a measure for uncertainty, which is the well-known NLL:

$$\text{NLL} = -\log(p_{\text{pred}})$$

Another frequently used measure for the aleatoric uncertainty (using not only the probability of the predicted class) is entropy, which you already encountered in

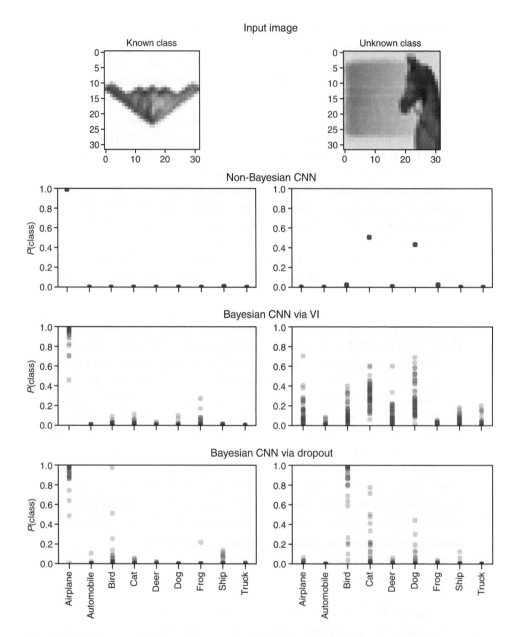

Figure 8.17 Upper panel: images presented to train CNNs included an image from the known class *airplane* (left) and an image from the unknown class *horse* (right). Second row of plots: corresponding predictive distributions resulting from non-Bayesian NN. Third row of plots: corresponding predictive distributions resulting from BNN via VI. Fourth row of plots: corresponding predictive distributions resulting from BNN via MC dropout.

chapter 4. There's no epistemic uncertainty when working with a non-Bayesian NN. Here's the formula:

$$\text{Entropy: } \mathbf{H} = -\sum_{k=1}^{9} p_k \log(p_k)$$

UNCERTAINTY MEASURES IN A BAYESIAN CLASSIFICATION NN

For each image, you predict T multinomial CPDs: $\text{MN}(p_1(x, w_t), \ldots, p_9(x, w_t))$ (see table 8.3 and the third and fourth rows in figure 8.17). For each class k, you can determine the mean probability $p_k^* = \frac{1}{T} \sum_{t=1}^{T} p_{kt}$. You classify the image to the class with the highest mean probability $p_{\text{pred}}^* = \max(p_k^*)$.

In the literature, there's no consensus on how to best quantify the uncertainty that captures both epistemic and aleatoric contributions; in fact, that's still an open research question (at least if you have more than two classes). Note that this mean probability already captures a part of the epistemic uncertainty because it's determined from all T predictions. Averaging causes a shift to less extreme probabilities away from one or zero. You could use $-\log(p_{\text{pred}}^*)$ as the uncertainty:

$$\text{NLL}^* = -\log(p_{\text{pred}}^*)$$

The entropy based on the mean probability values, p^*_k, averaged over all T runs is an even better-established uncertainty measure. But also, you can use the total variance (sum of the variances for the individual classes) of the multidimensional probability distribution to quantify the uncertainty:

- Entropy*: $\mathbf{H}^* = -\sum_{k=1}^{9} p_k^* \cdot \log(p_k^*)$
- Total variance: $V_{\text{tot}} = \sum_{k=1}^{9} \text{var}(p_k) = \sum_{k=1}^{9} \frac{1}{T} \sum_{t=1}^{T} (p_{kt} - p_k^*)^2$

USING UNCERTAINTY MEASURES TO FILTER OUT POTENTIALLY WRONG CLASSIFIED IMAGES

Let's see if these uncertainty measures can help us improve the prediction performance. You saw at the end of chapter 7 that the prediction performance in regression, quantified by the test NLL, is indeed better for a BNN than for a non-BNN, at least for the investigated simple linear regression task. But now, let's turn to classification. We could again look at the test NLL, but here we want to focus on another question. We want to check if we can identify uncertain examples and if removing those from test samples can enhance the accuracy. The idea is that the images of unknown classes should especially show high uncertainties. Hence, the accuracy can be improved if we manage to filter out these wrongfully classified images.

To check if we can identify wrongfully classified images, you can do a filter experiment (see http://mng.bz/MdmQ). For this, you pick one of the uncertainty measures

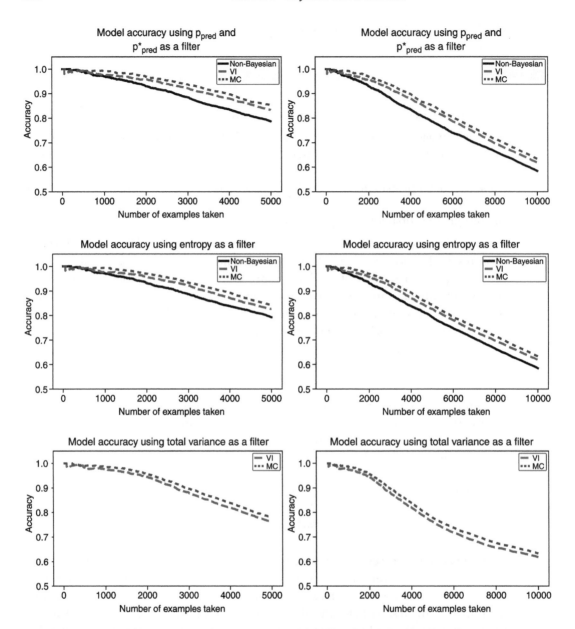

Figure 8.18 Accuracy decreases if more and more images that have higher and higher uncertainties are taken into account. The highest accuracy in each plot corresponds to the accuracy when only the most certain test image is taken into account (100% accuracy). Then images are added with increasing uncertainty measures. The solid curves correspond to the non-Bayesian CNN, the dotted curves to the MC dropout Bayesian CNN, and the dashed curve to the VI Bayesian CNN. The left column shows the curves when the 5,000 thousand most certain images are taken into account; the right column shows the curve for the entire test data set of 10,000 images. In the last row, only the Bayesian CNNs can be used for filtering because in a non-Bayesian CNN, no variance can be computed.

and then rank the classified images according to this measure. You start with classifying test images with the lowest uncertainty and determine the achieved accuracies with the three CNN variants. Then you add images in the order of their uncertainty (smallest uncertainties first) and determine after each added image, again, the resulting accuracies. You can see the results in figure 8.18. After adding the image with the highest uncertainty, all test samples are taken into account, achieving the following accuracies: 58% for the non-Bayesian CNN, 62% for the VI Bayesian CNN, and 63% for the MC dropout Bayesian CNN. This sounds quite bad, but keep in mind that 10% of all test samples come from the unknown class that must, by definition, lead to wrong classifications.

When restricting the test sample only to known classes, you achieve test accuracies of 65% for the non-Bayesian CNN, 69% for the VI Bayesian CNN, and 70% for the MC dropout Bayesian CNN (see http://mng.bz/MdmQ).

Let's come back to the question: Are the uncertainties from BNNs more appropriate to identify potentially wrong classifications? The answer is yes! You can see that in figure 8.18, where the accuracy of the non-Bayesian CNN could be improved by turning to a Bayesian variant. Also, between the VI and MC dropout Bayesian CNNs, you can see a performance difference. MC dropout clearly outperforms VI. This is probably because the VI works with unimodal Gaussian weight distributions and MC dropout with Bernoulli distributions. You already saw in figure 8.17 that VI tends to yield bell-shaped and quite narrow predictive distributions, while MC dropout yields for the same example broader and asymmetric distributions, which partly look almost bimodal (distribution with two peaks). We hypothesize that in the near future, VI will achieve the same or better performance as MC dropout when it becomes possible to easily work in VI with more complex distributions instead of Gaussian. The switch from non-Bayesian to Bayesian NNs is easy to do, regardless if you choose to do VI or MC dropout, and allows you to flag potentially wrong classifications and achieve better prediction performance in regression and classification.

Summary

- Standard neural networks (NNs) fail to express their uncertainty. They can't talk about the elephant in the room.
- Bayesian neural networks (BNNs) can express their uncertainty.
- BNNs often yield better performance than their non-Bayesian variants.
- Novel classes can be better identified with BNNs, which combine epistemic and aleatoric uncertainties compared to standard NNs.
- Variational inference (VI) and Monte Carlo dropout (MC dropout) are approximation methods that allow you to fit deep BNNs.
- TensorFlow Probability (TFP) provides easy-to-use layers for fitting a BNN via VI.
- MC dropout can be used in Keras for fitting BNNs.

Glossary of terms and abbreviations

Abbreviation/Term	Definition/Meaning
Aleatoric uncertainty	Data-inherent uncertainty that cannot be further reduced. For example, you can't tell on which side a coin will land.
API	Application programming interface.
Bayesian mantra	The posterior is proportional to the likelihood times the prior.
BNN	Bayesian neural network. An NN with its weights replaced by distributions. Solved with VI or MC dropout.
Bayesian probabilistic models	Probabilistic models that can state their epistemic uncertainty by characterizing all parameters of a distribution.
Bayesian view of statistics	In the Bayesian view of statistics, the parameters θ are not fixed but follow a distribution.
Bayesian theorem	$P(A|B) = P(B|A) \cdot P(A) / P(B)$. This famous formula tells how to invert a conditional probability.
Bayesian learning	$P(\theta|D) = P(D|\theta) \cdot P(\theta) / P(D)$. This formula tells you how to determine the posterior $P(\theta|D)$ from the likelihood $P(D|\theta)$, the prior $P(\theta)$, and the marginal likelihood (a.k.a. evidence) $P(D)$. It is a special form of the Bayesian theorem with $A = \theta$ and $B = D$, where θ is the parameters of a model and D the data.
Backpropagation	Method to efficiently calculate the gradients of the loss function with respect to (w.r.t.) the weights of an NN.
Bijector	TFP package for invertible (bijective) functions needed for normalizing flows (NF).
CIFAR-10	A popular benchmark data set containing 60,000, 32×32 color images of 10 classes.
CNN	Convolutional neural network. An NN especially suited for vision applications.
Computational graph	A graph that encodes all calculations in an NN.

Abbreviation/Term	Definition/Meaning
CPD	Conditional probability distribution. We also sloppily call the density $p(y|x)$ of an outcome y (e.g., the age of a person) given some input x (e.g., the image of a person) a CPD.
Cross entropy	Another name for negative log likelihood (NLL) in classification tasks.
Deterministic model	A non-probabilistic model that returns no distribution for the outcome but only one best guess.
Dropout	Dropout refers to randomly deleting nodes in an NN. Dropout during training typically yields NNs that show reduced overfitting. Performing dropout also during test time (see *MC dropout*) is interpreted as an approximation of a BNN.
DL	Deep learning.
Extrapolation	Leaves the range of data with which a model was trained.
Epistemic uncertainty	Uncertainty of the model caused by the uncertainty about the model parameters. This can, in principle, be reduced by providing more data.
fcNN	Fully connected neural network.
Glow	A certain CNN network based on NF that generates realistic looking faces.
ImageNet	A famous data set with 1 million labeled images of 1,000 classes.
Jacobian matrix	The Jacobian matrix of a multidimensional function or transformation in several variables is the matrix of all its first-order partial derivatives.
Jacobian determinant	The determinant of the Jacobian matrix. It is used to calculate the change in volume during transformations and is needed for NF.
Keras	Keras is a high-level NN API that we use in this book in conjunction with TensorFlow.
KL divergence	A kind of measure for the distance between two probability density functions (PDFs).
Likelihood	The probability $p(D|\theta)$ that sampling from a density specified by a parameter value θ produces the data.
Loss function	A function that quantifies the badness of a model and that which is optimized during the training of a DL model.
MAE	Mean absolute error. The MAE is a performance measure that is computed as the mean of absolute values of the residuals. It is not sufficient to quantify the performance of probabilistic models (here the NLL should be used as performance measure).
MaxLike	Maximum likelihood.
MaxLike learning	A likelihood-based method to determine the parameter values θ of a model (for example, the weight in an NN). The objective is to maximize the likelihood of the observed data $P(D|\theta)$. This corresponds to minimizing the NLL.

Abbreviation/Term	Definition/Meaning
ML	Machine learning.
MC dropout	Monte Carlo dropout. This refers to dropout during test time. A method that is interpreted as an approximation to a BNN.
MNIST	More correctly, the MNIST database of handwritten digits. A data set of 60,000, 28×28 gray-scaled 10 classes (the digits 0–9).
MSE	Mean squared error. The MSE is a performance measure that is computed as the average of the squared residuals. It's not sufficient to quantify the performance of probabilistic models (here the NLL should be used as a performance measure).
NF	Normalizing flow. NF is an NN-based method to fit complex probability distributions.
NLL	Negative log-likelihood. Used as a loss function when fitting probabilistic models. The NLL on the validation set is the optimal measure to quantify the prediction performance of a probabilistic model.
NN	Neural network.
Observed outcome	The observed outcome or y_i value that is measured for a certain instance i. In a probabilistic model, we aim to predict a CPD for y, based on some features that characterize the instance i. Sometimes y_i is also bewilderingly called the "true" value. We don't like that expression because in the presence of aleatoric uncertainty, there is no true outcome.
PDF	Probability density function. The PDF is also sometimes referred to as probability density distribution. See *CPD* for a conditional version.
PixelCNN++	A certain CNN model capturing the probability distribution of pixel values. The "++ version" uses advanced CPDs for performance.
Posterior	The distribution $p(\theta|D)$ of a parameter θ after seeing the data D.
Posterior predictive distribution	The CPD $p(y|x, D)$ given the data D that results from a Bayesian probabilistic model.
Prediction interval	Interval in which a certain fraction of all data are expected, typically 95%.
Prior	The distribution $p(\theta)$ that is assigned to a model parameter θ before seeing any data D.
Probabilistic model	A model returning a distribution for the outcome.
Residuals	Differences between the observed value y_i and the deterministic model output $\hat{y}_i$ (the expected value of the outcome).
RMSE	Root mean squared error. The square root of the MSE.
RealNVP	A specific NF model called real non-volume preserving.
softmax	An activation function enforcing the output of the NN, which sums up to 1 and can be interpreted as a probability.

Abbreviation/Term	Definition/Meaning
softplus	An activation function, which after its application, ensures positive values.
SGD	Stochastic gradient descent.
Tensor	Multidimensional array. This is the main data structure in DL.
TF	TensorFlow is a low-level library used in this book for DL.
The big lie of DL	The assumption $P(train) = P(test)$, meaning that the test data stems from the same distributions as the training data. In many DL/ML applications, this is assumed but often not true.
TFP	TensorFlow Probability. An add-on to TF facilitating probabilistic modeling of DL.
VGG16	A traditional CNN with a specific architecture that ranked second place in the ImageNet competition in 2014. It is often used with weights that, after training on the ImageNet data, extracted features from an image.
VI	Variational inference. A method for which it can be shown that it yields an approximation to a BNN.
w.r.t.	Acronym meaning *with respect to*.
WaveNet	A specific NN model for text to speech.
ZIP	Zero-inflated Poisson. A special distribution for count data taking care of an excess of the value 0.

index

Numerics

1D loss function 74

A

AffineScalar bijectors 179
Akaike Information Criterion (AIC) 132
aleatoric uncertainty 129, 264
API 264
artificial NNs (neural networks) 7, 26–28
autograd library 89
automatic differentiation 79–80
autoregressive models 160

B

backpropagation (reverse-mode
    differentiation) 80–90, 264
  dynamic graph frameworks 88–90
  static graph frameworks 81–88
banknotes, identifying fakes 30–38
batch dimension 57
Bayesian approach 201–207
  Bayesian models 202–205
  for coin toss example 215–218
  for probabilistic models 207–228
    coin toss as Hello World example for Bayesian
        models 213–222
    prediction with Bayesian models 208–212
    training with Bayesian models 208–212
  MC dropout as approximate 245–251
    classical dropout during training 246–249
    during train and test times 249–251
  VI as approximate 232–243
    applying to toy problem 238–243

overview 233–238
  with TensorFlow Probability 240
Bayesian Information Criterion (BIC) 132
Bayesian learning 209
Bayesian linear regression models 224–228
Bayesian mantra 212
Bayesian models 202–205
  coin toss as Hello World example for 213–222
    Bayesian approach for coin toss
        example 215–218
    MaxLike approach for coin toss
        example 214–215
  prediction with 208–212
  training with 208–212
Bayesian probabilistic classification 16
Bayesian probabilistic curve fitting 20–21
Bayesian theorem 212
Bayesian view of statistics 208
Bernoulli distribution 101, 106
big lie of DL 267
Bijector class 174
bijector package 170, 264
binary classification 99–105
binomial experiments 96
binom.pmf function 96
BNNs (Bayesian neural networks) 229–263
  case studies 252–263
  classification with novel classes 256–263
    filtering out classified images with uncertainty
        measures 261–263
    uncertainty in classification models 259
    uncertainty measures in Bayesian classifica-
        tion NNs 261
    uncertainty measures in non-Bayesian classifi-
        cation NNs 259–261
  extrapolation 252–256

BNNs (Bayesian neural networks) *(continued)*
  MC dropout as approximate Bayes
      approach 245–251
    classical dropout during training 246–249
    during train and test times 249–251
  regression 252–256
  VI as approximate Bayes approach
      232–243
    applying to problems 238–243
    overview 233–238
  VI with TFP 243–245
broadcasting 68

C

categorical cross entropy 99
cdf(value) method 135
CelebA data set 191
chain rule 80, 83
chaining flows 177–181
change of variable technique 170–175
CIFAR-10 264
classes 105–109
classical dropout 246–249
classification 8–16
  Bayesian classification 16
  binary 99–105
  KL divergence as MSE pendant in 110
  loss functions for 99–110
    cross entropy 109–110
    KL divergence 109–110
    NLL 109–110
  non-probabilistic 14
  of images
    deep learning approach to 12–14
    traditional approach to 9–12
    with fcNNs 38–44
  probabilistic 14–16
  with examples not in training
    filtering out classified images with uncertainty
        measures 261–263
    uncertainty in classification models 259
    uncertainty measures in Bayesian classifica-
        tion NNs 261
    uncertainty measures in non-Bayesian
        classification NNs 259–261
  with more than two classes 105–109
closed-form solution 69
CNNs (convolutional neural networks)
  architecture of
    biological inspiration for 50–51
    overview 44–47
  building 52–56
  edges and 47–50
  for image-like data 44–56

for ordered data 56–61
for time-ordered data 59–61
coin toss example
  as Hello World for Bayesian models 213–222
  Bayesian approach for 215–218
  MaxLike approach for 214–215
computational graphs 81, 264
computer vision 8
conditional probability distribution (CPD) 100–
    101, 106–107, 110, 119, 122, 125, 129–130,
    132–133, 138, 143, 147–148, 151–152, 154,
    158–159, 161, 206, 210–211, 224, 226, 251,
    254, 256, 259, 265
constant variance 136–139, 142
continuous data
  linear regression models with constant
      variance 136–139
  linear regression models with nonconstant stan-
      dard deviation 140–144
  modeling with TFP 135–144
convex problem 77
convolution 45
Convolution1DReparameterization 244–245
Convolution2DFlipout 245
Convolution2DReparameterization 244–245
Convolution3DReparameterization 244–245
count data
  modeling with TFP 145–156
  Poisson distribution for 148–153
  ZIP distribution for 153
coupling layers 187
cross entropy 109–110, 265
crossentropy function 32
cumulative distribution function (CDF) 162
curve fitting 16–21, 62–90
  backpropagation in DL frameworks 80–90
    dynamic graph frameworks 88–90
    static graph frameworks 81–88
  Bayesian 20–21
  gradient descent method 69–78
    loss with one model parameter 69–73
    loss with two model parameters 73–78
  Hello World in 63–69
  non-probabilistic 17–18
  probabilistic 18–20
  training DL models 78–80
    automatic differentiation 79–80
    mini-batch gradient descent 78–79
    SGD variants 79

D

D-dimensional bijector function 183
decision boundary 33
deep NNs (neural networks) 13, 79

DeepL 4
DenseFlipout 245
DenseReparameterization 244–245
deterministic model 265
differentiation, automatic 79–80
dilated convolutions 160
discretized logistic mixture 162–164
DL (deep learning) 265
   advantages of 22
   disadvantages of 21–22
   frameworks for 80–90
   overview 6–8
   training models 78–80
      automatic differentiation 79–80
      mini-batch gradient descent 78–79
      SGD variants 79
dropout 265
dynamic graph frameworks 88–90

E

eager execution 89
edge lovers' notebook 49–50
edges 47–50
embedding 58
end-to-end training 37
entropy 109
   See also cross entropy
epistemic uncertainty 198, 201, 265
epochs 32
exp function 140
extrapolation 198, 265

F

faces, sampling 188–193
fcNNs (fully connected neural networks) 26–44
   artificial NNs (neural networks) 26–28
   classifying images with 38–44
   implementing NNs 28–38
      software tools 29–30
      tensors 28–29
      to identify fake banknotes 30–38
feature expansion 33
feature maps 46
feature representation 12
fitting 7, 11, 225
flexible probability distributions 159–164
   discretized logistic mixture 162–164
   multinomial distribution as 160–162
flows
   chaining 177–181
   networks to control 183–188
   See also NFs (normalizing flows)

frameworks
   backpropagation in 80–90
   for dynamic graphs 88–90
   for static graphs 81–88

G

Gaussian CPD 137, 139, 142, 144, 148
Gaussian distribution 125, 132, 138, 158, 176–178, 222, 232, 238, 243, 245, 253, 259, 263
generative adversarial networks (GANs) 168
Glow 188–189, 265
Google Colab 29–30
GPUs (graphic processing units) 30
gradient descent method 69–78
   intuition of 70–71
   loss with one model parameter 69–73
   loss with two model parameters 73–78
   mini-batch 78–79
   stochastic 79
   update rule in 71–73

H

Hello World
   for Bayesian models, coin toss example as 213–222
      Bayesian approach for 215–218
      MaxLike approach for 214–215
   in curve fitting 63–69
heteroscedasticity 111, 122
hidden layer 33
high-dimensional spaces 181–183
homoscedasticity 121
hyperplane 33

I

image-like data 44–56
ImageNet 198, 200, 256, 265
images, classifying
   deep learning approach to 12–14
   filtering out with uncertainty measures 261–263
   traditional approach to 9–12
   with fcNNs 38–44
input_feature dimension 57

J

Jacobi matrix 181, 183–184, 187–188
Jacobian determinant 265
Jacobian matrix 265
joint likelihood (jointlik) 218
Jupyter notebooks 30

K

Kant 58
Keras 29, 31, 57, 79–80, 87, 102, 104, 117, 134,
    142, 164, 251, 265
KL (Kullback-Leibler) divergence 109–110,
    234–235, 237, 239, 265
    as MSE pendant in classification 110
    cross entropy and 109

L

learning rate 71
likelihood approach
    building loss functions with 93–127
        deriving loss functions for classification
            problems 99–110
        deriving loss functions for regression
            problems 111–127
    MaxLike approach 94–99
linear regression models
    Bayesian 224–228
    fitting 65–69
    with constant variance 136–139
    with nonconstant standard deviation 140–144
linear relationships 111–119
log_det_jacobian(z) method 182
logistic regression 28, 31
log_prob(value) method 135
long short-term memory networks (LSTMs) 59
loss
    with one model parameter 69–73
        intuition of gradient descent 70–71
        update rule in gradient descent 71–73
    with two model parameters 73–78
loss functions
    building with likelihood approach 93–127
    fitting linear regression model based
        on 65–69
    for classification problems 99–110
        binary classification problems 99–105
        cross entropy 109–110
        KL divergence 109–110
        NLL (negative log likelihood) 109–110
        with more than two classes 105–109
    for regression problems 111–127
        NNs with additional output for regression
            tasks with nonconstant variance 121–127
        NNs without hidden layers and one output
            neuron for modeling linear
            relationships 111–119
        NNs without hidden layers and one output
            neuron for modeling non-linear
            relationships 119–121
loss_kl component 240

loss_nll component 240
LSTMs (long short-term memory networks) 59

M

machine learning (ML) 6–7, 13, 21, 63, 94, 131,
    200, 266
MADE (Masked Autoencoder for Distribution
    Estimation) 185
Markov Chain Monte Carlo (MCMC) 231
max pooling 53
MaxLike (maximum likelihood) approach 94–99,
    214–215, 265
MaxLike learning 117
MC (Monte Carlo) dropout 232, 255, 257, 259,
    263, 266
    as approximate Bayes approach 245–251
    during train and test times 249–251
mean absolute error (MAE) 144, 265
mean squared error (MSE) 67–68, 76, 83, 85,
    110–111, 117, 119–121, 126, 133, 137, 144,
    146, 266
mini-batch gradient descent 78–79
mini-batches 30
MNIST notebook 39–40, 42, 52, 55–56, 99, 108,
    159
model parameters
    loss with one 69–73
        intuition of gradient descent 70–71
        update rule in gradient descent 71–73
    loss with two 73–78
model uncertainty 201
model.evaluate function 104
model.summary() method 244
multinomial distributions 106, 160–162, 257

N

natural language processing 8
negative log likelihood (NLL) 104, 109–110, 118,
    122, 124, 126, 129–130, 132, 139, 143, 155,
    166, 225–226, 238–239, 261, 266
NFs (normalizing flows) 158, 166–193, 266
    chaining flows 177–181
    change of variable technique for
        probabilities 170–175
    fitting to data 175–177
    networks to control flows 183–188
    overview 168–170
    sampling faces 188–193
    transformations between high-dimensional
        spaces 181–183
NLL (negative log likelihood) 104, 109–110, 118,
    122, 124, 126, 129–130, 132, 139, 143, 155,
    166, 225–226, 238–239, 261, 266

NNs (neural networks) 6, 13, 266
    architecture of 25–61
        CNNs for image-like data 44–56
        CNNs for ordered data 56–61
        fcNNs 26–44
    artificial 26–28
    implementing 28–38
    models to identify fake banknotes 30–38
    software tools 29–30
    tensors 28–29
    with additional output 121–127
    without hidden layers and one output neuron
        for modeling linear relationships between
            input and output 111–119
        for modeling non-linear relationships
            between input and output 119–121
non-Bayesian DL (deep learning) 198–201
non-Bayesian NNs (neural networks) 259–261
nonconstant standard deviation 140–144
nonconstant variance 121–127
non-linear relationships 119–121
non-probabilistic classification 14
non-probabilistic curve fitting 17–18
Normal distribution 113–114, 116, 119, 124, 134,
    136, 145, 158
novel classes
    filtering out classified images with uncertainty
        measures 261–263
    uncertainty in classification models 259
    uncertainty measures in Bayesian classification
        NNs 261
    uncertainty measures in non-Bayesian classifica-
        tion NNs 259–261

O

observed outcome 266
one-hot encoding 40, 58, 108
ordered data
    CNNs for 56–61
    overview 58

P

parametric models 11
PixelCNN 161–162, 164–165
PixelCNN++ 158, 161–162, 166, 266
Poisson distribution
    extending to ZIP distribution 153–156
    for count data 148–153
posterior distribution 206, 211, 233, 235, 266
Posterior predictive distribution 266
prediction 208–212
prediction interval 266
predictive distribution 211

prior distribution 211, 218, 266
probabilistic classification 14–16
probabilistic curve fitting 18–20
probabilistic models 4–6
    advantages and disadvantages of 22–23
    Bayesian approach for 207–228
        coin toss as Hello World example for Bayesian
            models 213–222
        prediction with Bayesian models 208–212
        training with Bayesian models 208–212
    defined 266
    for prediction 130–132
probabilities 170–175
probability density function (PDF) 266
probability distributions, flexible 159–164
    discretized logistic mixture 162–164
    multinomial distribution as 160–162

Q

QuantizedDistribution function 163–164
quant_mixture_logistic function 164

R

random variable 96
rate parameter 150
RealNVP 186–188, 266
receptive field 53
regression 252–256
    loss functions for 111–127
        NNs with additional output for regression
            tasks with nonconstant variance 121–127
        NNs without hidden layers and one output
            neuron for modeling linear
            relationships 111–119
        NNs without hidden layers and one output
            neuron for modeling non-linear
            relationships 119–121
    with nonconstant variance 121–127
regularization 223
regularizers 237
ReLU (Rectified Linear Unit) 41
residuals 66, 266
RMSE (root mean squared error) 151, 266
RNNs (recurrent neural networks) 59
RSS (residual sum of squared errors) 67

S

sampling faces 188–193
Scale-Invariant Feature Transform (SIFT) 10
shared weights 47
simple linear model 65
SinhArcsinh bijectors 179

skewness parameter 179
softmax function 35, 39, 99, 105, 266
softplus function 140–141, 179, 238, 267
source distribution 175
static graph frameworks 81–88
stochastic gradient descent (SGD) 32, 78–79, 83, 93, 102, 111, 117, 123, 267

T

target distribution 175
Tensor 267
TensorBoard 81
tensors 28–29
TF (TensorFlow) 29–30, 57, 79–84, 87, 89, 102, 267
tfb.Exp() function 176
tfb.Permute() method 187
tfd.Distribution 137
tf.distributions.Distribution 136
tf.distributions.Normal 136
tfd.Normal() method 136
tfd.Normal(0,1).prob(z) 170
@tf.function decorator 89
TFP (TensorFlow Probability) 128–156, 245
  defined 267
  modeling continuous data with 135–144
    linear regression models with constant variance 136–139
    linear regression models with nonconstant standard deviation 140–144
  modeling count data with 145–156
    extending Poisson distribution to ZIP distribution 153–156
    Poisson distribution for count data 148–153
  overview 132–134
  probabilistic prediction models 130–132
  VI with 243–245
tfp.bijector package 175, 178
tfp.layers.DenseReparameterization class 243
tfp.layers.DistributionLambda layer 136–137
tf.train.GradientDescentOptimizer() function 87
The big lie of DL 267
time-ordered data
  architecture of 59–61
  CNNs for 59–61
  format of 57–58

timestep dimension 57
training
  classical dropout during 246–249
  models 78–80
    automatic differentiation 79–80
    Bayesian 208–212
    mini-batch gradient descent 78–79
    SGD variants 79
transformations 181–183
transformed distribution 175

U

unbiased estimate 78
uncertainty measures
  filtering out classified images with 261–263
  in Bayesian classification NNs 261
  in classification models 259
  in non-Bayesian classification NNs 259–261
unnormalized posterior (unnorm_post) 218
update rule 71–73

V

VAEs (variational autoencoders) 168
variational approximation 235
variational distribution 232, 234
variational parameters 234–235, 237
VGG16 network 199, 267
VI (variational inference)
  applying to problems 238–243
  as approximate Bayes approach 232–243
  overview 233–238
  with TFP 243–245

W

WaveNet 158, 160–162, 164, 166
weights decay 223
with tf.GradientTape() construction 89
w.r.t abbreviation (with respect to) 70

Z

ZIP (zero-inflated Poisson) distribution 153–156

DL with Python, 2nd edition
by François Chollet

ISBN 9781617296864
400 pages (estimated), $59.99
Spring 2021 (estimated)

DL with Pytorch
by Eli Stevens, Luca Antiga, and Thomas Viehmann
Foreword by Soumith Chintala

ISBN 9781617295263
520 pages, $49.99
July 2020

Grokking Deep Learning
by Andrew W. Trask

ISBN 9781617293702
336 pages, $49.99
January 2019

For ordering information go to www.manning.com

RELATED MANNING TITLES

Math for Programmers
by Paul Orland

ISBN 9781617295355
650 pages (estimated), $49.99
November 2020 (estimated)

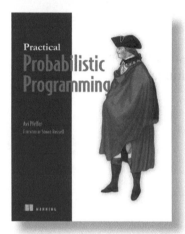

Practical Probabilistic Programming
by Avi Pfeffer
Foreword by Stuart Russell

ISBN 9781617292330
456 pages, $59.99
March 2016

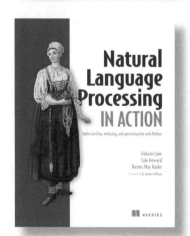

Natural Language Processing in Action
by Hobson Lane, Cole Howard, Hannes Max Hapke
Foreword by Dr. Arwen Griffioen

ISBN 9781617294631
544 pages, $49.99
March 2019

For ordering information go to www.manning.com